THE WISDOM OF SYRIA'S WAITING GAME

BENTE SCHELLER

The Wisdom of Syria's Waiting Game

Syrian Foreign Policy Under the Assads

HURST & COMPANY, LONDON

First published in the United Kingdom in 2013 by
C. Hurst & Co. (Publishers) Ltd.,
41 Great Russell Street, London, WC1B 3PL
© Bente Scheller, 2013
All rights reserved.

Distributed in the United States, Canada and Latin America by
Oxford University Press, 198 Madison Avenue, New York, NY 10016,
United States of America.

The right of Bente Scheller to be identified as the author of
this publication is asserted by her in accordance with the
Copyright, Designs and Patents Act, 1988.

A Cataloguing-in-Publication data record for this book
is available from the British Library.

ISBN: 9781849042864

www.hurstpublishers.com

This book is printed on paper from registered sustainable
and managed sources.

CONTENTS

ACKNOWLEDGEMENTS

I would like to express my gratitude to all those who made it possible for me to complete this book. There are a number of people inside Syria who were of great support in my research and who in endless discussions went through data with me, flipped around ideas, and gave me their opinion on developments. For some of them, this is not the time and place to be mentioned, but I want to express my gratitude to them anonymously at least.

Furthermore I want to thank the following people for their stimulating support: Maan Abdul Salam, Robert Bain, Nadja Engelhardt, Christina J.C. Friedrich, Yassin Haj Saleh, Anna Korpijaakko, Aliya Mawani, Frida Nome, Serap Ocak, Prof. Dr Volker Perthes, Omar Sheikhmous, Joshua Stacher, Petra Stienen, Robert Vitalyos, Kari and Dag Wollebæk, Razan Zeitouneh. I am particularly indebted to Wael Sawah, Ambassador Nikolaos van Dam and my husband Christoph Reuter for their incredibly helpful support and for being my most critical readers. I would also like to thank Michael Dwyer and his team for believing in this book and making it happen. Moreover, I would like to give my special thanks to my family: my parents Heidrun and Volker Scheller, my late grandparents Edith and Alfred Cöster, my brother Malte and his partner Wolfgang. Without their patience, support, and belief in me it would have been difficult to carry out this work.

Brian O'Rourke has done a great job editing this. Despite the efforts of committed proofreaders to eliminate all mistakes, I'm sure I managed to make some more. For these, of course, I assume full responsibility.

Bente Scheller   August 2013

INTRODUCTION

"No government in the world kills its people, unless it's led by a crazy person," Syrian President Bashar al-Assad said in a December 2011 ABC TV interview. In a blunt denial of responsibility for the violence in his country, he, by constitution the highest leader of the armed forces, claimed that he did not have command over the army, and thus could not be held responsible.[1] Over two years later, more than 100,000 people have lost their lives per UN estimates, millions have fled from their homes, and hundreds of thousands have been arrested or disappeared. Despite the imbalance in military might the opposition has taken control over vast parts of the country, and as of early 2013 is challenging the regime even in the heart of Damascus. The regime has made no effort to seek a political solution. Moreover, looking at the patterns of destruction, the indiscriminate and deliberate violence against civilians, as well as the targeting of infrastructure, it seems that despite vehemently clinging to power, Bashar al-Assad has given up on the idea of governing. Does this mean that Syria, according to the definition of its own president, is run by a crazy person? How does it reason, and what does it mean for other countries' foreign policy towards Syria? How should they deal with a regime that seems to have realized it will not last, yet which continues with a policy of violence and destruction?

These questions seem even more pressing after several hundred people died by chemical weapons on 21 August 2013 in areas surrounding Damascus. This while a team of UN inspectors was less then 10 miles away in the heart of the Syrian capital on a mission to investigate allegations of the use of chemical agents earlier in 2013. While evidence pointing to the Syrian regime's involvement in the attacks in Eastern Ghouta was overwhelming, it was a puzzle to many observers: how could the regime deploy chemical weapons so brazenly before the eyes of an international investigation team?

At first glance it may seem anachronistic to write about a regime whose days are apparently numbered—and to write about its foreign policy while all eyes are on the internal developments in the country. But to understand the regime's strategies and habits, which derive from its experiences in dealing with internal as well as external crises, permits precious insight into how foreign policy was executed. The resilience of Bashar al-Assad to any international initiatives and pressure shows the limits of international diplomacy, even though the longer the conflict goes on, the clearer it is that the Syrian revolution is turning into a regional and international matter. Foreign interests inside Syria have come to play an increasingly visible role, and international concern not only about Syria's future but also its regional impact is growing. In the beginning, it was Bashar al-Assad who chose, as Lebanese scholar Fawaz Traboulsi puts it, a "strategy of externalization"[2] of the crisis, portraying the uprising as an external fabrication. When admitting that there were actually protests taking place, the government blamed them on "foreign agents" and "terrorists," while on other occasions the official Syrian Arab News Agency would deny that what was seen in the international media was real, claiming there was an international conspiracy in which Qatar would fabricate Hollywood-style clips, staging protests set in models of Syrian cities in film studios.[3]

The Syrian revolution came as a surprise for the Syrian government, for observers, and even for the traditional Syrian opposition: most thought that the Arab Spring would not have any repercussions in Syria, which had experienced a bloody clampdown on an Islamic-led uprising in the early 1980s, and in which an authoritarian system seemed to have depoliticized society by repressing dissidents. Yet after other Arab dictators were swiftly ousted, the mood gradually changed towards thinking that Bashar al-Assad would also not last for long. But the death knell for the Syrian regime has often rung prematurely. When Hafez al-Assad died in June 2000, analysts questioned whether Bashar al-Assad would be able to establish his own power base, and the regime's downfall was predicted after 2005, when Syria's international relations had reached an all-time low over Syrian regional politics. At the start of the current crisis, however, Syrian activists had high hopes for success, which were partly based on the expectation that they would receive support from outside—they were part of an authentic popular uprising, and even though it is difficult to verify most of the material, through Syrian and international human rights reports and Youtube videos of protests and violence it is not difficult for the world to get an idea of the atrocities taking place in Syria.

Sovereignty and intervention: shifting "red lines"

In theory, a sovereign state is free to do what it pleases on its own territory. This means that it also has a "right to do wrong." There are limits to this, however. Syria has signed and ratified the International Covenant on Civil and Political Rights, and the current handling of the situation in the country obviously violates this Covenant. In addition, there has been a great deal of discussion in recent decades about humanitarian grounds that might justify foreign intervention, and the responsibility to protect. As Henry Shue puts it: over the course of time, some actions have been "removed from the list of wrongs" that sovereigns are free to commit (Shue 2004). Given the number and level of atrocities committed in Syria every day, one might assume that the tipping point had been reached long ago. Instead, the international community has watched the Syrian regime cross one "red line" after the other. It was widely known at the beginning of the revolution that the regime had ordered the shooting of peaceful protestors. In June 2012, the UN for the first time confirmed aerial attacks on civilians by helicopter, and in July 2012 even with fighter jets. In August 2012, US President Barack Obama said the use or transport of chemical weapons constituted a red line, which was obviously interpreted by the Syrian regime as a carte blanche to use anything short of this: in October 2012, Human Rights Watch documented the use of cluster bombs, and in November the use of incendiary weapons.[4] Activists from Aleppo claimed that the latter had also been used to set the historical bazaar in Aleppo ablaze in September 2012. Since December 2012, the regime has also been launching SCUD missiles from Damascus, hitting areas in the north and particularly Aleppo. That was also the time when the first allegations of chemical weapons use were levelled. In March and April 2013, more suspected cases became public. The US administration acknowledged that chemical weapons had been used in Syria but said it was waiting for "more details" before altering its strategy towards the regime. They were not the only ones to be hiding behind a supposed lack of evidence. Reporters for the German magazine *Der Spiegel* in touch with activists who had collected samples were unable to find any institution that would analyze them. And even after French reporters spent two months in Syria documenting the use of chemical weapons, including tested samples, the international community remained reticent (Rémy 2013).

While the images of scores of civilians and particularly children who died in the attack on 21 August 2013 caused international outrage, it was not clear at first whether the UN inspectors would be allowed to examine the case. Only after five days did the Syrian regime give its consent, and even then the inspectors were subject to a series of disruptions—for example mortar shelling close to their hotel and sniper fire at a regime checkpoint—thus limiting the time they were able to spend in the respective areas. While the Syrian regime's first reaction to the massacre was to pretend nothing had happened, the picture at an international level was mixed: Russia was the first to claim chemical agents had been used, but by the rebels. The Iranian president Hassan Rouhani via Twitter urged the international community to use "all its might" to prevent the use of chemical weapons, and former Iranian president Akbar Hashemi Rafsanjani even claimed it was the Syrian government that had been using them. It seemed as though Assad's allies were not happy.[5] However, both opposed military intervention. While at first there were some strong statements by the United States and Great Britain indicating swift action, as soon as the UN inspectors had left Syria both started to row back. A poster at a protest in the town of Dael on 23 August read: "It is more merciful to die from chemical weapons than to wait for your help."

No country for an intervention

Whoever expected that in light of the overwhelming evidence the regime would be held accountable for its actions soon learned that the world's patience with Damascus was longer than with Tripoli. That an intervention has not yet been seriously considered until the end of August 2013 is due to various reasons, the most important being the complexity of international interests in Syria, which has led to an impasse in the UN

INTRODUCTION

Security Council. With the negative experience of military interventions in Iraq and Afghanistan, the international community has become hesitant to use force, and in the only instance of Western intervention in the Arab Spring, namely Libya, Russia felt it had been betrayed. The situation in Syria is fundamentally different from Iraq and Afghanistan, however: even after two and a half years of war, there is a strong and committed popular movement, which is evident not only in the persistent protests but also in the efforts to organize life in the liberated areas. Efforts to engage the Syrian regime in a peace plan presented and headed by UN Special Envoy Kofi Annan, and later on by Lakhdar Brahimi, have failed. The regime paid lip service to the plans but could hardly be said to have complied with any of their conditions. At the same time, the Syrian regime masterfully undermined the opposition's credibility by playing on domestic and international fears of Islamism and Islamist terrorism.

The international community (i.e. the United States and Europe) gravely mistook the specific character of the Syrian regime and continue to bank on negotiations, while Damascus pretended to be interested in negotiations purely in order to buy time to quell the initially peaceful, and then military, uprising with brute force.

When looking at the reasons why the international community was and is at the time of writing hesitant to throw its weight behind the revolution, it is also necessary to examine the opposition itself, which despite significant progress in unifying, remains diverse not only in composition but also in terms of its vision. More than forty years of authoritarian rule have shaped the Syrian political landscape in a particular way. Similarly, the "traditional" opposition in Syria, admirable for their perseverance over many years, can hardly be said to have attracted and integrated younger activists. The backbone of the current protests is mostly formed by young and/or disenfranchised people who have not previously been politically active. Inside Syria, in areas either liberated or contested, an impressive grassroots movement has emerged to take care of services no longer delivered by the government, and which has also begun organizing to discuss the political future of the country and/or a new constitution.[6]

In November 2012, the Syrian National Coalition was formed in Doha under the leadership of Mo'az al-Khatib, Riad Seif, and Suhair al-Atassi. It is the largest coalition formed to date and joins all of the opposition groups together. A visit of Mo'az al-Khatib to northern Syria before resigning on 22 April 2013 was widely welcomed by local residents. The National Coalition is perceived as a more comprehensive entity than the previously established Syrian National Council (SNC), which became part of the National Coalition, yet the main task now is still to be done: to earn respect inside Syria, the National Coalition will need to show that it can deliver what is needed there and that it is recognized internationally in a way that allows it to assume the functions of a transitional governmental body. While the Local Coordination Committees perform rather well on the ground, and steps have been taken for a unified military command, this does not yet encompass a nationwide structure that can be relied upon for the moment of political transformation. This is not only a question of choice: the liberated territories continue to be subject to daily aerial bombardments and, due to the massive destruction of infrastructure and a lack of electricity, among other severe problems, there are practical impediments with regard to communication and coordination.

Under these conditions, it is difficult to achieve the level of unity Western countries deem essential for throwing their full weight behind the revolution, especially in light of growing concern about Salafist movements. The helplessness of the international community has led to a general feeling of abandonment among revolutionaries and civilians, since it appears that it has failed to explore all of the available possibilities on the political or the humanitarian level, and Western inertia has helped to produce some of the developments it was most afraid of: a strong role for Islamist actors, and foreign influence in the country that cannot be controlled.

A debate replete with myths

A number of renowned scholars have been studying Syria for decades—Volker Perthes, Eyal Zisser, Nikolaos van Dam, Raymond Hinnebusch, Anoushiravan Ehteshami, Radwan Ziadeh, Rime Allaf, and Joshua Landis, to name just a few, have extensively studied and analyzed different aspects of Syrian history and policy. More recent publications by Carsten Wieland, Stephen Starr, or Fouad Ajami have examined Syrian domestic politics, civil society, and the revolution. However, Syria still remains an understudied subject, an outcome due in part to the opaque nature of its political system and decision-making process. This renders the public debate on the Syrian revolution and how to handle it polarized, and replete with myths. There is the leftist myth of Syria as a spearhead of anti-imperialism, which comfortably ignores the fact that Syrian foreign policy has mostly been pragmatic, particularly with regard to the United States where Syria was a welcome and cooperative partner in the "war against terrorism," receiving alleged terrorists kidnapped in third countries sent by the United States for interrogation to Syria.

Another myth is that of the Syrian regime as protector of the minorities. It is true that Syria—historically but also recently—provided shelter to victims of war and persecution in their home countries and managed to integrate some, like the Palestinians, to a considerable degree. Yet when it comes to Syrian minorities, the picture is mixed: the official adherence of the regime to secularism glossed over the fact that members of the Alawite community under Assad were privileged, for example, and stressing the Arab nature of the Syrian state served to deny Syrian Kurds full citizenship rights. In the current crisis the Syrian government has used fear of minorities as a tool, suggesting that the fate of the Christian minority in particular was dependent on regime survival, while at the same time instigating sectarian tensions and violence. In government controlled areas, it has recruited special units among civilians that are similar to the infamous *Shabiha* militias, but not involved in fighting. Instead, they man checkpoints. This is something Syrian playwright and activist Mohammad Al-Attar sees as a highly divisive issue: "It means giving civilians power over civilians. By recruiting among the minorities and arming them, it makes them more exposed and they believe that there is a need to defend themselves and their community. These units were created with the sole aim of dividing the population and encouraging tensions at the civic level.[7]

Against a personalistic approach

Syrian propaganda has focused strongly on the presidents. Statues of the president, posters of Hafez al-Assad, Bashar, or the "trinity" with the deceased Basel al-Assad were omnipresent, and Syria was often referred to as "Assad's Syria," which was even the official reception slogan at Damascus International Airport. Patrick Seale's works have focused on Assad's struggle for Syria (and the Middle East), and several recent publications, such as those by Flynt Leverett or David Lesch, have also chosen to explain Syrian politics with a highly personal approach. It would be consonant with this simply to blame the prolonged crisis of the country on an irrational leader or to depict Bashar al-Assad as a tragic figure who was willing to reform but who was hindered by circumstances. This might lead one to conclude that the present crisis could be solved easily, by removing a leader, rather than by changing the system. But this is not what the protesters demand. I argue, therefore, that Syrian behavior in this crisis is best understood by looking at the institutional framework and analyzing the past crises of the Syrian government. A look into the Syrian politics of recent decades reveals that various approaches, from radical policy shifts to patient persistence, have largely determined Syrian politics and that the regime's approach to the present situation might follow a narrow path consistent with previous experience. Even though it would appear that such a path may no longer result in the regime's survival, it is still worthwhile to open this broader analytical framework.

From years of hope to despair

This book analyzes two decades of Syrian foreign policy—the last ten years of Hafez al-Assad's rule and the thirteen years of Bashar al-Assad's. It traces how Syria has, step by step, lost all of the gains made after an auspicious new beginning in 1990/1, when, after a period of international marginalization, Syria was welcomed back into the international scene. During these twenty-two years the Syrian government has passed through very different phases, some of them characterized by hope for change in the Middle East, some by despair about a lack of progress. Regional and international developments have posed severe challenges to the Syrian government. It has experienced sanctions before, but never has the political situation been so uncomfortable and threatening—facing domestic pressure and international isolation at the same time—to the political elite as now.

That Syria has, despite its central importance in the Middle East, been the "odd man out" throughout most of its history is only partly due to the Syrian government's inability to make use of political opportunities. A country of limited power, it has also been subject to changing trends in international relations. For that reason, I do not focus exclusively on Syrian foreign policy but also on the way other states' behavior towards Syria has developed. On more than one occasion, namely in the Middle East peace process and in the so-called "war on terrorism," the Syrian government has felt that its cooperation has not been rewarded. Syria has experienced this kind of disappointment in its relations with the United States and Europe, which, from a Syrian point of view, have offered incentives but, upon Syrian compliance, have simply imposed further conditions instead. This explains why neither incentives nor pressure from outside seem to work particularly well with Syria: history has taught the Syrian government that cooperation is not rewarded, and that, when under pressure, the most rational choice is to remain inactive and wait for better times. Two very interesting examples of this can be found in the chapters on Lebanon and Iraq. The depth of the nadir in relations with international and regional actors after Syria's siding with Iraq in 2003, and after the assassination of former Lebanese Prime Minister Rafiq Hariri in 2005, brought the Syrian government under considerable pressure but the international attitude changed after a few years—without any change in Syrian policy.

To understand the reasoning behind the Syrian government's policy of denial and ignorance, it is important to analyze how the Assad regime has survived deep crises before, a goal which I attempt in this book. When looking at previous decades of Syrian foreign policy—and the policies of other states vis-à-vis Syria—what might appear irrational, or, as hinted at in the opening to this chapter, as "crazy," is not so absurd since the goal of gaining time has paid off in the past, and thus the decision to play a "waiting game" could be viewed as a rational option for the regime in the current crisis. Especially in light of the increasing militarization of the conflict, which is drowning out the "voice of reason," as Syrian analyst Wael Sawah points out, the perception both internally and externally of the revolution as an uprising against a dictatorial regime is on the wane—a fatal dynamic for the civil activists and advocates of democratic change who originally started the uprising (Sawah 2013).

When it comes to the question posed earlier—why would Bashar al-Assad dare to use chemical weapons in the presence of a team of investigators?—the answer might be a combination of factors. One reason why I have chosen to refer extensively to Assad's interviews and speeches is that he is one of the very few from the Syrian regime to speak out publicly at all. A second reason is that over the time of the conflict it becomes ever more clear that for him its resolution cannot come from negotiation or reconciliation but by one side winning over the other. And he is becoming ever more cynical in his way of arguing his case while losing territory. When in June 2013 he was asked about the use of chemical weapons, Assad referred to the—until then—low number of casualties blamed on nerve agents and claimed "it makes no sense to use chemical weapons to kill the same number of people that could be achieved by using conventional weapons." But one could argue that the relatively low number of victims early on fits well with the overall strategy visible during the revolution: increasing the number of victims and the severity of the atrocities step by step to inure international observers to the violence. This worked well for him when it came to conventional warfare, and it could have worked the same even for chemical agents, something German journalists Hans Hoyng and Christoph Reuter dubbed "Assad's Cold Calculation." (Hoyng/Reuter 2013).

The chemical attack might also have been a sign that Assad realized that his prospects of survival were not good: it came shortly after the last supply route for the besieged pro-government part of Aleppo had been cut by the rebels, a similar situation occurring also in Deir ez-Zor. Despite heavy shelling for months, rebels in Damascus suburbs were not about to give up, and by August 2013 had managed to advance further into the heart of the city. So it might have been a last ditch effort by the regime to end the struggle in areas considered vital for its security by any means. German intelligence reported having intercepted a phone conversation between a Hezbollah functionary and Iran in which the former said Assad had "lost his nerve" and "made a big mistake by ordering the chemical weapons attack" (Gebauer 2013).

Whether the "waiting game" is a chosen option in the current crisis, or simply the only solution coming to the minds of the ruling cast of Bashar al-Assad's family and the top security establishment, also depends on structure of decision-making within the inner circle of power: Hafez al-Assad was the sole relevant power in Syria during his reign, which enabled him to change course even against all traditions and qualms. His son and successor has neither the power, nor the strategic mind, to exert all of the options his father had at his disposal. He instead relies on one option alone: to defeat the opposition militarily, even when this means that Syria will be destroyed. In addition to this comes the structure of decision-making: as hinted at even by Bashar himself, it is not clear who is in charge in Damascus. Most probably, decisions are taken collectively by the ruling circle, whose members deeply distrust each other—which makes any changes to the already trodden path highly unlikely.

Parallel foreign policies

An important factor to be considered in terms of Syrian foreign policy is its pattern of establishing "parallel" foreign policies with non-governmental armed actors in other countries in order to pressure its neighbors. The most prominent example of this is the Syrian relationship with the Kurdish PKK, which nearly drove Turkey and Syria to war in 1998, and which was only settled by a credible, simultaneous military threat from Turkey and Israel. At the beginning of the revolution, the Syrian regime has revitalized its relations with the PYD, the Syrian Kurdish branch of the PKK, allowing it to establish its control over parts of Syria's north, and at the same time using it as a less than subtle threat against Ankara. Other countries in the region have been subject to similar strategies: in Lebanon, Syria has always had good relations with Hezbollah; in the Palestinian territories, it has supported not only anti-Israel but also anti-Arafat groups; and after hosting the Iraqi opposition to Saddam, Syria encouraged fighters against the post-Saddam government in Iraq and allowed them to pass through Syrian territory. This willingness to play the spoiler rather than to work constructively with neighboring states to form alliances or otherwise enhance Syrian security seems erratic. But the government has learned that it will normally get away with it. During the revolution, Syria has tried to use some of its allies in Lebanon or among the Kurds to create unrest in neighboring countries and to remind these states that its close relations with armed non-state actors provide an additional source of leverage over their domestic and foreign policies.

In this book I make use of extensive material regarding Syria's relations with these groups—material that can explain the flare-up in PKK activities after the Turkish government adopted a confrontational course with Bashar al-Assad in 2011, and which gives an idea of the relevance of the recent peace agreement of the Turkish government with the PKK.

I try to answer important questions for policy-makers and decision-makers alike in order to contribute to a better understanding of the Syrian government's reasoning in other crises. I start with an overview of the Syrian political structure and its relevance for its foreign policy, looking also into the linkages between domestic and foreign policy. The chapters analyze Syria's relations with core actors—on the international level, the United States, and in the region its neighboring states and Iran. Since actors such as the Gulf States have not played a significant role over most of the studied period, even though they have come (back) to the scene in light of the revolution, I have not dedicated single chapters to them but tackle their engagement in the conclusions and outlook, where I also cast light on those domestic and external constraints that any future government will need to deal with. They might be relevant actors for the future Syria, also taking into consideration that the current developments are often framed within a regional struggle, but data for analyzing their actions are too meager for the time being.

This book is the outcome of long-term research and a PhD project, as well as a vast number of interviews and discussions I had with Syrian and international analysts, observers, activists, journalists, and diplomats between 2001 and 2013. It is of immediate relevance in the current situation in which knowledge about this central regional player in the Middle East is still limited, and in which the question of Syria's future for the region is growing ever more pressing.

1

THE LINKAGE BETWEEN DOMESTIC AND FOREIGN POLICY AND THE REBELLION OF 2011

Authoritarian rulers can largely act independently of public opinion and do not have to take domestic considerations into account in their foreign policy. The Syrian government was therefore used to the fact that its domestic politics hardly affected its foreign relations. On single issues there were complaints by other states, such as the constant reminders emanating from the European Union to respect human rights or its requests to release specific political prisoners. This did not overly trouble the Syrian regime, however, because the only serious external pressure it ever became subject to was due to its foreign policy, and particularly its involvement with terrorist groups in other states. For much of its history the Syrian regime was thus able to decide the degree to which it would link its foreign and domestic policy, and it did so in basically three different ways: first, to boost its legitimacy and its claims to leadership not only in Syria but the region, it promoted itself as the "beating heart" of pan-Arabism. This was mainly and continuously done by Hafez al-Assad—regardless of the fact that Syria's closest partners in the 1980s were non-Arab states like the Soviet Union and Iran, while relations with theoretically like-minded states such as Iraq were openly hostile. Secondly, at certain times it used its foreign policy in a populist manner in order to appeal to the "Arab Street." Steadfastness with regard to Israel was part of this under Hafez al-Assad, while Bashar also applied it with regard to the Iraq War in 2003—at the expense of relations with Jordan and other Arab states that supported the intervention. Third, in times of external crisis it invoked foreign policy to silence the internal opposition, blaming it for jeopardizing Syrian security or accusing it of cooperating with foreign interests, which also was mainly a tactic employed by Bashar al-Assad.

In contrast, the Syrian government has excluded issues that genuinely have both domestic and external dimensions from discussion. Identity-related questions, such as the Kurdish issue, that might imply supra-state loyalties have always been taboo, and the regime has hidden sectarian differences under an official cover of adherence to secular values.

At the beginning of the revolution, the Syrian government tried to externalize the conflict, blaming it on a foreign-sponsored conspiracy. With the government's increasingly violent suppression of the largely peaceful protests, internal developments in Syria started to affect its foreign relations, which led to a double crisis—internally and externally—which the regime had never before experienced. At the time of writing the Syrian government has established control over some strategic points in the area stretching from Damascus over Homs to the coast—an area many suspect will become "Alawitistan" should the country fall apart. The government has lost control, however, of the whole of the north and the few spots it holds are heavily contested: in August 2013, for example, rebels cut the last supply route to Aleppo's government controlled area; the same was true of Deir ez-Zor in the east. The provincial capital of Raqqa has fallen to the rebels, who have advanced in the southern province of Daraa, and only nine airports remain active. Even the coastal area, a regime stronghold, is far from quiet. On the international level, the regime has been subject to sanctions imposed by the United States, Europe, and most importantly of all, the Arab League.

In this chapter I analyze the relationship between foreign and domestic politics. I start with an overview of the institutions and the role of the bureaucracy, political participation, and socio-economic developments under Hafez and Bashar al-Assad before the revolution. In a second step, I look at civil society and the opposition before the revolution, and dedicate a third part of the chapter to the political developments since the beginning of the revolution.

POLICY AND THE REBELLION

Formal and informal power structures

Hafez al-Assad focused on institution-building and development and in 1973 promulgated a new constitution. He built an authoritarian, centralist, and hierarchical system, with the military, the security services, and the Ba'th party as the main pillars of power, over which he presided. According to the constitution, the president is the primary decision-maker, the primary source of power, the highest military commander, and the secretary general of the Ba'th party. The president nominates and dismisses the Cabinet.[1] The heads of the different security services report directly to the president. This guaranteed the president a high degree of autonomy since all of the institutions from which a challenge to his rule might emerge were firmly under his control. Through this process of institution-building, Hafez al-Assad created a degree of internal stability that allowed for the development of a Syrian foreign policy (Perthes 1995, p. 4).

Alongside his control over the institutions of governance, the president maintained an informal circle of advisors consisting partly of high-ranking officials but also including other trusted individuals, such as family members. Loyalty was the most important criterion for membership of this group, and once someone had become part of the core circle they tended to remain there for a long time. This could best be seen in case of the key formal office-holders under Hafez al-Assad, all of whom also stayed into the first years of Bashar's rule: Minister of Defense Mustafa Tlass, who retired after thirty-two years in office in 2004; Abdel Halim Khaddam, vice president from 1984 to 2005; and Farouk al-Sharaa who served as foreign minister for twenty-two years and was promoted to vice president in 2006.[2] In his first years in power Bashar left central positions untouched and later on stuck to the same family and loyalty-oriented pattern of recruitment as his father.[3] Bashar al-Assad also retained the same personal secretary that Hafez al-Assad chose in the 1970s.

A major difficulty in understanding the Syrian political processes was always to discern who actually belongs to the political leadership and the decision-making procedures, since the formal position of an individual did not necessarily correspond to his or her de facto importance. Syria expert Eyal Zisser described this as a "dual power system"—the formal system of government is paralleled by an informal system in which power is exerted through the heads of the security services, senior army officers, members of the president's family, and other persons with access to influential officials (Zisser 1998, p. 8).

This is partly also reflected in the role some of the institutions subsequently assumed. Hafez al-Assad, coming from a military background in the Air Force, relied heavily on his former companions there, which resulted in a much broader role for Air Force Intelligence. Along with the Palestinian Branch of the General Security—officially only in charge of monitoring Palestinian activities in Syria—the Air Force Intelligence became the most notorious of the agencies when it came to the brutal persecution of the internal opposition; many of those arrested by either of these branches disappeared or were returned to their families after having been tortured to death, the latter serving to scare citizens away from potentially suspicious activities.

Different members of the security institutions also played a role in foreign policy, a fact Syrian scholar Radwan Ziadeh underlines, while the role of the foreign minister in the policy-making process was reduced to carrying out presidential decisions:

The unspoken aspect of Syrian foreign policy is in the role played by military and security organizations in making foreign-policy decisions. It is generally not mentioned in the media, though all the political players, observers and even foreign diplomats are aware of it; some even assume that the military and security organizations in fact make the final decisions. (Ziadeh 2011, p. 80)

Political participation

Elections in Syria—whether the presidential referendum or the parliamentary elections—left little room for surprise in terms of their results. In the presidential referendum, held every seven years, the Regional Command of the Ba'th party nominated a single candidate, and results were always above 97 per cent.[4] In the parliamentary elections the Ba'th party and a number of smaller parties formed the "Progressive National Front" (PNF), running a joint list in elections with the majority of seats reserved for them.[5] A smaller number was reserved for "independent" candidates. The parliament did not act independently of the president, but merely served to rubber stamp policy.

That also meant, however, that there was no routine mechanism to monitor public opinion. In the absence of legal outlets for public discontent, political participation was possible only in the space defined by the government. The autonomy of the government from its citizens came at the expense of a permanent feeling of insecurity. It is in this context that former US Special Envoy Dennis Ross recalled how two of Hafez al-Assad's confidants came to the president to inform him about the death of his son Basil. He saw from their faces that something had happened. As Ross relates: "At this point, Hafez al-Assad had been ruling Syria for twenty-four years. And yet, Assad's first instinct … was to ask if it was a coup. This was not a man who felt secure. This was not a man immune to a sense of conspiracy" (Ross 2004, p. 141).

Political stagnation

Avoidance of change was understood by Hafez al-Assad as a guarantor of stability and continuity. The downside was the political stagnation that befell Syria in the 1980s.[6] With a few exceptions, the ruling elite had grown older while ruling over an increasingly youthful society, and personal continuity in the higher ranks of institutions blocked promotions. With a birth rate of 2.5 per cent/year, the gerontocratic elite in 2000 already faced a population in which an estimated 41 per cent were under the age of fifteen (CIA World Fact Book 2000). While averse to change, Hafez al-Assad was interested in creating ideal conditions for a smooth succession, and in the late 1990s he cut back the power of some influential officials. Maybe the clearest example of this was the transfer of the Lebanese portfolio to Bashar from Vice President Khaddam in 1998, a move designed to shift the balance of power away from Khaddam and toward his son.[7] He also changed the leadership of different intelligence services, replacing functionaries who could question Bashar's legitimacy.[8]

The top political priority for Hafez al-Assad was security, understood as regime security, but also national security. Regime survival was and is Syria's top priority, and this defines what is perceived as a security threat: "The over-riding, all-pervading objective has been the maintenance of the regime: not out of any particular sense of responsibility to the populace at large, not in the service of any particular grand vision, but simply as an end in itself" (George 2003, p. 9). Any other topic, including the economy, was of secondary importance, and thus he did not allow economic interests to shape Syrian foreign policy, regardless of the situation of the Syrian people. Though this partly explains why the regime was able to endure the sanctions imposed in the 1980s, Hafez al-Assad was also highly successful in obtaining external revenues from his foreign policy choices: in the 1970s, Syria received funding from the Gulf States because of its "frontline status" in the conflict with Israel, and in the 1980s it received discounted Iranian oil for its support in the Iran–Iraq War. The 1991 Gulf War provided a new opportunity for mobilizing payments from the Gulf States, even though the result was less durable than might have been expected.[9] In the early 1990s, the rise in oil prices helped Syria to overcome its economic crisis and, recognizing the inevitability of economic reform, Hafez al-Assad introduced investment law no. 10 in 1991, which was intended to ease and encourage foreign investment and a limited liberalization in Syria. Political developments on the international and regional level reduced the opportunities for rent-seeking over the 1990s.

Ideology and pragmatism

Hafez al-Assad always promoted pan-Arab solidarity, but he was acting more on pragmatic than ideological grounds.[10] Too much adherence to ideology would have limited his freedom of action. Flexibility, however, was required to adapt strategically to newly arising problems and crises. Therefore, regarding intra-Arab issues, Hafez al-Assad did not hesitate to override public opinion. His interventions in Jordan and Lebanon against the PLO and his support for the non-Arab side in the Iran–Iraq War and the 1991 Gulf War are illustrative examples of this.[11] In these cases, Hafez al-Assad opted for what he deemed to be the strategically better choice in terms of the national interest.

The only foreign policy issue for which Hafez al-Assad ever argued that he needed to take domestic public opinion into consideration was Syrian–Israeli relations. The peace negotiations were of special delicacy for the Syrian government. Having always asked for a "just and comprehensive peace," and presenting himself as "most steadfast" vis-à-vis Jerusalem, it was important for Assad to maintain this image in the peace process. The best accounts of this are given by Henry Kissinger, James Baker, and Dennis Ross.[12] While tacitly preparing the Syrian public for the prospects of peace he stressed that he would not move ahead without the knowledge and consent of the population (al-Assad 1993). Assad explained to Baker in dramatic terms what might happen if he acted against public opinion: "We will lose Arab domestic public opinion ...

This would not only be adventurism, it would be a form of suicide. It is one thing to adopt a suicidal policy if it brings benefits to the people, but it is truly foolhardy if there is no positive result" (Baker 1995, pp. 456f).

Baker rejected the notion that Hafez al-Assad had to take into account what other Syrian officials, let alone the Syrian public, thought. When the Syrian president said that he could not decide a point without consultations within state institutions and the Progressive National Front, Baker noted: "It was, I knew, the ultimate brush-off; there was no one in the Syrian Arab Republic with whom Assad needed to consult, except himself." Kissinger, who had negotiated the Syrian–Israeli disengagement agreement of 1974, and Ross, on the other hand, take the Syrian president's concern for public opinion seriously: "[B]ecause Assad genuinely worried about how he was perceived, he worried that any gestures toward Israel might be perceived as personal weakness in a way that could be exploited by potential rivals; he was dead set against giving anything away" (Ross 2004, p. 142).

Bureaucracy

The Syrian bureaucracy was never considered a reliable entity and therefore was not power-relevant. It was heavily overstaffed and inefficient. Relevant qualifications were of secondary importance to party membership or personal networks. The strong parallel network of interests and influence made it risky to take decisions that might interfere with the personal interests of influential personalities. Whenever there was a conflict between what legislation demanded and the personal interests of a high-ranking personality, the employee in charge risked his position (Perthes 1995, p. 143). Individual initiative was rare and unwelcome. The administration could not serve any filtering function. Routine decisions had the potential to reach the highest levels of decision-making, and not even ministers had the backing of the government if they took legally correct but undesired decisions (Perthes 1995, p. 144).

The higher administrative levels were flooded with matters of minor importance. The lack of dynamism in the lower ranks was matched by the unwillingness of superiors to delegate work and their interest in handling even routine decisions in all their details (Perthes 1995, p. 143). As a consequence, chief administration officials were so overwhelmed by the sheer number of issues that there was little room to develop long-term strategies. In his June 2011 speech, Bashar al-Assad finally gave this problem some attention, calling upon ministers to leave micro-management to their subordinates for the sake of improved performance (al-Assad 2011c).

These general impediments also haunted Syrian foreign policy-making. According to James Baker, who as Secretary of State dealt with the Syrian government within the Middle East peace process, "no detail in our discussion could ever be too small" for Assad to take care of it personally (Ross 2004, p. 142). This made it difficult for the system to react to challenges, not to mention policy planning. It also contributed to Syrian policy as such becoming much more reactive than active

Ethnic and religious diversity

The Syrian regime has always prided itself on the peaceful coexistence of groups with various ethnic and religious backgrounds. Sunni Arabs form the majority of the population with an estimated 70 per cent. Among religious minorities, Christians, who comprise around 10–12 per cent of the population, are the largest minority group, but are subdivided into a variety of different churches, followed by Alawites (7–8 per cent), and smaller numbers of Druze and Ismailis.[13] The largest ethnic minority is the Kurds, with an estimated 2 million people (10–11 per cent of the total population). Moreover, Syria has a history of open doors for refugees from neighboring countries. In the early twentieth century a considerable Armenian minority arrived in the country, at that time fleeing from persecution in the crumbling Ottoman Empire. The 1948 Palestinian refugees number about 400,000 today, and in recent history, the largest community, of about 1 million refugees, came from Iraq after the war in 2003.

The Syrian state defines itself as secular. Article 35 of the constitution guarantees freedom of faith and of religious rites. Only the head of state by the constitution has to be a Muslim. Any mention of differences was taboo because of its presumed potential to cause unrest: the government printed Muslim and Christian textbooks and provided religious instruction; the religious holidays of Muslims and Christians were public holidays; and religious buildings were exempted from paying taxes and received free electricity. The secular strategy of the regime even extended to descriptions of groups such as Hamas or Hezbollah as "nationalist," rather than using their self-reference of "Islamic" (Ibrahim Hamidi in al-Hayat, 2004).

POLICY AND THE REBELLION

As a legacy of the French mandate, in the first decade after independence minorities had a strong presence in politics and in the military. The rise of Arab nationalism in the 1950s and the Syrian–Egyptian unification of 1958–61 led to a purge of minority members in key positions, a change that particularly affected the Kurds.[14] Regardless of its rhetoric, under the Assads there has always been political discrimination. When Hafez al-Assad, himself a member of the Alawite minority, assumed power he strongly relied on other minorities. Particularly in sensitive areas such as the "saraya ad-dif'a," a special defense squad to protect the capital and the government from domestic threats, he preferred members of minorities to the Sunni majority, and by defining the state as the "Syrian Arab Republic" he ultimately denied Kurds full citizenship rights.[15]

Kurds in Syria

The most sensitive domestic issue, however, has been Kurdish affairs, due to its relationship with foreign policy, particularly after the 1991 Gulf War and the ensuing Kurdish quasi-autonomy in northern Iraq. This elicited fear that separatist tendencies could affect Syrian territorial integrity. The Kurdish community was not recognized as an integral part of Syrian society. While the Armenian population was allowed to use and teach their own language, Kurds were not. Unlike the Palestinian refugees, Kurds were not eligible for careers in the military and administration. The government seems to be more at ease with integrating foreigners—especially when they are Arabs—than in accepting a genuinely resident non-Arab community.[16]

Kurds in Syria live mainly in the north-eastern border region, in Qamishli and Hassake, along the Turkish border, and in Ifrin and its surroundings—areas President Hafez al-Assad never visited. In its determination to avoid territorial disintegration, the Syrian government has opted for a repressive rather than an integrative course with respect to Syrian Kurds. Most unfortunate in this context was the fate of a group that currently comprises around 200,000 Kurds, the so-called "Maktumin." This group does not have Syrian citizenship, which goes back to an unannounced census in 1962: whoever on the day of the census was not at home was stripped of Syrian citizenship, whether or not others in their family were considered Syrian citizens.[17] While on an individual basis the citizenship could be recovered, a systematic approach to solve this problem has never been implemented.[18] Without citizenship, this group is deprived of civil rights. The only official document that stateless Kurds can obtain in Syria is a kind of birth certificate—a paper confirming that their existence is known to the Syrian authorities. They do not have travel documents and are prevented from owning land or businesses. They are excluded from higher education and thereby from many professions.

This has increased Kurdish opposition. As Syrian expert Montgomery writes about the contradictory Syrian practice of demanding loyalty while carrying out a discriminatory policy:

In a somewhat paradoxical relationship, the Syrian state denies the national identity of the Kurds, which cannot be accommodated within the legitimizing rhetoric of Arabism, and seeks to incorporate Kurds within the state as Arabs and as individuals. ... Because the Kurds also have trans-state as well as sub-state loyalty, this, in turn distinguishes them as a potential threat to the identity and security of the state (Montgomery 2005, p. 70).

Despite his discomfort and mistrust of the Syrian Kurds, until 1998 the Syrian government supported the Kurdistan's Workers Party (PKK) in Turkey and had close relations with its leader Abdullah Öcalan. This was a strategic choice to pressure Ankara. Similarly, in the 1990s, Syria gave safe haven to a variety of Iraqi opposition groups, among them activists from the KDP and PUK, with the aim of weakening Saddam Hussein. This means that Syrian concern regarding Kurdish aspirations is a product not only of its domestic but also its foreign policy: with the Syrian government's policy of supporting Turkish and Iraqi Kurdish groups against their respective governments, it seems logical to assume that other states could do the same with Syrian Kurds.

From father to son

The system that Hafez al-Assad created, with institutions tailored to his needs and to be ruled over by him in an authoritarian and highly personal style, raised questions regarding what would come after him, particularly after his son Basil, groomed as a successor, died in a car accident in 1994. Over the 1990s it became clear that he wanted to keep rule "in the family," preparing for his second son, Bashar, to take over. When Hafez al-Assad died in 2000, Bashar's inauguration was observed with a mixture of concern as to whether he would be able to fill this position and hope that—due to his Western education—he would become a political reformer. Even though Bashar lacked authority, experience, and the military and political credentials to move into his father's position, and a constitutional change lowering the president's minimum age was required, due to his father's preparations there was no open challenge to his becoming president.

Verbally, Bashar al-Assad focused on continuity. In his inaugural speech in front of the People's Assembly, he said that development could only take place based on the achievements of his late father. With regard to foreign policy, he invoked pan-Arab unity, explained the Syrian stance on the Middle East conflict, mentioned the issue of Lebanon, and briefly called upon the United States to engage for peace.

With regard to government officials, Bashar al-Assad continued his father's restructuring of political personnel through co-optation, removal through retirement, and promoting hardliners to positions in which their formal status was upgraded but their de facto influence diminished.[19] Launching the broadest retirement program since 1970 and promoting lower- and middle-rank personnel proved an effective method for Bashar al-Assad to create his own base of loyalty. In 2003/4, Bashar al-Assad appointed more than thirty new ambassadors. Especially those in important locations, such as Washington, London, and the United Nations, had the reputation of being not only highly qualified but excellent communicators. The best example was perhaps the Syrian ambassador to the United States, Imad Moustapha. In contrast to his predecessors, he often appeared on television discussing political issues in public and ran his own blog, supporting the image that Bashar al-Assad wanted to create for Syria: a country which was catching up with modernity.[20]

In the administrative sector there were only minor reforms. After 2000, Bashar al-Assad allegedly signed a vast number of reform-oriented laws and decrees, many of which were never implemented. Some observers believed that this was due to deliberate hindrance by backward-oriented elements within the apparatus.[21]

Divisive economic reforms

Bashar al-Assad inherited a Syria facing daunting economic problems.[22] Thus much of his efforts were dedicated to revitalizing the ailing economy. The priorities were privatization and a stronger integration of Syria into the world economy, which mainly resulted in a reduction in subsidies without creating new jobs. He recognized the importance of qualifications for performing meaningful reforms and removed the criterion of party membership for appointment to certain positions. Expert expatriates like Abdullah Dardari, Nabras Fadel, and Issam Za'im were brought back to the country, and they subsequently worked toward a gradual modernization. Fadel soon stepped down, complaining about the Syrian intelligence's interference with his work, and Za'im was forced to leave his post as minister of industry in 2003 due to a decision he made in favor of foreign investment that conflicted with individual domestic interests.[23] Cases like this had a stultifying effect on the rest of the administration and showed that even if there was political will to implement change, it had its limits. On the Corruption Perceptions Index published by Transparency International, Syria fell in the rankings from 66 (2003) to 129 (2011).[24] If the aim was to attract more foreign investment in the rankings, this was problematic since investors need a reliable base on which to operate.[25] The lack of (a) transparency, (b) the rule of law, and (c) an independent judicial system was, accordingly, an internal matter with an external dimension.

The awarding of licenses turned into a tool for patronage under Bashar. The political and business spheres increasingly merged, with major companies being run by the "sons and daughters of the Ba'this' nomenklatura," who chose business careers rather than following their fathers in political or military careers.[26] Instead of broader participation and a wider distribution of power among more actors, what was happening was the concentration of power through the blurring of distinctions between the political and economic elite. At the same time, the loss of illicit trade revenues from Iraqi oil after 2003 and the absorption of a massive wave of Iraqi refugees imposed an additional burden on the Syrian economy, a situation compounded further by US sanctions imposed after 2005.

The widening gap in the distribution of wealth became an important social question. The growing number of young people created increasing pressure on the economy. The official rate of unemployment in 2010 was 8.3 per cent. And even those who were in employment were often guaranteed only minimal living standards: "Official data suggests that nearly 70 per cent of the workforce earns less than US$ 100 a month, with some 40 per cent of public-sector employees taking second jobs to boost their income," the Economist Intelligence Unit's country profile stated in 2010 (EIU Country Profile 2010, p. 31). With inflation and increasing prices for housing in particular, as well as for consumer goods, the situation became more and more difficult for large segments of the Syrian population in the years before the revolution.

The government failed to address socio-economic problems systematically. It raised state employees' salaries several times before the revolution while at the same time trying to decrease reliance on state employment. In the absence of job alternatives, the government's announcement in 2004 that engineers would no longer have guaranteed state jobs caused protests. A further important reason for social discontent was to be found in the ability of privileged individuals to pursue their interests more recklessly and to flaunt their privileges more openly than was possible under Hafez al-Assad.

Managing external crises at home

In the Syrian population there is a sense of belonging to a wider Arab nation, an awareness of the injustice the Palestinian people has experienced, a perception of Israel as an aggressive state and of the United States as Israel's main sponsor, and a sense of victimhood and a responsibility to defend a cause to which no Arab can be indifferent. As Volker Perthes argues, one of the reasons that identification with these issues is so high is that they have remained vivid in the Syrian memory through constant repetition on the news and in political speeches (Perthes 2000). Government rhetoric highlighting resistance and a common Arab cause against perceived external conspiracies has therefore always appealed to large segments of the Syrian population.

The most crucial issue with a connection between foreign and domestic policy for Bashar al-Assad has been the 2003 Iraq War, which forced Bashar to choose between international cooperation and public opinion. Syria felt threatened by the assertive US policy in light of the Iraq War, and by the prospects of a prolonged presence of American troops in the neighboring country. In this situation the regime did not want to risk internal destabilization. As is discussed in detail in the chapter on relations with the United States, Syrian officials not only opposed the war but adopted an overtly hostile attitude to the US administration—a stance that earned them applause in the Arab arena. While jeopardizing its ties with other Arab countries and the United States, Syrian foreign policy in this case strengthened the Syrian regime domestically. Only by taking into consideration the domestic dimension can one understand why Syrian officials became so explicit in their criticism and did not—as did other states in the region—simply lie low.

More than just appealing to its domestic audience, in times of external crisis, the Syrian regime has requested support from all domestic actors. Thus during the 2005 crisis—see the chapter on Lebanon—the president emphasized that critics were traitors who would be held responsible:

One example, a person raises his voice in harmony with voices coming from outside his country and lowers it also in harmony with outside voices. This person belongs to the outside. How can he be a patriot and connected to the outside. Those who raise their voices should do that according to certain principles and according to national principles. Voices should be raised within the same house not in harmony with outside voices. I do not allow anyone to raise his voice from the outside and be called a patriot. We will deal firmly with unpatriotic cases, because these cause confusion at times of crises. (al-Assad 2005c)

Regardless of this tough rhetoric, internal repression has not automatically increased in periods when the Syrian regime has faced intense external pressure. After the war in Iraq in 2003, when fears were high that Syria could be next in line for a US-led wave of regime change and the power constellation on the international and regional level rendered the Syrian government vulnerable, the regime refrained from adopting an overly assertive domestic course. This has been confirmed by human rights lawyer Razan Zeitouneh at various points in time, among them the tense period after the assassination of former Lebanese Prime Minister Rafiq Hariri. According to Zeitouneh, in the two months following the incident there was a lessening of pressure, manifested by the smaller number of summons from the security services.[27] The peak in the wave of arrests came a year later, when international attention had decreased.

The Iraq War brought two other factors with a foreign element to the domestic agenda: the Kurdish issue and Islamism. Kurdish autonomy in Iraq and the even stronger self-consciousness of Iraqi Kurds after 2003 served to influence Syrian Kurds and became an issue in March 2004. At a soccer match between the Kurdish soccer team al-Jihad and the Arabic team al-Fatwa in Qamishli, fans of the two teams clashed: the al-Fatwa fans had allegedly provoked the Kurds by praising Saddam

Hussein. Several people died in the clashes. Later, an Assad statue was vandalized and several official buildings attacked, stormed, or set on fire. In response, Syrian police arrested several thousand Kurds, some of whom remained in prison for a year. This showed how nervous the Syrian regime was about developments in Iraq.[28]

Interestingly, the Syrian government did not claim that this incident was a result of foreign powers' efforts to stir up unrest. In an interview with al-Jazeera, the Syrian president declared with uncommon clarity that investigations had confirmed the absence of external involvement (al-Assad 2004b). Realizing that the Kurdish issue had the potential to get out of control, the government tried a different strategy, making hasty promises to work on a solution (al-Assad 2004b). In June 2004 the Syrian government announced that all unofficial Kurdish parties would be disbanded. The Kurdish leaders did not protest publicly but continued their activities, and the Syrian government did not enforce its decision. For the time being the Kurdish issue seemed to have vanished from the agenda, and it was to return only with the onset of the revolution.

With a growing trend in the region towards greater conservatism and sectarianism, the Syrian government on the one hand felt a need to highlight its Islamic credentials. It did not abandon its rhetoric of secularism, but the president tried to show increased religious commitment, for example by highly publicized visits to mosques during Ramadan. In 2003, legislation was changed to allow military personnel to pray while on duty. Yet in practice the Syrian regime has remained suspicious of religious activity and has sought to control Islamist trends in Syria by following a strategy of incorporating religious instruction. The official institution for religious study for foreign students was the Grand Mufti Sheikh-Ahmad-Kuftaro Center. With the "Qubeissiyat," a religious women's circle was established to extend control to women's activity (Khatib 2011).

Far more problematic for the regime was its decision to recruit foreign fighters in Syria and abroad. Busloads of "volunteers" travelled to Iraq from and via Syria. One of the religious personalities allegedly involved on a massive scale in their recruitment in Syria was Mahmoud al-Aghasi, also known under his *nom de guerre* Abu Qaqa, acting as a sheikh in Aleppo. Rumor later spread that he was cooperating with Syrian authorities by providing them with data on those who went to Iraq, thus contributing to their arrest in case of return. The regime was interested in using them to pressure the United States in Iraq, but it was also afraid that they could become active in Syria. In 2005, the minister for religious endowments removed Qaqa from his post, but he was reinstalled soon afterwards—allegedly by the security services. Abu Qaqa was assassinated in Aleppo on 28 September 2007, under circumstances that remain unclear.[29] Thus despite its efforts to utilize Islam to gain more credibility in the eyes of Syria's Sunni population, the regime's tight control over Islamist organizations, and its attempts to use Islamists as part of its policy towards Iraq, have ultimately proven highly counterproductive.

Operating in "grey areas": "traditional" opposition and civil society

In the beginning of Bashar's presidency there were some steps towards a political opening. In November 2000, 600 political prisoners were released, leaving the number of political prisoners—according to a Syrian human rights activist—between 500 and 1,000.[30] The two most notorious prisons, Tadmor and Mezzeh Airport, were closed down. There was a brief period of relative openness and tacit governmental encouragement to speak out. This was soon curbed, however, and political freedoms remained at the mercy of the government. The regime made occasional concessions but these were never formally guaranteed through legislation. By preserving its ability to interfere arbitrarily with the personal freedom of any individual, the Syrian regime retained its grip on the population.

Syria does not have any official legislation regarding political parties, thereby limiting political participation to the Ba'th and a few other, affiliated legal parties. The opposition and civil society were confined to operating in a "grey area" of partially tolerated illegality. As a reaction to Bashar al-Assad's call for constructive criticism, improvement, and renewal of old ideas and the introduction of new ones (al-Assad 2000), discussion forums for political and economic issues emerged, mainly in Damascus and Aleppo.

Even though only small groups of intellectuals and activists were involved, the regime soon feared a loss of control, closing the forums and arresting some of the leading figures. In January 2001, the Syrian minister of information explained to journalists that the newly emerging civil society organizations were tools of the foreign embassies that supported them, stating: "Neo-colonialism no longer relies on armies" (*al-Hayat*, 30

January 2001). One month later, the president underlined this suspicion in an interview in order to justify the government's clampdown:

When the consequences of any action affect stability at the level of a country there are two possibilities: one that the actor is an agent who is working against the interests of the state and he is either ignorant or doing it without intending to do so. The result is that in both cases the person will be serving the enemies of his country. ... Here the person will be held fully responsible regardless of his intentions and backgrounds.[31]

In particular the arrest of two members of parliament strained recently improved relations between Syria and Western states, and the calls for their release remained unanswered.[32]

The "traditional" opposition consisted mainly of outlawed political parties, intellectuals, and civil society activists, many of which had served long sentences in prison. Under the leadership of Hassan Abdul Azeem a group of six opposition parties referred to as the "National Democratic Rally" was active, and there are also Kurdish parties of various sizes. Dissidents often chose to work on civil society matters and established non-governmental organizations (NGOs). This did not protect them from governmental persecution, however.

It was decreed that only registered NGOs were eligible for financial support from abroad and that meetings of foreign representatives with projects in Syria could be held only in the presence of a Syrian official. In theory, NGOs can obtain licenses at the Syrian Ministry for Labor and Social Affairs, but authentic civil society organizations in many cases have not been registered. Instead, the government invented a do-it-yourself approach, establishing "quasi"-NGOs (QNGOs) that were run by relatives of regime members. The largest umbrella organization was "Syria Trust," run by the first lady Asma al-Assad; organizations that formed part of this coalition were thus referred to as "First Lady Organizations." As analyst Ammar Abdulhamid states:

NGOs such as the Syrian Young Entrepreneurs Association, MAWRED, FIRDOS, and a host of others are good examples of this. Publications such as Syria Today, sites such as Cham Press, Syria News are all attempts to crowd out the real independent civil society organizations.[33]

In the Syrian government's specific understanding of pluralism, the existence of one organization of this kind was considered sufficient to fulfill the requirements of pluralism.[34] Legal foreign funding thus remained the privilege of QNGOs.

Despite the odds, in several instances the opposition groups tried to overcome their differences and sign common petitions. The "Statement of the 99" of September 2000 and the "Statement of the 1000" published in January 2001 were the first significant petitions, demanding political reforms and asking for the abolition of martial law. This was also the first time in Syria that dissidents had expressed their views publicly without an immediate government reaction.[35] Soon after the "Statement of the 1000," however, the Syrian president declared his disapproval of the attempt by opposition groups to communicate publicly and "through foreign channels."[36] The signature of the "Damascus Declaration" in October 2005 was a historic step since it included the whole range of Syrian society, Arab and Kurdish groups, Islamists, and secular groups, inside and outside Syria.[37] The declaration asked for a gradual, peaceful transformation and outlined its ideas for this. The regime's decision to respond with arrests and the dismissal of its signatories might be an indication of the broad resonance that the declaration found within Syrian society.[38]

In an unprecedented move, 150 Syrian intellectuals in 2005 for the first time signed a foreign policy-related petition to Bashar al-Assad, addressing the sensitive issue of Lebanon and asking for new political solutions. A similar resolution was signed by Syrian and Lebanese intellectuals in 2006. The Syrian regime, not fond of voices of dissent and even less so when they touched upon sensitive foreign policy matters, persecuted the individual signatories. Repression by the Syrian government made opposition activity extremely difficult. The opposition has also contributed to its own weakness, however, by allowing the regime to have such a powerful influence on relations among its different groups. As Syrian analyst Wael Sawah candidly remarks: "In the Bible, God created Man in his own image; in Syria, it is the government who created the opposition in its own image."[39]

Indeed, in some regards the resemblance is striking: Syrian opposition leaders have aged together without recruiting from the younger generation. They do not trust each other, and until 2011 much of their discussions revolved around questions like Arab nationalism, the Arab–Israeli conflict, and anti-Americanism. Instead of developing political programs for addressing the most pressing socio-economic questions and scenarios for change, opposition groups spent much of their time on matters about which there is actually no dissent with the government, such as the Syrian position towards Israel or the rejection of foreign intervention in the region.[40]

In some cases, the opposition has used the congruency of its views with those of the government cleverly. In 2002, it organized pro-Palestinian demonstrations and in 2003 anti-war protests—since both were core points of populist governmental policy, the authorities could not forbid the protests. At the same time it was embarrassing for the government that it was the opposition that had organized the events. Thus it organized parallel mass protests to drown out the opposition.[41]

Fertile ground for a revolution

During his first ten years in office, it became clear that Bashar al-Assad was not willing to implement profound changes. A tacit political opening was nipped in the bud; administrative reforms were half-hearted and failed to produce visible results. Significant reforms took place only in the economic sector, where an ever more bluntly displayed nepotism enhanced societal divisions and marginalized increasing sectors of the Syrian population.

The government's policy with regard to Islamism antagonized secularists, while its manipulative use of Islamism in external relations diminished its credibility in the eyes of the domestic Islamic constituency.

There was also a lack of success stories in foreign policy that could have made up for the regime's domestic shortcomings. While the Syrian government earned some popularity from its stance in the 2003 Iraq War, the forced withdrawal from Lebanon in 2005 showed the limits of Syria's external power, a fact that was also underlined by several instances in which Israel bombarded sites in Syria. The alliance with Iran was strong but not popular. In a material and an immaterial sense, Bashar's system of governance was simply unable to offer Syrian citizens what they needed and desired.

The "intifada of dignity"

The revolution showed that neither external observers nor the Syrian government itself were aware of the level of discontent. The initial small-scale protests in Syria failed to acquire much momentum until March 2011. A history of forty years of authoritarian rule, a small, well-known "traditional" opposition, which was not sure whether this would be the right time, and the tight control of the security services all seemed to indicate that Syria would remain calm. In an interview with the *Wall Street Journal* in February 2011, Assad himself expressed confidence that there would not be an uprising due to the close connection between the Syrian government and its people. Furthermore, the Syrian population had experienced the impact of the toppling of the Iraqi regime and the ensuing sectarian violence as no other country in the region.

The revolution was sparked by children in the southern city of Daraa; inspired by what they saw on TV from other Arab countries, they sprayed anti-governmental graffiti and were arrested and tortured. Their fathers asked for their release but were humiliated by the local authorities, thereby fueling conflict with some of the most important families in Daraa. In the ensuing, large protests, the military shot indiscriminately at the crowd, killing people, and the central government responded half-heartedly. The case of thirteen-year-old Hamza al-Khateeb, who was arrested on the street and subsequently died from horrific torture, led to widespread outrage, especially when the government failed to investigate the case properly.

In the beginning, the demands of the protesters stopped short of asking for regime change, instead focusing on bringing to account those responsible for jailing and torturing the children in Daraa, on reforms, and on reining in corruption and nepotism. The Syrian efforts to regain control or at least scare the population into obedience have relied exclusively on the security forces. There has never been any visible political strategy for finding a solution, no dialogue, no mediation. The self-confidence of the regime, and its failure to recognize how serious the situation had become, was well illustrated on 30 March 2011, when Bashar al-Assad gave his first public speech since the onset of the revolution in the Syrian parliament, where the MPs laughed along with the president at his own jokes and applauded him.[42] Bashar al-Assad tried to belittle the incident, and was seen giggling even though people had already been killed. Furious at the president's failure to take their concerns seriously and encouraged by the successful public protests in hardline countries like Tunisia, Libya, and Egypt that had removed long-term authoritarian rulers, the rebellion spread all over Syria in what human rights activist Haitham al-Manna calls an "intifada of dignity" (Oudat 2011). It is unclear if the protestors' demands could have been settled had the situation been handled differently. The failure to address people's concerns in an appropriate manner, however, and the brutal response to peaceful protests, added fuel to the flames while introducing new dynamics to the protests.

The unprofessional handling of the crisis made things much worse for Syria on the international level as well. For weeks, President Assad ignored UN expressions of concern over the deteriorating situation. He called Secretary General Ban Ki-moon to promise an end to the violence only when it seemed that a resolution against Syria would be passed the next day. Due to the Chinese and Russian opposition to a resolution, a presidential statement by the UN was passed instead. And despite his hasty promises, the violence did not end. The Arab League peace plan, which Syria formally accepted on 2 November 2011, met with a similar reception. The very next day it became obvious that nothing had changed. Even after the Arab League's observer mission was allowed in, the Syrian regime did not stop its military operations. A member of the Revolutionary Committee of Homs stated that immediately before the arrival of the observers, the city was attacked by tanks "as if they wanted to flatten everything" (Haj Yahya 2012). In his interview with Barbara Walters on ABC News in the beginning of December, Bashar al-Assad left no doubt about his disrespect for the United Nations, saying it had no credibility and that he was merely considering it a "game": "It's a game you play. It doesn't mean you believe in it" (al-Assad 2011d).

Initial international sympathy with the revolution was based to some extent on the use of the creative means with which some of the groups gained additional coverage. Protesters wrote "Freedom" or "Democracy" on thousands of ping pong balls which they threw on the streets of the Damascene quarter of Muhajireen at night, from where they rolled down-hill right towards the presidential residence. When the authorities blocked the central place around the clock tower in the Khalidiya quarter of Homs where the protests had started, citizens built their own fake clock tower: "If we cannot go to the clock tower, the clock tower comes to us."[43] On the internet, satirical cartoons and serials like Masasit Mati's "Top Goon" appeared, brilliantly ridiculing Bashar al-Assad—something that nobody had dared to do before.[44] The citizens of the hitherto unknown Syrian village of Kafranbel became world famous with their cartoons and protest banners, many of which were directed at the international com-munity, mocking all sides for their mishandling of the crisis.

THE WISDOM OF SYRIA'S WAITING GAME

The previously described social disparities fueled part of the protests. As Syria expert Frida A. Nome explained in autumn 2011:

Many of those who are out on the streets now are people who in a material sense do not have so much to lose. This is one reason why so far Damascus and Aleppo are not so affected. People there are still relatively well off. Some have privileges from the government. They are not rich but can make their living, there is business, and there used to be tourism.[45]

At the same time, the protesters made it clear that economic improvements were not their main aim. After the first casualty in Daraa, governmental advisor Boutheina Shaaban announced a package of decisions and services the government had agreed upon. The protesters responded by inventing a rhyme in Arabic which translates to English as: "We don't want bread, we want dignity."[46]

The regime continued, however, to think it could appease the protesters with half-hearted reforms. After roughly a decade of talking about it, in summer 2011 a new law regarding political parties was announced that would no longer favor the Ba'th party. In the dramatic events of the year and after the killing and arrest of thousands of people, this seemed like a ridiculously small concession. The president nevertheless did not want to give the impression that the announced reforms were a reaction to the protests:

If there was no sedition wouldn't we have done these reforms? If the answer is yes, it means that the state is opportunistic, and this is bad. If we say that these things were made under the pressure of a certain condition or popular pressure, this is weakness. And I believe that if the people get the government to bow under pressure, it will bow to foreign pressure. (al-Assad 2011a)

He also added that the reforms that had been announced were nothing new but were based on the decisions of the Ba'th Party Regional Conference in 2005, the reason being "that the content of the decisions is not related to the crisis, it is related to our need for reform" (al-Assad 2011a).

At the beginning of the revolution, some of the opposition groups that were requesting negotiations regarding a transition were in touch with the office of Vice President Farouk Sharaa, who invited opposition leaders to attend a conference in June 2011. While some groups and individuals declined this invitation, other renowned opposition members like Tayeb Tizzini decided to attend. As Syrian scholar and opposition member Wael Sawah relates:

The conference produced good recommendations, but these were not followed by the Syrian government. Sharaa after the conference was sidelined, and the Syrian government's disrespect for the conference's recommendation undermined the credibility of those opposition members who believed in and advocated for negotiations about transition.[47]

Governmental advisor Boutheina Shaaban, who had also been in touch with the proponents of negotiations, was holding a series of meetings with senior opposition member Louay Hussein, but contact decreased after the opposition's conference in the Semiramis hotel in Damascus in July 2011; discussions continued for a while over the phone but had ceased altogether by autumn 2011.[48] A speech by Bashar al-Assad at Damascus University in June 2011 showed that the government did not consider a political solution appropriate:

They say that the security-based solution has failed, and consequently the state should proceed in the direction of the political solution. In fact, we in the state think that the solution should be political. ... But what identifies the method of solving the problem is not the state's view but the nature of the problem itself. It is not the state which wanted, desired, or forced those who are involved in acts of destruction; neither can we deal with those politically. This is not reasonable. (al-Assad 2011c)

With its outright refusal to even consider engaging in negotiations with the opposition, the government closed the door for a peaceful solution and contributed to divisions within the opposition.

Bashar al-Assad decided to hold a referendum on amendments to the constitution in February 2012, to be followed by parliamentary elections in May 2012. While previously, the regime's interest in elections had served the purpose of providing a façade of popular democracy to conceal the authoritarian nature of the regime, on this occasion, in contrast, they were designed to cover up the erosion of power, as part of the pretense that the regime was not facing an extraordinary situation in the country but could simply do business as usual.

The military coordination and strategy

Bashar al-Assad, according to Syria expert Eyal Zisser, "lacked interest in politics and the military" before being groomed for regime succession (Zisser 2007), when he was forced into a fast-track military career. It can be assumed that, for military expertise, he relied upon members of the "inner circle" with a more solid military background. One might expect that at times of deep crisis it would become clear who the decisive persons at the head of a system are. But this is not so in the Syrian case. Already in the 2005 crisis, when asked whether he was fully in charge, Bashar al-Assad answered irritably:

They [the people who claim he was not in charge, B.S.] say I am a dictator. So they should chose [sic]. You cannot be a dictator and not be in control. So if you are a dictator you are in full control, and if you are not in control you cannot be a dictator. (al-Assad 2005e)

When Bashar in his famous December 2011 ABC interview said that nobody was in command of the army, he might have unintentionally revealed the truth. Elite troops were pulled together to protect the presidential palace in Damascus and were sent to hotspots of the conflict; for the rest of the army it seems that no powerful players, openly or behind the scenes, orchestrated what was going on in Syria, but the regime simply gave the military and security services a free hand to act as they liked. This was supported by a 2011 Human Rights Watch report based on interviews with more than sixty Syrian army defectors who said they were ordered to quell the revolution "by all means necessary."[49]

From the outset, soldiers were given orders to shoot a certain number of protesters. The scale of violence constantly increased. Snipers turned central city roads into death zones, and as early as April 2011 tanks began to be deployed to several cities. From July 2012 on, aerial bombardments with fighter jets, first indiscriminately, and then deliberately, targeted civilians. In August 2012 Human Rights Watch reported on bakeries and people queuing in front of them becoming a major target, and a terrible case, involving more than ninety casualties in the village of Halfaya, made it to the headlines in December 2012.[50]

The government followed a strategy of gradual escalation. In contrast to Hafez al-Assad's brutal suppression of the uprising in Hama, where tens of thousands of people died within a few days, the death toll in the current crisis was initially kept at a low-level before increasing to over 1,000 victims a week from the end of 2012, thereby slowing the response from the international community. This strategy was also apparent on the domestic level in the regime's efforts to militarize the revolution through its deliberate targeting of pacifist elements within the Syrian resistance. In September 2011, for example, the activist Ghiath

Mattar, who had become famous for offering flowers and water to the Syrian army when it invaded the city of Daraya, was arrested by the security services. Days later, his body was dumped at his family's home—there were indications that he had been tortured to death. Activists in many instances defied getting dragged into a spiral of violence and revenge. After more than 200 victims died in a massacre in Daraya in 2012, protesters went out on the street carrying signs reading: "No matter what you do, we will not stray from our course. We will take you to trial in Free Syria."

Peaceful activism was a thorn in the side of the Syrian government since it contrasted with the regime's narrative of terrorists against which they had to fight. The Lebanese researcher Doreen Khoury, who carried out an in-depth study of Syria's grassroots activism and local forms of administration, came to the conclusion that the worst militant groups of the uprising were often not targeted by the regime because their radicalism and disrespect for the population played into the hands of the Syrian government:

Activists from the Damascus suburbs reported that regime forces often did not target FSA divisions who exhibited unsavory heavy-handed tendencies with locals, such as looting and imposing a "protection" levy on locals whose resentment was made worse by militias coming from different regions. By behaving like the hated "shabiha", these militias were considered by the regime as accomplishing its aim: turning local opinion against the opposition.[51]

Security in the revolution was first handled by the intelligence services and the Syrian army. When it became apparent that the Syrian army was unable to extinguish the sparks of revolution, the regime gave a free hand to several thousand private "mercenaries," mainly but not exclusively stemming from the Alawite community in the coastal areas. These militias, referred to as *Shabiha* (meaning specters), armed groups acting on behalf of the Syrian government and often entering villages along with the military, were perhaps the most important factor in escalating violence and instigating sectarian violence. As Yassin Haj Salah explains in his groundbreaking article on their background, the phenomenon of these mafia-like gangs is not new but entered a new dimension in the revolution (Haj Saleh 2012). The Shabiha were actively recruited and offered a good salary. In early January 2012, the financial auditor of the Ministry of Defense, Mahmood Suleiman Haj Haddad, defected and spoke about the regime's expenses for the Shabiha, saying they had been given 2 billion Syrian Pounds (roughly US$36 million). As one witness from Homs related:

In a company for metal works in Homs, according to a Sunni employee in early summer, the Alawite workers stopped showing up. Instead of getting 10,000 Syrian Pounds monthly salary, they now got 2,000 SP per day plus the opportunity to loot.[52]

Governmental funding was not their only source of income, however: private businessmen supported them, with payments often being made through real estate agencies (Nakkash 2013), and they were allowed to loot, with the goods later sold on what were dubbed "Sunni markets" in Homs and even Tartous.

In Homs in 2011, initiatives of elders and representatives of the different religions came together to demonstrate that they would not let the government drive a wedge between them.[53] Yet with the overwhelming amount of violence that the city experienced, this kind of initiative was unable to produce lasting results.

The regime, obsessed with its own survival, has given up the state's monopoly on the execution of force by tolerating and encouraging (if not ordering) the Shabiha's actions. Even in the unlikely event of regime withdrawal to a kind of Alawite state, it would not be in control and in power, but would instead find itself presiding over a mafia state with powerful, uncontrollable actors who are bound to follow only their private interests. The *Shabiha* have become most notorious through a number of massacres in Sunni villages in mixed confessional areas where they entered the villages after army raids and slaughtered civilians. Their sense of impunity became particularly obvious in the fact that they often not only film the atrocities they are involved in but have sold many of these videos to the Free Syrian Army in order to earn a few hundred dollars.[54] The merciless fighting by the Shabiha seems to be based on a realistic, although suicidal, assumption: for them, there is no future after any transition. Therefore, they are likely to fight for the regime with any means and until the end, which will be their end as well.

The opposition of the 2011 rebellion

During the rebellion in 2011, the question of outside support—a constant issue of dissent within the "traditional opposition"—became less controversial. This is mainly because the traditional opposition has begun to recognize the importance of outside support for the strength of the opposition as a whole: "The question of external support which attracted a lot of criticism in the past is now different because the more support you get the greater the action you will be able to take."[55]

Throughout the rebellion, Salafists, though limited in number, gradually became more visible. While some observers saw them as having hijacked the Syrian revolution, it may be more accurate to say that they hijacked media attention—partly due to their agenda, but to no lesser extent because of a special focus on them that blew their significance out of proportion. For groups advertising their Islamic credentials it was much easier to acquire funding, mainly from private donors in the Gulf States.

For the external opposition, which in early 2013 comprised a mix of the "traditional" opposition and representatives who have been long-term exiles, the current resistance to the regime has proven to be grossly inefficient—partly due to its members' internal disputes, but also its inability to cope with the rapidly changing situation on the ground, because of a lack of commitment to work with the emerging committees and local leaders, but partly also due to external meddling. For a long time, the French and the US government believed that having a "strong leader" would strengthen the opposition, when in fact it enhanced divisions and competition between long-standing opposition members, each considering themselves to be the most appropriate choice of leader—instead of strengthening the working ability first of the "Syrian National Council," which was later expanded (under US pressure) to the "National Coalition." Another example of foreign meddling is the rigid favoring of the Muslim Brotherhood by the government of Qatar, which has repeatedly announced that it will cut or increase its funding of local opposition groups depending on their support for Muslim Brotherhood candidates. This has upset Saudi Arabia, which is fearful of Qatar's dominance over any future authorities in Syria. Turkey in turn was—until early 2013—less concerned about the influx of foreign jihadis from their border into northern Syria than about any Kurdish aspirations.

Regime disintegration

During the conflict, the Syrian army has thinned out, through losses, but mainly through defections. According to an IISS study released in March 2013, the Syrian army has shrunk to half of its original size, with only half of its members being trusted by the regime. This is not something that Bashar al-Assad would admit to:

The armed forces have wrote [sic] down the epics of heroism thanks to their cohesion, steadfastness and national unity which reflected those of the people, thus doing citizens proud and keeping them safe. (al-Assad 2013a)

In contrast to the Libyan uprising, hardly any prominent political figures changed sides. This might be partly explained by the regime's precautions. In the summer of 2011, it was leaked that state officials who were not working in the foreign ministry had to return their diplomatic passports, among them Farouk al-Sharaa, Abdullah Dardari, and Mustafa Miro. This could not be confirmed independently, but when asked why those three specific individuals were requested to do so, one Syrian analyst said:

I am convinced that some officials are not happy with the security solution which leads to the killing of the Syrians. I am pretty sure that Sharaa and Dardari are among them. Miro, on the other hand, being the son of al-Tal, a city that is entirely against the government, is afraid because of the wealth, which he had illegally accumulated.[56]

Another reason may be the fear of the regime taking revenge on the families of defectors. In July 2012, rumor had it that Vice President Farouk al-Sharaa had defected and fled to Jordan, something that seemed to be supported by the fact that his hometown in Daraa was bombarded heavily for days before a visibly aged Sharaa made a TV appearance at the funeral of senior officials assassinated on 18 July in Damascus.

The assassinations on 18 July 2012 might actually have been the toughest blow to the inner circle of the regime, since, along with the president's brother-in-law Asef Shawkat and senior intelligence officer Hisham Bkhtiar, two central figures from the security establishment were also killed.

Foreign and domestic policy in light of the rebellion

When talking about external pressure on Syria in the wake of the protests in March 2011, Bashar al-Assad underlined that the strength of Syria had always been its unity, with the citizen as the link between foreign and domestic policy. The regime in these cases has always presented itself as the protector and defender of the Syrian people against external hostilities. When not giving in to external pressure, Bashar al-Assad said he that always referred to the will of the Syrian people:

When pressures intensified, I used to tell them that even if I accept this the people will not. And if the people do not accept it, they will reject me. And if they do, that means political suicide for me. (al-Assad 2011a)

This passage is clearly revealing—instead of arguing on the basis of Syrian interests, Bashar al-Assad mentions his own interest in staying in power.

Whereas Bashar al-Assad accused the revolutionaries of being "enemies of the homeland" (al-Assad 2013a), the Lebanese scholar Fawaz Traboulsi sees the timing of the revolution as an act of patriotism: "The Syrian peoples' greatness lies in the fact that it never failed in its patriotism. It did not rise up against regime and country when they were under threat during the American invasion of Iraq. It rose up once the armies of the US and her allies had withdrawn" (Traboulsi 2013).

For the Syrian activists inside Syria, the support of outside powers has become more and more important. Due to the hesitance of Western states to provide financial and material support, private and official sponsors from the Gulf States have played a major role, supporting mainly conservative and Islamist groups. At the same time, the Syrian government has become ever more dependent on its allies, Russia and Iran, to support it financially, as well as with military expertise and equipment.

Interestingly, during 2011 the protesters increasingly questioned the regime's relations with Israel. The protesters were mocking "Assad" (meaning lion) at home, and "arnab" (meaning rabbit) on the Golan, indicating that despite the government's fierce rhetoric against Israel, it had never taken action against the latter but was now using its military against its own people. In this situation, it was certainly not helpful for the regime that Israeli journalists referred to Assad as "Israel's favorite dictator" (Masalha 2011).

Kurds and the rebellion

Since 2003, on several occasions rumor had it that the stateless Kurds were about to be given citizenship and that a renewed census or another examination of Kurdish documents was planned. The government's handling of this issue was tactical. In times of high external pressure, any move by the Syrian government that would benefit its Kurdish population could serve as a conciliatory gesture that would stabilize the Syrian regime. The issue was thus kept on hold for a situation in which Syria had a dire need to demonstrate its good will:

The issue of granting citizenship to the Kurds that were deprived of it is something with which the Syrian government in a given moment can gather support. It is on and off the agenda because the regime does not want to give it just like that. They want to save it for an occasion in which they can get something from it.[57]

In March 2011 it seemed that this moment had come. Bashar al-Assad announced that the government would grant Syrian citizenship to stateless, registered Kurds (not mentioning the "Maktumin"), and some actually obtained this status (al-Assad 2011a, ICG Report 2013). Hence the regime clearly intended to keep the Kurds from joining the revolution.

Furthermore, at the beginning of the revolution the Assad regime revitalized its ties to the PKK, and it has given the PYD, the Syrian Kurdish party affiliated with the PKK, control over parts of northern Syria, particularly Ifrin. As analyst Bakr Sidki writes:

The head of the PKK in Syria, Saleh Muslim, returned to Damascus. Long pursued by the Syrian security agencies, he had lived for years in the Qandil Mountains in the far north of Iraq. It was said that a deal had been struck between the Kurdish party and the Syrian regime, marking a resumption of relations that had been suspended for thirteen years, since Öcalan's expulsion from Damascus in the autumn of 1998. (Sidki 2012)

Initially the participation of the Kurdish community in the revolution was comparatively minor. One Western diplomat in March 2011 explained:

Our Kurdish contacts had told us that in March, huge protests against the regime would start but they were not going to take part in them. One reason they mentioned was that they did not want to give any pretext to the regime to characterize this as a foreign movement. Another probably was that on previous occasions they had felt neglected by Arab groups.[58]

In October 2011 pro-revolutionary Kurdish leader Meshal Temmo was assassinated by masked men assumed to be acting on behalf of the Syrian government. When Temmo had been released from a Syrian prison shortly before his death, intelligence general Ali Mamlouk personally met him and told him that the regime would not object to greater Kurdish autonomy so long as the Kurds would in turn refrain from joining the uprising. Temmo did not follow the advice.[59] In the north-eastern areas, "Popular Defense Units" (YPG) organized by the PKK-affiliated PYD took control, established checkpoints, and persecuted revolutionaries. PYD fighters clashed with Islamist forces in Ras al-Ain in early 2013 until a truce was negotiated by Michel Kilo, a Christian leader of the "traditional" opposition. Although clashes between Kurdish groups in March and April 2013 make it difficult to get a clear picture of where Kurdish activists groups are heading (Van Wilgenburg 2013) the truce has been adhered to by both sides for months and seems to have been strengthened by the political breakthrough between the Turkish government and PKK leader Öcalan to end the civil war.

Turkey's role in supporting the Syrian uprising also served as an important factor in the initial Kurdish resistance. Due to Ankara's difficult relationship with the Turkish Kurds, all Syrian Kurdish parties boycotted the Syrian opposition summit held in Antalya on 31 May 2011, and only two Kurdish parties participated in the August convention in Istanbul at which the Syrian National Council was formed. The agreement between the SNC and the National Coordination Committee was especially criticized by Kurdish leaders for not containing any provisions regarding Kurdish rights in Syria.[60] On 18 January 2012, Fouad Alyko, a prominent member of the Kurdish Yekiti party, announced that none of the parties of the National Kurdish Council supported the Syrian opposition because of their refusal to include Kurdish rights in a new constitution (al-Watan, 19 January 2012).

While the Kurdish community has been discriminated against under Hafez and Bashar al-Assad, Kurdish groups remain anxious as to what can be expected from any future Syrian government. Relations with other opposition groups have been unstable, a situation fuelled by the mistrust that has permeated Syrian society for most of the Assad reign. Kurdish groups fear that Arabs will not advocate for their rights and might continue to consider them as "second class citizens." Arab groups are afraid of Kurdish separatist tendencies. Kurdish reluctance to support the revolution fully is likely to create conflict after the transition since this will give Kurdish parties little say in a future government. Having said that, it remains to be seen how the new rapprochement between the Syrian opposition and the Kurdish groups will develop over the longer term.

THE WISDOM OF SYRIA'S WAITING GAME

Whistling in the dark—the impact of sanctions

After two years of domestic protests and violence, the regime finds itself under considerable economic pressure. Two of the most important previous sources of income, tourism and oil exports, have nearly dried up. International sanctions on money transactions with the Syrian Central Bank have made it difficult for Syria to purchase much-needed goods. With the destruction of harvests and the impossibility of working the lands in some of the most fertile areas, shortages in the Syrian crops have unexpectedly forced Syria to import wheat, which due to international sanctions on the Syrian banks has become increasingly difficult. Sanctions are not new to the Syrian government; from the 1980s on Syria had been subject to different sanction packages imposed by different actors, the most recent of which being the sanctions the United States imposed in 2004 under the Syria Accountability Act. Those imposed since 2011, however, are different in that they are more encompassing and wide ranging; in contrast to the past, the Arab League has also been involved in their formulation and implementation. Asked about the impact of the current sanctions on Syria, President Bashar al-Assad gave a confusing answer. On the one hand, he said that Syria was not isolated, and having been under sanctions for the last thirty to thirty-five years, it would not be affected anyway. At the same time, he argued that other states were not implementing sanctions because this would make Syria collapse, which was not in their interest:

Nobody can … isolate Syria because of our position. That happened in 2005 and they couldn't, Bush tried to isolate Syria, Chirac, Blair, everybody. They couldn't, we have a role to play. We are related to two different problems. If they isolate Syria, Syria will collapse and … everybody will suffer, so they don't have interest to isolate Syria, we're not isolated. We've … been under … embargo for the last 30, 35 years, it's not something new, but it's fluctuating, up and down depending on the situation, those country that you're talking about, they have little influence on the situation in Syria. In reality, we're not isolated here. It's not implemented. They're going to suffer, the countries around Syria … suffer. (Bashar al-Assad 2011d)

Conclusion

Bashar al-Assad has been acting within the framework of institutions established by his father, and, despite an initial tacit political opening, he has effectively followed the path of authoritarian rule. The changes made in personnel in the years 2000–11 were simply designed to strengthen his position; they were attempts to improve Syria's image rather than a change of policy. Institutional inertia was one reason for this, but more important was the lack of a political will for extensive reforms. Al-Assad's focus was on economic reforms, the success of which, instead of strengthening his power, has been a major factor in preparing the ground for the revolution. With the aim of consolidating his power base, he focused on a small circle of beneficiaries, thereby ignoring the needs of the majority of Syrians.

In contrast to his father, in the case of the Iraq War he chose public opinion over foreign relations, thus putting Syria's security at risk in order to assure popular support. Yet at first glance, his way of dealing with the current domestic crisis—as a security threat, not a political challenge—has clearly been informed by the example of Hafez al-Assad, who ended the uprising in the 1980s by military means. However, although there is evidently a significant degree of "continuity," it has become obvious in this chapter that, in a number of respects, Bashar al-Assad has strayed from his father's path: he has relinquished the state's monopoly on the use of force by establishing the Shabiha, militias outside a command structure that would allow the state to control them. Rather than focusing militarily on protecting the center of power and Syria's borders, he has instead tried to retain some kind of control in all of the provinces, while withdrawing in mid-2012 from the northern border. This has created an opening for foreign fighters—making his allegations regarding the involvement of foreign interests in Syria a self-fulfilling prophecy. Another dangerous step has been the release of thousands of criminals and Islamist fighters first sent to Iraq and arrested on their return in the first months of the revolution, a step also taken in order to support his narrative of fighting terrorists, and with consequences that are beyond the control of the government.

The conditions of control and decision-making in general differ remarkably under Bashar al-Assad from those during his father's reign: under Hafez al-Assad, there was one person—and one person only—in control of decision-making, which enabled him to undertake radical policy shifts. Under Bashar, it is not clear who really takes decisions: he alone? Unlikely. Perhaps, then, it is the circle of seasoned generals, leading elite units of the army and the intelligence services, who distrust each other? His family, in particular his mother Anissa, as it is often speculated? Most probably a form of collective decision-making in one way or another is taking place, which surely has an effect on the regime's ability to change course (i.e. diminishing any chance to leave the beaten track).

Although it can only be speculated upon, given the authoritarian nature of the system, there is a possibility that Assad was not briefed on the real level of protests happening in other parts of the country, especially in the beginning, and it is this which led him to underestimate the size of the revolution. Furthermore, in his close circle of advisors—as far as can be judged—military and not political experts were of crucial importance, thus diminishing the prospects of a political resolution right from the start: those regime members in touch with parts of the opposition, Vice President Sharaa and advisor Boutheina Shaaban, were marginalized in the early months of the revolution, while his brother Maher, his brother-in-law Asef Shawkat, and the heads of the security services were part of the inner circle. On the international level, well-respected diplomat and Syrian Foreign Minister Walid al-Mouallim has hardly been visible. In any case, as the examples from the administration and bureaucracy have shown, the system under Hafez and Bashar al-Assad was not designed to encourage political initiative, and this has in turn prevented the kind of adaptation that might have led to a political solution.

The increasing overlap of the political and economic elites has left the regime's greatest support in the current crisis among the business elite, mainly in Damascus and Aleppo—apart from those enrolled with the regime to the extent that they feel they have nothing to gain in a new system, and perhaps the opposite. It is questionable, however, with the continuation of the crisis, and business opportunities being severely affected by the level of infrastructure and the burden of sanctions, whether this support can still be relied upon.

The government's tactic might be due to the Syrian regime's fear of external intervention. The regime's strategy of having a limited but constantly rising number of casualties every day, of gradually using more lethal forms of armament has, in a tragic sense, been successful: not only has the world's reaction been more muted than in other international cases with a single, large-scale massacre, but it has also developed a tolerance to the use of conventional but banned weaponry. Despite the fact that the majority of victims are civilians dying at the hands of the government, there is hardly any discourse on the "responsibility to protect."

POLICY AND THE REBELLION

As with other crises, the Syrian government has chosen to ignore external pressure and wait for international attention to focus on another conflict or change. While it is clear that there is no "way back" to the pre-revolutionary setting, at the time of writing it seems that this strategy has, once again, so far functioned rather well. The revolution has become militarized and "changed in flavor," with a democratic opposition that remains shattered and growing violent and extremist participation on the ground. The longer the conflict goes on, the more skeptical the international community will grow regarding the Syrian opposition's ability to take over, to establish control and governance over a devastated country, and regarding its orientation. As the Dubai-based analyst Taufiq Rahim commented regarding Assad's speech on 16 April 2013: "He's feeling the wind in his sails." (Syria Deeply, 20 April 2013).

2

FROM PUSH TO SHOVE

SYRIA AND THE UNITED STATES

Throughout the cold war, Hafez al-Assad had skillfully exploited the superpowers' desire for regional influence to his advantage, and despite Syria being on the US list of state sponsors of terrorism, relations between the two countries were neither close nor openly hostile. However, Assad wished to see the end of US export sanctions on his country, and this necessitated being taken off the list. From the Syrian point of view, Iraq's assault on Kuwait in 1990 was a golden opportunity to improve relations with the United States. There was no love lost between the Syrian and the Iraqi regimes; they had long been viciously opposed to one another to the point of attempting to assassinate each other's leaders.[1] Assad therefore decided to join the international coalition against Iraq, killing two birds with one stone: advancing his regional strategy by weakening his strongest adversary, and opening a new page in Syrian–American relations. For the United States, the Syrian change of position was valuable. They saw the decline of the Soviet Union as an opportunity to become more involved in the Middle East, and Washington, thus able to point to the participation of an Arab government notoriously critical of American policy, could improve the legitimacy and the overall image of the campaign.

In spite of its initial interest, US engagement in the Middle East in recent decades has been neither constant nor consistent. Rather, it has changed depending on the American administration's global priorities, specific interests in the region, and the success of its engagement. Relations between Syria and the United States were never based on bilateral interests, but formed part of the broader picture of regional developments and interests, and even during instances of cooperation they were never free of mistrust.

Looking at Syrian–American relations between 1990 and 2013, five different phases are apparent: (1) from 1990 to 1997, the years of hope and cautious optimism, in which, with the start of the Middle East peace process, the most comprehensive effort ever to solve the Middle East conflict was undertaken, which silently petered out when the peace process became stalled; (2) from 2001 to 2002/3, when the United States refocused on the Middle East as part of the "War on Terror" and cooperated with Syria until both fell apart over the 2003 Iraq war; (3) the years between 2003 and 2010, which were characterized by more downs than ups in both states' relations because of Syrian regional policy; (4) 2010 to mid-2011, when the United States tried to re-engage with Bashar al-Assad; (5) and finally, as a result of the Syrian government's violent repression of the Syrian revolution, hostility between the Syrian regime and the US administration, which shifted its focus to the Syrian opposition.

A new start: hope and skepticism in American–Syrian relations

In his address to Congress on 11 September 1990, a month after the Iraqi assault on Kuwait, President George H. Bush declared: "Recent events have surely proven that there is no substitute for American leadership. In the face of tyranny, let no one doubt American credibility and reliability" (Bush 1990). Seeking to bolster the legitimacy of his administration's policy choices, Bush highlighted the broad participation in the international coalition to oust Iraq from Kuwait, adding: "From the outset, acting hand-in-hand with others, we've sought to fashion the broadest possible international response to Iraq's aggression. The level of world cooperation and condemnation of Iraq is unprecedented" (Bush 1990). In responding to Iraq's aggression against Kuwait, the United States was keen to ensure that the confrontation would not be characterized as pitting "the West" against Arabs or Muslims. To this end, America courted the Arab states, conscious that their public support and participation would be necessary to lend credibility to its efforts.[2] This need on Washington's part created an opportunity for Syria, resulting in a win–win situation for both.

The Gulf Crisis in 1990 was an opportunity Hafez al-Assad seized in a visionary way. Iraq had already demonstrated its expansionist regional policy when it became involved in Lebanon, supporting the anti-Syrian move of President Michel Aoun, and this was now confirmed through the invasion of Kuwait. Syria wanted to clip Iraq's wings, but more importantly Hafez al-Assad saw that it needed a profound change to make up for the major loss Syria suffered through the decline of the Soviet Union.

For Damascus, the decision to join the coalition against Iraq came with a high price tag. Assad recognized that the move to force his archrival out of Kuwait would likely lead to a strong and lasting US military presence in the region. Therefore, Syria attempted to solve the problem without external interference, calling on Iraq prior to January 1991 to withdraw voluntarily from Kuwait and thereby avoid precipitating a war that would only harm Iraq, Syria, and the entire Arab region.[3] These efforts made little impression on Saddam Hussein, who used his position to try and influence the regional balance of power by offering to withdraw from Kuwait in exchange for an end to all forms of occupation in the region, with explicit reference to Syria's dominant role in Lebanon.[4]

Syria's participation in the coalition was relatively symbolic. Damascus moved its troops to the Gulf but they did not participate in combat—Syria's value as an Arab state was more in helping to change the international perception of the war. Syrian cooperation was particularly desirable for Washington given that Damascus was well known for its complex and somewhat distant relationship with the United States and its consistent criticism of US engagement in the region—unlike some of its neighbors. To Washington, Syria's participation was important in signaling that the war against Iraq was not a war between the "West" and the "Arab world." Syria could be satisfied with its regional and international reward: the Gulf States expressed their gratitude for Syrian support in the form of financial assistance to shore up the ailing Syrian economy. From Damascus's perspective it had demonstrated that it was a key regional actor and the United States now owed it a favor.

While regional and international attention was focused on the Gulf crisis, Syria established and solidified its rule in Lebanon, ousting the

Iraqi-backed government of Michel Aoun in October 1990. In recognition of Syria's support in the war against Iraq, the United States turned a blind-eye to the fact that Syria was establishing its hegemony in Lebanon. The war shifted the regional power balance significantly, leaving a previously strong Iraq isolated and subject to UN sanctions, and Damascus in the happy position of having its main rival for regional leadership virtually eliminated.[5] Furthermore, Washington vowed to undertake a new peace initiative to resolve the Middle East conflict.

Launching the Middle East Peace Process

The United States recognized the importance of resolving the Arab–Israeli conflict in order to bring peace and stability to the region over the longer term:

Our objective must be clear and straightforward. It is not simply to end the state of war in the Middle East and replace it with a state of non-belligerency. This is not enough; this would not last. Rather we seek peace, real peace. And by real peace I mean treaties. Security. Diplomatic relations. Economic relations. Trade. Investment. Cultural exchange. Even tourism. (Bush 1991)

The 1991 Madrid Conference would certainly not have been convened but for strong US interest. While all parties were in principle willing to participate, the details of the prospective conference were not easy to settle, and the United States had to engage in determined shuttle diplomacy to bring it about. Even in the early stages of discussion, the characteristics of Hafez al-Assad's style of negotiation became evident as he presented his demands as non-negotiable, making concessions only when there was no other possible option. While he was interested in negotiating, it was clear that he did not want to do so at any price:

Assad's negotiating style was extremely cautious and suspicious. We used to say he was the Frank Sinatra of the peace process, because he wanted to do it "My Way." He would not go to Jerusalem, he would not meet with Israelis, he would not let his negotiators meet secretly with Israelis. Before engaging in serious direct negotiations, he insisted on knowing what their result would be. (Indyk 1999a)

It can be assumed that Assad was testing the waters to determine just how much room he had to maneuver. On several occasions he overplayed his hand and later backed down, thereby creating considerable strain in US–Syrian relations (Ross 2004, p. 79). He refused to participate in the multilateral track and urged all parties to proceed at the same pace. At the same time, Assad was careful not to be held responsible for the failure of the negotiations. Had it been up to him, the process would have had more diverse sponsorship. Hafez al-Assad was well aware that American support for the peace process was essential due to the strong ties between Washington and Jerusalem, but he was still somewhat reluctant to trust the United States.[6] He made it clear that though he had misgivings about the process, his willingness to engage stemmed from a perceived positive change in American attitudes:

It is a mistake to suggest that we joined the peace process because of the Soviet collapse. In fact we went to Madrid when Gorbachev was still in power. The Soviet collapse had not yet taken place. What persuaded us to go to Madrid was evidence of new American seriousness, and in particular the text of the American initiative that struck us as fair.[7]

The Israeli–Syrian track of the peace process required strong US intervention since both parties were reluctant to take negotiations into their own hands (Kissinger 2001). Despite concerted US efforts, the negotiations produced little in terms of results. Syria expected that sufficient American pressure on Israel would force it to make concessions in the peace process; as Secretary of State James Baker III put it:

Like many Arab leaders, Assad harbored the simplistic notion that the United States could simply deliver Israel whenever we wished because of her dependence on American financial and security commitments. I knew just how false that impression actually was.[8]

The negotiations provided an unprecedented opportunity for high-ranking Syrian and US officials to spend long periods of time together and to get to know each other better, but this did not result in increased confidence between the parties. Hafez al-Assad enjoyed the reputation of being a tough but reliable negotiator, yet his behavior during the negotiations, including reneging on previous commitments, reinforced doubts on the American side regarding Syria's sincerity in entering the process.[9] Indeed, even Hafez al-Assad's negotiating style, akin to a physical and verbal war of attrition involving hours of lectures on Syrian and Arab history, which he tended to win based on years of experience, was designed to create the most uncomfortable conditions for talks.[10] The mistrust was not only one-sided, however, and Assad's back-tracking and haggling over details was likely indicative of his fears of giving up too much and getting too little in return. The failure of each to grasp the actual needs and capabilities of the other has, in many ways, characterized the relationship between Syria and the United States over time. The United States has always found Syrian efforts to comply with its demands half-hearted or "too little, too late," whereas Syrians, on the other hand, tend to feel that they have cooperated effectively with the United States without getting much in return. Damascus welcomed President Bill Clinton's 1992 election victory, which heralded a period of active US engagement in the Middle East. In describing President Clinton Hafez al-Assad noted:

You know I liked President Bush. But President Clinton is a real person. He speaks to you with awareness and understanding. He knows our problems better and he is committed to solving them. I haven't felt this from an American president before. (Ross 2004, p. 140)

As Ross points out, for someone who had met a series of US presidents, including Nixon, Carter, and Bush, this was a remarkable statement. And yet, despite this promising beginning, the Clinton era yielded little in terms of concrete progress on the peace process. Syria and Israel came close to concluding an agreement in 1993 and again in 1995.[11] After that, this track was abandoned until 2010.

Terrorism and the Peace Process

Syrian support for Palestinian militant groups was not considered a major obstacle during the initial years of the peace process. At that point in time all of the rejectionist groups had offices in Damascus and even when, as a reaction to the rapprochement between Israel and the PLO they expressed their opposition by forging the "Alliance of Palestinian Forces," also referred to as the "Damascus 10," it did not cause a storm of protest.[12] Only in 1994 did American pressure on the Syrian government to issue public condemnations of Palestinian suicide bombings increase. Despite having promised to do so, when President Clinton arrived in Damascus in October 1994—the first visit of a US president to Syria in twenty years—during the joint press conference Hafez al-Assad chose not to condemn a suicide attack that had just taken place in Tel Aviv. The Americans declared the visit a "disaster," and the incident went on to have a lasting negative impact on Syrian–US relations, as well as on the peace process (Ross 2004, p. 151). On the one hand, it would have been in Syria's interests to create goodwill in Israel; but on the other, the domestic cost of such a gesture would have been extremely high—a point that Israel and the United States failed to recognize.[13] Following this incident, Syrian support for Palestinian groups did not become a major issue again until 2001.

American–Syrian relations after 11 September 2001

It was only with the attacks of 11 September 2001 that the US administration turned its sights once again to the Middle East—but this time with a different agenda. Fighting terrorism became the policy priority in the United States. The terrorist attacks changed the administration's view on the nature of security threats emanating from the Middle East. Prior to 9/11, the United States had sought to secure its interests in the region—namely, access to resources, geostrategic interests, and the security of Israel—by playing off regional actors against one another. But the terrorist attacks against the United States changed the game completely. Instead of engaging in negotiations, it raised demands, and Washington did not leave any doubt that it was fully prepared to employ military means if states would not cooperate in the "war on terrorism." While human rights and democracy had hitherto not featured prominently in US diplomacy in the region, they were now invoked selectively in order to bring about systemic changes by any means.

The United States accepted Syria's offer of cooperation against al-Qaeda, despite the fact that Syrian support for terrorist groups had long been a major source of contention in US–Syrian relations—that the regime remained on the US list of state sponsors of terrorism, or that Syria had sponsored foreign terrorist groups over many decades, and continued to host anti-Israeli Palestinian groups, was thus temporarily ignored in the broader interests of the War on Terror.

Syria described itself—with reference to the Islamist uprising of the early 1980s—as one of the first victims of Islamist terrorism, and regarded the War on Terror as a matter of shared interest. As Bashar al-Assad later noted: "For us, September 11 was a good opportunity. The need to cooperate was very self-evident, and it was in our interests. It was also a way to improve relations" (Hersh 2005, p. 337).

From the outset, President Bush was uncompromising in his rhetoric, using biblical allusion to depict the world through a simplistic black-

and-white paradigm: the fight of "good" against "evil." Bush promised to "rid the world of the evil doers," and depicted the threat as "a new kind of evil. And we understand. And the American people are beginning to understand. This crusade, this war on terrorism is going to take a while" (Bush 2001a). His use of the word "crusade" raised suspicions that he regarded fighting terrorism as part of a broader Muslim–Western conflict—ironically using much the same rhetoric as radical Islamist voices in their discourse about the West. The United States was referred to as a "nation under attack," with terrorists having "declared war" on the country and its values.[14] The response of the US administration was a "War on Terror" and an ultimatum from President Bush to countries across the globe: "Either you are with us, or you are with the terrorists. From this day forward, any nation that continues to harbor or support terrorism will be regarded by the United States as a hostile regime."[15]

Momentum around the War on Terror grew, and the United States was soon leading an internationally sanctioned attack on Afghanistan to oust the Taliban regime and target al-Qaeda leaders suspected of being in hiding there. As time went on, doubts began to surface about the effectiveness of the military approach adopted by the United States in dealing with terrorism. International skepticism increased even more when the American administration identified military action against Iraq as the next project in the War on Terror. Saddam Hussein's reluctance to comply with the demands of the international community and his evasion of the sanctions regime had long been a thorn in Washington's side. Soon after 11 September, the United States began to build a case against the Iraqi regime, accusing it of being involved in international terrorism (Cheney 2001). Washington ramped up its rhetoric on so-called "rogue states" and the so-called "Axis of Evil." Syria was not identified specifically as part of this nefarious group, but was closely associated with it as a "state supporter of terrorism." The State Department's country reports on terrorism noted that Syria had not been directly involved in any act of international terrorism since 1986.[16] However, it remained on the list due to the presence of Palestinian rejectionist groups in Damascus, as well as the Syria–Hezbollah relationship. As US scholar Stephen Zunes noted:

That alone is grounds for keeping Syria on its list of terrorist nations, despite the fact that this is a stricter criterion for keeping the country on the State Department's list of state supporters of terrorism than for any other government. (Zunes 1997, p. 2)

Syrian Cooperation on al-Qaeda

As had been the case ten years earlier when it had sought to build a coalition to oust Iraq from Kuwait, the United States took pains to avoid giving the impression that the War on Terror was about a Western–Muslim or Western–Arab divide: "The enemy of America is not our many Muslim friends; it is not our many Arab friends. Our enemy is a radical network of terrorists, and every government that supports them."[17]

Syria offered intelligence and helped foil several planned attacks on American citizens.[18] The United States brought terror suspects to Syria for interrogation, among others the Canadian citizen Maher Arar and the German Mohammad Haydar Zammar. The practice of rendition flights did not make headlines in the Arab world, but having suspects interrogated in countries with notoriously poor human rights records further damaged the credibility of the United States in civil society circles and highlighted the apparent hypocrisy of US campaigns for democracy and human rights in the Middle East.[19]

It was not long, though, before the scope of the War on Terror was broadened, and the Israeli government seized the opportunity to draw more attention to its own challenges by attempting to link Hamas and Hezbollah with al-Qaeda. "We have to make Hezbollah al-Qaeda No. 2," an Israeli parliamentarian said, trying to explain how other states could be convinced of the imminent threat posed by Hezbollah.[20] The efforts of pro-Israel lobby groups in the United States to build on this idea in turn resulted in a broadening of the scope of the War on Terror. This created friction between Syria and the United States due to differences in which organizations they considered terrorists. "Our war on terror begins with al-Qaeda, but it does not end there. It will not end until every terrorist group of global reach has been found, stopped and defeated,"[21] was a maxim formulated early on by the US administration. "Syria has spoken out against al-Qaeda. We expect it to act against Hamas and Hezbollah as well," President Bush added in a speech in April 2002.[22] The dilemma became obvious: countering al-Qaeda necessitated engagement with Syria, and Syria was willing to cooperate. In contrast, Syria insisted on the Palestinian groups being treated as legitimate actors and as an entirely separate case. This dilemma resulted in an ambiguous and somewhat incomprehensible US policy toward the country. In December 2001, during the vote for new members of the

UN Security Council, the United States did not oppose Syria's election, and on several occasions US government officials praised Syrian cooperation in combatting terrorism while emphasizing that American lives had been saved due to information provided by Syrian intelligence (Blanford 2002). For this reason, the Syrian president and senior officials reacted with irritation in the face of increased US pressure and public demands to end support for Palestinian groups.

The 2003 Iraq War as a decisive point in the Syrian–American relationship

The war in Iraq turned out to be a make-or-break issue between Syria and the United States. In the lead-up to the war, Syria found itself in the uncomfortable position of being the only Arab country in the UN Security Council. It hesitantly supported Resolution 1441 and portrayed this as a diplomatic victory. Foreign Minister Farouq al-Sharaa said the resolution "stopped an immediate strike against Iraq" and thus Syria, by its own definition, had defended the Arab cause (NYT, 11 November 2002). When it became obvious that Washington would circumvent the UN and move ahead without a UN mandate with a "coalition of the willing," Syria felt that it had been tricked and became more outspoken in opposing the war. The stronger the US criticisms of the Syrian position became, the more vociferous Syria grew in its frustration with the United States—not out of any sympathy for Saddam Hussein, but, as the Syrian government said, out of solidarity with "the Iraqi people."[23]

Boutheina Shaaban, at that time head of the foreign media department in the Syrian foreign ministry, stressed that Syria shared some of the United States' concerns about the situation in Iraq but that it did not agree with the American strategy of eliminating the problem by military means.[24] Other Syrian officials were more outspoken and even insulting. In a widely reported incident, the then minister of foreign affairs, Farouq al-Sharaa, labeled the US administration "exceptional"— "Perhaps there have been similar administrations in the past, but never one at the same level of violence and stupidity."[25] While opposition to the war was not uncommon, no other state was so openly critical, a fact that contributed to the rapid deterioration in Syrian–American relations at the time. The rapid advance of coalition forces and the fall of Baghdad came as a shock to many Syrians, who had banked on protracted resistance in the Iraqi capital. The seemingly easy victory raised fears within the Syrian regime that it could be next.

United States demands—the visit of Colin Powell to Damascus in 2003

The degree to which US–Syrian relations had suffered as a result of the war became evident during US Secretary of State Colin Powell's visit to Syria in May 2003. Syria welcomed the visit as a chance to re-establish dialogue with the United States.[26] But it was not a friendly meeting. Powell made it clear that Washington expected a change of attitude from Syria; the US asked that Syria seal off its eastern border to stem the flow of foreign fighters into Iraq. Washington also insisted that Syria establish diplomatic relations with the new Iraqi government, transfer any Iraqi funds to the Iraq Development Fund, and prevent officials of the former Iraqi regime from entering Syria. Furthermore, Powell made it clear that it was time for the Syrian government to close the offices of the Damascus-based Palestinian groups and expel their leaders. Powell expressed satisfaction at having extracted a "promise" from the Syrian president to close the offices. Bashar meanwhile chose to handle the issue in a way that was characteristic for his rule—on the surface complying while at the same time looking for a back door. The offices simply redefined their role. As a representative of Islamic Jihad in Damascus criticized the American demand, saying: "This is just talk, it's a storm in a cup because we are merely media offices."[27]

All of the groups denied having been ordered to close their offices, but Hamas representative Osama Hamdan said that some of them were considering closing doing so in order to ease the pressure on Syria (Blanford 2003). They kept a low profile and some of their leaders temporarily moved to Lebanon or the Gulf region, also giving interviews with by-lines indicating they were outside Syria. Though it can be assumed that they did this on the orders of Syrian officials, the Syrian regime deliberately avoided giving the impression that it was complying with US demands so as not to tarnish the government's image in the eyes of the Arab street. In the meantime, the US administration was waiting for a clear signal from the Syrian president that he would comply with its demands. As relations with the United States deteriorated even further, Palestinian groups resumed their public activity in Syria and their leaders returned to Damascus.[28]

THE WISDOM OF SYRIA'S WAITING GAME

The US position on Israeli incursion on Syrian territory in October 2003

The stricter position of parts of the US administration on Syria led to a more lenient stance on Israel's behavior in the region. In October 2003, the Israeli army bombed a deserted training facility belonging to Palestinian groups in the Syrian village of Ain Saheb. The Syrian government denounced the strike and tried to obtain a UN Security Council Resolution condemning this violation of its sovereignty. It was the first Israeli attack on Syrian territory since 1973, and was presumably made in retaliation for a suicide bombing in Haifa for which Islamic Jihad claimed responsibility. The Israeli ambassador to the United Nations declared in a letter to the Security Council and the General Assembly that the Israeli action was "no different than the forcible measures recently taken by other States against terrorist groups and their state sponsors, with the support of the international community."[29] The United States assured Israel of its right to self-defense and asked both sides, especially Syria, to exercise self-restraint. The US ambassador to the UN, John Negroponte, mentioned on this occasion that the United States believed Syria was "on the wrong side of the war on terrorism" (BBC, 6 October 2003). While it was clear that retaliation was not an option, Foreign Minister Al-Sharaa warned against escalation:

Syria is not incapable of establishing a balance of resistance and deterrence that would oblige Israel to refine its approach. Syria has demonstrated extreme restraint fully aware that Israel is attempting to fabricate all kinds of pretexts, gleaned from different quarters, to export its internal crisis to the region as a whole and expose the region to a new escalation and a new conflagration.[30]

The resolution did not pass at the Security Council due to US opposition; perhaps the ultimate sign that Syria had failed to seize the foreign policy opportunities presented by its UN Security council membership:

A two-year stint on the United Nations Security Council proved unproductive: Syria did not cultivate relations with key powers, nor recover the status it had enjoyed in the nineties. Tellingly, Syria even failed to promote a discussion on a draft resolution condemning Israel's violation of its sovereignty in a controversial strike—a unique situation for a member of the Security Council. (Allaf 2004)

In 2004, there were two assassination attempts targeting Hamas members in Damascus. The first, in September 2004, resulted in the death of a senior official and wounded three bystanders. The second, in

December 2004, missed its target.[31] The Israeli government did not take responsibility for either incident, although Israeli officials praised the September bombing (NYT, 27 September 2004).

Sanctions

Regardless of the fact that American officials had publicly praised Syrian cooperation with the United States on Islamist terrorist organizations, the regime was not removed from the list of state sponsors of terrorism, which meant that the imposition of sanctions was a straightforward process.[32] With relations deteriorating, this was what Congress ultimately focused on. The post-9/11 context created a receptive environment for anti-Syrian lobbying, which led in April 2002 to the introduction of the "Syria Accountability and Restoration of Lebanese Sovereignty Act" (SALSA), passed in 2003.

This was not in the interest of the State Department—particularly not while the Bush administration was trying to garner Arab support for the war in Iraq. President Bush's Middle East envoy, David Satterfield, noted at a press conference in Beirut in 2002: "I want to confirm that my administration disapproves [of the] Syrian Accountability Act and has made this clear to the congress. ... The bill harms the maneuverability of the US president which is why the US administration is opposed to it" (BBC 4 September 2002). Yet the Syria Accountability Act gained wide support in Congress, placing pressure on President Bush to pursue a harder course with Damascus. After delaying as long as possible, on 12 December 2003 Bush eventually signed the document—although he only chose to implement one of the six measures provided for in the Act, largely for symbolic purposes, this still dealt a further blow to Syrian–American relations.

The Bush administration's growing discontent with Syrian policies—considered as being unhelpful at best and as overtly hostile with regard to Iraq—led to a much tougher US stance toward Syria in many areas. Whereas it was simply aggressive rhetoric that had soured Syrian–American relations prior to the 2003 war, it was now Syrian behavior that pitted Washington against the regime: the influx of foreign fighters to Iraq via Syrian territory, revelations that more than 70 per cent of Saddam Hussein's illicit arms procurement had taken place through Syria and to the benefit of members of the political elite, and the issue of

Iraqi assets in Syria. In addition to these new concerns, several topics the United States had previously ignored (such as Syria's continued interference in Lebanon) or which it had left to one side (like the Palestinian offices in Damascus) were now brought to the table and used to pressure Syria.

President Bush stated that Syria posed "an unusual and extraordinary threat to the national security, foreign policy, and economy of the United States," and declared "a national emergency to deal with that threat."[33] On 11 May 2004, the US Department of the Treasury, under the provisions of the USA Patriot Act, designated the Commercial Bank of Syria a "financial institution of primary money laundering concern."[34] Further sanctions subsequently led to the assets of certain Syrian individuals and government entities considered to be involved in activities hostile to the United States becoming frozen.[35] Syrian politicians denounced the sanctions and claimed that they would do much more harm to the United States than to Syria. This was of course an exaggeration, but it is evident that the situation encouraged Syria to explore new business opportunities with Russia, China, and other states. Diplomatically, US–Syrian relations became even more strained after the assassination of the former Lebanese Prime Minister Rafiq Hariri in February 2005. Convinced that his assassination had been ordered by Syria, the United States withdrew its ambassador and left the post vacant until 2010.

Mending Syrian–American ties: 2009–11

When President Barack Obama took office in January 2009, expectations were high that there would now be new opportunities to mend the Syrian–US relationship. Indeed, in 2009 President Obama's administration began stretching out the feelers towards the renewal of peace talks. In February 2010, there was a visible sign of a major improvement in relations with Syria: on 17 February 2010, Robert Ford was appointed to be the first US ambassador to Syria since 2005, and a month later, Under Secretary of State for Political Affairs William Burns traveled to Syria to explore the revival of both states' relations.

Even though this never paid off, Syria remained hopeful that one day it might be asked for help with the regional "troublemakers" with which it had good relations. Maybe this is what drove Bashar al-Assad to invite Iranian President Mahmoud Ahmadinejad and Hezbollah Secretary

General Hassan Nasrallah for dinner in Damascus only a week later, on 25 February 2010, this being the time a Nasrallah visit to Damascus was reported. This was an obvious provocation, particularly because Hezbollah's official TV station, while not explicitly mentioning Hamas, insinuated that the meeting had included the organization.[36] During the meeting Ahmadinejad stressed that resistance was the best way to "liberate lands" (*Haaretz*, 26 February 2010).

Obama subsequently started a new initiative for Syrian–Israeli peace talks, a process that was interrupted due to the beginning of the Syrian revolution (NYT, 12 October 2012).

From reformer to rogue

The United States was initially hesitant with regard to the Syrian revolution. The Obama administration expressed its confidence in Bashar al-Assad's ability to handle the situation. In a CBS interview at the end of March 2011, US Secretary of State Hillary Clinton referred to Bashar al-Assad as a reformer and underlined that she saw no need at that point to intervene militarily. The United States could not ignore what was taking place, though. Ambassador Robert Ford visited the city of Hama on 7 July 2011 and was warmly welcomed by the protesters. The Syrian government was enraged, and when an angry mob of Assad supporters attacked the US embassy a few days later, Syrian security forces reacted only slowly. In August 2011 Obama called for Assad to step down. In 2011, the US ambassador was recalled, a move paralleled by the Syrian government's recalling of Ambassador Imad Moustapha from Washington.

Altogether, the United States seemed to be without a strategy and vision for Syria. The record of Bashar al-Assad's obstructive policies with regard to American interests was longer than the list of positive points of cooperation. The US had supported opposition groups before but did not seem to expect the Syrian protesters' perseverance—nor did the US administration have a great deal of faith that the opposition had the requisite skills to take over.

If ten years ago George W. Bush had tried to force regime change in countries that were not prepared to bring it about themselves, Obama now failed to recognize what was a truly popular revolution and to act in time. The Syrian regime benefited from a general hesitance to intervene in light of the negative experience in Afghanistan and Iraq. Aware that the American public was not interested in running into another potential disaster, Bashar al-Assad could assume that a military intervention was unlikely to occur before the US elections in November 2012, and he did not miss a chance to repeat what would make a Western audience hesitant about toppling him: that his secular regime was under threat of Islamist terrorism, and that the alternative to his reign was chaos.

Throughout the first two years of the Syrian revolution, the United States left no doubt that they did not plan to intervene militarily. In August 2012, President Obama declared the use of chemical weapons a "red line," without specifying what the consequences would be for crossing it. In practice, the Syrian regime simply viewed this as permitting the use of any other means, including cluster bombs and incendiary weapons. Allegations have and continue to be made that chemical weapons had been used, and in April 2013 this was confirmed by European officials. Even in light of this, the US administration seemed to continue its "wait-and-see" approach.

Conclusion

Syrian–American relations have been determined by US interests in the region and the role Syria could potentially play in achieving or impeding them. The principal points of agreement and disagreement between the two states do not center on bilateral matters, but on regional and international interests. US foreign policy towards Syrian cannot be detached from Israeli interests, which also has to be taken into consideration when looking at Washington's position towards the Syrian revolution: Israel has long considered Assad a guarantor of stability with calculable risks. The increasing disintegration of Syrian authority and control, the growing strength and visibility of Islamist actors on the ground, and concerns regarding chemical weapons use have played a role here.

The US administration—and its related institutions—has consistently sent mixed signals when dealing with Syria—on the one hand denouncing Syrian behavior and on the other suggesting deeper engagement as a means to solve regional problems. The Syrian regime, based on its awareness that US priorities can change, has often chosen to push Washington to the limits, and despite moments of massive US pressure, it has not really needed to give in—as the period between 2003 and 2010 clearly demonstrates. In the absence of any change in Syrian policy, the US administration took a new initiative to engage the regime in 2010.

There are numerous occasions on which Bashar al-Assad has played dumb in the face of allegations and accusations, regardless of how strong the evidence may be. In proliferation of material to Iraq, for example, or later on the crossing of foreign fighters into Iraq. In other cases his promises to take action were followed by the eager search for a back door—as in the case of the Palestinian offices in Damascus. He has paid lip-service without actually complying, mostly to win time in order to reduce external pressure. Early on in the rebellion it became obvious that he was following the same evasive strategy, including bluntly lying at the United Nations and committing to a plan that he did not intend to implement. In all these cases, the Syrian regime has learned that it can get away with this type of behavior and use the intervening time to establish facts.

This should have taught the United States that the Syrian regime would not change its behavior in the revolution unless it was faced with a credible threat. Assurances that the United States was not considering an intervention and the setting of a (shifting) red line without indicating what would be the consequences of crossing it was therefore the least helpful strategy the US administration could have possibly adopted.

3

SYRIA, ISRAEL, AND PALESTINE

When Arab regimes from Bahrain to Tunisia were challenged by popular uprisings in early 2011, Israel was quick to signal a readiness to re-engage with Syria to reach a peace deal. Previous Israeli governments had largely dismissed the Syrian track, assuming that the regime, however intractable, would remain stable and in control. With unprecedented changes sweeping the region, Israel's strategy changed; it suddenly became preferable to deal with "the devil you know" rather than worry about potential successors. This was captured in an article in *Ha'aretz* dubbing Bashar al-Assad "Israel's favorite dictator" (Maslaha 2011). On 1 February 2011, Israeli Defense Minister Ehud Barak warned against a military confrontation with Syria. Disappointment at the lack of progress in the indirect talks, he said, could develop into a comprehensive war (al-Jazeera, 2 February 2011). A month later, he said that if Syria was serious, Israel would be ready to enter into peace talks. This differed from Prime Minister Netanyahu's hesitant approach to dealings with Syria. Any enthusiasm was short-lived, however, since Damascus gave no sign that it was considering negotiations. Furthermore, in the beginning of June 2011 protesters tried to cross the Syrian–Israeli border into Israel, and several people were killed in the ensuing clashes.

Yet as 2011 progressed the Israeli government became more and more isolated. A mob protesting the killing of Egyptian soldiers from Israeli territory broke into Israel's embassy in Cairo, leading to the evacuation of Israeli diplomats. The previously smooth working relations between Israel and Turkey, which had already suffered a heavy blow in 2010 due to an Israeli attack on a Turkish flotilla carrying goods to Gaza, froze in September 2011 when Israel refused to apologize for the incident.[1] In March 2013, the Israeli government apologized to Turkey. At the same time, Israel came under domestic pressure from protesters seeking greater social justice in Israel, and diplomatic pressure from the Palestinian request for UN recognition of its statehood.

The many issues faced by the Israeli government and its diminishing confidence in the Syrian regime's ability to remain in power, as expressed in June 2011 by Defense Minster Barak, ended considerations of a renewal of peace talks with Syria (al-Jazeera 3 February 2011).

After a long period of silence, in January 2012 Israel's chief of staff, Benny Gantz, made a surprising announcement: "The day the Assad regime falls, this is expected to hurt the Alawite sect. We are getting ready to take in Alawite refugees in the Golan Heights," he told the Knesset's Foreign Affairs and Security Committee (israelnationalnews.com), a bizarre plan that would effectively guarantee bad relations with any future Syrian government. On 19 January 2012 the Israeli journalist Aner Shalev in *Ha'aretz* criticized the inability of the Israeli government to adapt to the changes in the Middle East and develop a policy toward Syria:

The world of tomorrow does not interest us, even if it may contain possibilities and dramatic change ... The present Israeli leadership consists of the people of yesterday, who look forward to the past, swim against the tide of history and hastily flee from any change. The familiar is preferable to what is good and right ... We must admit, this is the Syrian people's finest hour. It is not our finest hour. (Shalev 2012)

The antagonism between Syria and Israel dates back to the 1948 war. The two were involved in direct military confrontations in 1948, 1967, and 1973, and encountered each other indirectly during the Lebanese Civil War. Mutual suspicion that each sought to establish regional hegemony with plans for a "Greater Israel"[2] or a "Greater Syria"[3] poisoned any prospect for a relationship, and was continuously used by each to discredit the other domestically. Until 1990, the situation between Syria and Israel could be described from a foreign policy perspective as unsatisfactory but stable. Their common border remained quiet, and the dispute over the occupied Golan Heights was, in effect, put on hold. Notwithstanding his uncompromising rhetoric, Hafez al-Assad had come to realize that the Golan could not be recovered militarily.

SYRIA, ISRAEL, AND PALESTINE

The Madrid Conference in 1991 was the first serious attempt in many years to find a comprehensive solution, and Syria used the opportunity to explore the possibility of reaching an agreement. This meant that the Syrian regime had to reconsider its public rejection of Israel and explain its decision to negotiate with the archenemy to a skeptical domestic audience. There were good reasons for entering the Madrid peace process. In the Arab world, interest in continuing a fruitless struggle had declined throughout the 1980s, and Syria did not enjoy the same support as "the defender of the Arab cause" as it had before. The loss of its primary sponsor, the USSR, coupled with heightened US engagement in the region, made it necessary for Damascus to adapt. Syria's recent rapprochement with the United States made it feel stronger. American commitment to renewed peace efforts in the region gave Hafez al-Assad confidence that he could rely on Washington's support for his position.

The convening of the Madrid Conference in October 1991 was an important step for regional politics. While the conference was marked by Syrian revisionist rhetoric and bouts of mutual Syrian–Israeli recriminations, the mere fact that the regime participated and agreed to settle the conflict on the basis of UNSCR 242 and 338 signaled Assad's pragmatism.[4] It also demonstrated that this was not an irreconcilable ideological conflict but one that was about negotiable issues—namely, territory and security. Assad was expected to be a tough negotiator who would not easily give anything up, but it was generally acknowledged that if he agreed to something he could be trusted to keep his word. For the Syrian president, the prospect of having to make concessions posed not so much a risk as a challenge:

Although his rule was not in question, following decades of maximalist rhetoric regarding return of the Golan (including its use to justify repressive government policies), a compromise position on return of that land could invite disruptive public opposition to Assad's regime as well as a personal loss of credibility.[5]

The various accounts of those in charge of the negotiations as well as interviews given by Syrian officials at the time provide valuable insight into the depths of Syrian foreign policy-making. Syria had never dedicated effort on such a scale to any other long-term project involving close and continuous contact with Western powers. For Syria, the conflict with Israel had always been viewed not only as a bilateral matter but also as part of a broader framework; in many ways, it was the cornerstone of Syria's pan-Arab and regional policy. Developments within the peace process forced the Syrian regime to reconsider its position on both fronts. The Israeli–Palestinian accord of 1993 and the Jordanian–Israeli peace agreement of 1994 clearly showed that Assad's regional power and influence had declined. Not only was he unable to prevent these actors from seeking separate peace deals with Israel, but he was not even informed—let alone consulted—before the accords were finalized. Instead of clinging to hazy pan-Arab ideals and adhering to the Syrian dictum of comprehensive negotiations, King Hussein and Yasser Arafat opted for a policy that at least allowed for a tangible improvement in their relations with the United States. The region's power balance was visibly shifting, and the prevailing pattern of Arab–Israeli interaction that had thus far consisted of conflict and crisis began to give way to the possibility of cooperation (Perthes 2000, p. 130).

Basic negotiating positions

There are several constants in Syrian foreign policy: the taking of a "principled stance"; insistence on a "just and comprehensive" solution to the Arab–Israeli conflict; the indivisibility of the Syrian–Israeli conflict from the broader Arab–Israeli conflict; and the conclusion of an "honorable peace." These are not only messages to Israel, but also to a wider Arab audience to demonstrate that Syria is the staunchest and most consistent advocate of Arab rights. The Israeli–Palestinian conflict remains an important tool for the Syrian regime to mobilize internal support and, in the name of "war," to suppress the aspirations of its own people. Syria practices a kind of "perceived victimhood," interpreting and amplifying any injustice perpetrated by Israel as a deliberate attack on Arab dignity and values. On the ground, Syria has shown more pragmatism than is evident in its official statements. While adamant on matters of substance at Madrid, Syria exhibited remarkable flexibility with regard to procedural questions in the lead-up to the conference. Despite its insistence on "comprehensiveness," it agreed to negotiate on a bilateral track focusing solely on bilateral issues. It also accepted the participation of other Arab states in a parallel multilateral track despite its vehement opposition to any discussions that might prejudice a final settlement of the conflict. Damascus's primary objective in the peace process was to improve bilateral relations with the United States and to develop closer ties with the US administration. Hafez al-Assad regarded

President Clinton as sympathetic to Arab interests and saw Madrid as an opportunity.[6]

The extent to which Syrian and Israeli decision-makers were familiar with their opponents' positions and capabilities is unclear (Astorino-Courtois/Trusty 2000, pp. 362f.). Both sides had years of confrontation to fall back on, and in this sense they were well prepared for negotiations. That said, Israeli expertise on Syria is much greater than Syria's on Israel. A vivid and dynamic scholarly and intellectual community in Israel studies and analyzes Syria. This is certainly not matched by similar interest and dedication in Syria, and Syria tends to exaggerate Israel's capabilities. Israeli intelligence, as well as the scope of Israel's cooperation with the United States on security matters, deepens Israeli insight into developments in Damascus.

Syrian demands for a comprehensive settlement

Syria introduced the notion of a "just and comprehensive peace" to the Arab–Israeli conflict because Hafez al-Assad was convinced that a united front would improve each Arab actor's chances for a favorable agreement. In his view, all of the participants in the peace process should move at the same pace and coordinate closely in order to pressure Israel to make concessions. From the Syrian point of view, the PLO—as well as Jordan and Lebanon—are only minor regional actors and, as such, are objects rather than subjects in the broader regional geopolitical competition. Within this framework, Syria behaves as though it has a "quasi-natural right to interfere" when secondary actors deviate from the Syrian course (Perthes 2000, pp. 145f.). This thinking stems from Hafez al-Assad's fear that Israel would try to drive a wedge between the Arab states and from his mistrust of the latter and their intentions. Again trying to perpetuate the image of Syria as the guarantor of Arab dignity and values, the Syrian president stressed that Syria had put its own interests last, saying, "Syria could have concluded a bilateral agreement with Israel a long time ago" (al-Assad 1993).

The Golan Heights—territory, water, and settlements

For Syria, the restoration of its sovereignty over the Golan Heights is of paramount concern. This Syrian territory was lost in the 1967 war, and the hitherto politico-ideological conflict thus gained a territorial component.[7] In 1973, Syria and Egypt initiated an unsuccessful military attempt to recover the Golan Heights and territory lost in the Sinai. While finally recognizing that the problem could not be solved militarily, Hafez al-Assad would go no further than a disengagement agreement, given his strict opposition to a separate settlement. In 1982, at the peak of Israeli–Syrian tensions in Lebanon, when world attention was focused on the Iran–Iraq War, Israel annexed the Golan Heights. Identity cards and residency permits were handed out, and the population of the Golan became eligible for Israeli citizenship. This annexation was never internationally recognized, but facts on the ground changed fundamentally as a result.

In addition to the political and territorial issues involved in the Golan conflict, there is also a strategic consideration. Syria wants access to Lake Tiberias—which is why it insists on a withdrawal to the 4 June 1967 line, though this line has never had the status of a border. In the partition plan between Syria and Palestine in 1923, Syria did not have access to the lake. This was obtained only through the conquest of additional territory in 1948. Even though UNSCR 242 states that Israel should withdraw from territories occupied in the 1967 war, Israel rightfully claims that the border demarcation should take place within the framework of a peace agreement.[8]

An Israeli withdrawal from the Golan would likely generate significant domestic opposition in Israel, given the number of its citizens who have settled in the area with the aim of bolstering Israeli claims to the territory. An estimated 14,000 to 20,000 Israeli settlers currently live in the Golan Heights.[9] In contrast to the former settlers in Gaza and those in the West Bank, the Golan settlers are more left-wing and remain in the area in order to focus on agriculture, alternative energy, and winemaking, rather than for ideological reasons. Relations between the settlers and the Syrian population are therefore noticeably more relaxed than they would otherwise be (Reuter 2000). Interestingly, in this context, it is worth mentioning that the Israeli citizens of the Golan Heights are seen in a different light to settlers in the West Bank/Gaza by the Israeli population, and are in fact never referred to as "settlers." This suggests that the idea that the Golan Heights is "Israeli territory" rather than "occupied territory" is much more prominent than in the case of the West Bank and Gaza Strip.

SYRIA, ISRAEL, AND PALESTINE

Security and normalization

For Israel, security guarantees are paramount. Giving up the Golan Heights would mean ceding a geographically advantageous position. Sophisticated military technology makes this less of an issue today, but during negotiations from 1992 to 1996 Israel maintained its demand for an early warning station on the Golan Heights. Syria signaled its willingness to agree to this demand provided that the station was manned by American and French personnel, as well as personnel of "a potential third party" (Israel). In exchange for territorial concessions, Israel wants Syria to establish a demilitarized zone, and on this point Syria expects reciprocity.

Normalization is a core Israeli demand that would entail lifting the Arab economic boycott of Israel, opening the Syrian market to Israeli products, permitting reciprocal tourism, and establishing diplomatic ties. Israel views these as necessary components of a peace agreement, for despite the Camp David Accord of 1979, peace with Egypt never became "warm," resembling more closely a bare absence of war. Syria's deep mistrust of Israeli intentions and fear of espionage have created distinct discomfort with the prospect of normalization. When the mere export of apples from the Golan Heights to Syria constitutes headline news, it is not difficult to imagine how high the psychological barriers to further economic or cultural exchange might be.[10] Syrian reservations are not only psychological, however; opening the Syrian market—and through it other Arab markets—to superior Israeli technology is likely to hurt the Syrian economy while at the same time increasing Israel's economic clout in the region (Perthes 2000, pp. 126ff.).

Syrian–Israeli relations under Shamir, 1991–2

On 30 October 1991 Itzhak Shamir reluctantly agreed to participate in the Madrid Conference. The high-level of mistrust that pervaded the conference made progress improbable—particularly between Israel and Syria. At Madrid, both Israel and Syria took pains to tarnish the image of the other.[11] Refusal to compromise on the Golan presented a serious obstacle to talks, as did the looming Israeli elections of June 1992 and a consequent lack of appetite for major foreign policy changes.

Under Shamir, Yossi Ben-Aharon was appointed chief negotiator with Syria. His account of the negotiations recalls the harsh tone set in the initial encounter and the intransigent Syrian position on the implementation of UNSCR 242 and 338. From the Syrian point of view, the resolutions did not oblige Syria to agree to normalization or anything else in return for the territory. Ben-Aharon bitterly remarked:

Throughout the exchanges with Syria, during both the Shamir and Rabin administrations, the Syrians harped incessantly on the preamble to Resolution 242, which mentioned the "inadmissibility of the acquisition of territory by force." However, when the Syrians presented their position on the border question, they demanded an Israeli withdrawal to the June 4, 1967 lines. This would have granted the Syrians slices of Israeli territory that they had conquered by force during the 1948 war. In Syrian eyes, it was inadmissible for Israel to claim (no less acquire) territory in a defensive war, but it was entirely legitimate for Syria to demand territory it had conquered in an unprovoked attack in 1948. (Ben-Aharon 2000, p. 5)

The Syrian delegation turned down any Israeli suggestion of starting with confidence-building measures or any security or territorial issues that were not entirely focused on withdrawal from the Golan. Unsurprisingly, these irreconcilable official positions led nowhere. At the same time this official contact was only one part of the Shamir government's dealings with Syria. The official formula for dealing with Syria at this time was "peace for peace" but there was an additional, secret parallel channel through which an emissary was authorized to signal the possibility of some territorial concession in the Golan as part of a settlement (Rabinovich 1998, pp. 42–3). The negotiations only gained real momentum after Rabin's electoral victory in June 1992.

Negotiations under Rabin, 1992–1995

Itzhak Rabin was a seasoned politician. He had been prime minister from 1974 to 1977 and had served as minister of defense from 1984 to 1990. During the 1967 war, Rabin had been chief of staff, and his actions during the war had made him a hero in the eyes of many Israelis. He was nicknamed "Mr. National Security" (Rabinovich 1998, p. 43) and enjoyed the confidence of broad segments of the Israeli public. Rabin displayed an uncompromising position on the Golan in the run-up to the elections, underscoring his commitment to hold onto this territory for security reasons: "To raise the thought that we descend from the Golan Heights would be tantamount to abandoning, I repeat, abandoning the defense of Israel" (Ben-Aharon 2000, p. 3). Nonetheless, he changed the previous government's formula of "peace for peace" to "land for peace," and later specified that the depth of an Israeli withdrawal from the Golan Heights would be contingent on the depth of the peace offered by Syria.[12]

The Syrian decision to open the way for Jewish emigration in 1992 was the first strong signal of its readiness to make concessions. Syria had always had a vibrant Jewish community to whose cultural heritage the Syrian government often liked to refer when making the point that its rejection of Israel was directed against the state, not the Jewish faith. Petrified by fear of Israeli espionage, successive Syrian governments imposed travel restrictions on members of the Jewish community— including travel within Syria—and excluded them from careers in areas considered sensitive.[13] The situation improved under Hafez al-Assad, but he would not permit the several thousand remaining members of the Jewish community to leave the country, claiming that their emigration to Israel would strengthen the enemy state.[14] In 2013, the Jewish community in Syria is estimated to number a mere fifty to 250 members. In finally allowing the Jewish community to leave the country, the Syrian government voluntarily relinquished a tool that it could have used in the negotiations as a gesture of good will to the new prime minister. However, the revocation of exit permits a year later—as well as their reinstatement shortly thereafter—demonstrated that the Syrian government was still handling this issue in an arbitrary manner (Darrah 2007, p. 42).

Rabin appointed Itamar Rabinovich to succeed Yossi Ben-Aharon. Rabinovich, a scholar and Syria expert, had previously served as Israeli ambassador to Washington. It was evident to Rabin that progress could not be made on all fronts at the same pace, so he decided to focus first on Syria and Palestine, as Lebanon was too dependent on Syria to act alone and Jordan was less likely to conclude a peace agreement first because of the number of Palestinians in the country.

The format and substance of the Syrian and Palestinian negotiations were entirely different. Israel's conflict with Syria was mainly about territory and security. The long-lasting reign of Hafez al-Assad had brought stability and continuity to Syrian foreign policy, and despite the authoritarian character of the Syrian regime and its general hostility to Israel, there were few surprises to deal with.

In contrast, the Palestinians did not have an established structure or functioning institutions and lacked a clearly defined territory. The PLO, recognized by the Arab League as the only legitimate representative of the Palestinian people, was a difficult partner for Israel to engage with; Arafat and a small group of leaders resided in Tunisia, presiding over what Israel regarded as an amorphous entity. The issues at stake were much more complex and difficult to settle than a mere territorial conflict. There was no agreement whether the objective of negotiations was one or two states. Israel claimed the city of Jerusalem as its indivisible capital. Palestinian terrorism and the intifada had created a perceived necessity within Israeli society to deal with the Palestinian question, yet at the same time Arafat enjoyed little credibility in Israel, with Arab leaders, and with broad segments of the Palestinian population.[15]

It was perhaps the presence of these obvious stumbling blocks that led Hafez al-Assad to misjudge the situation. Apart from his personal challenges with the Palestinian leadership, he could not envisage a Palestinian–Israeli deal being concluded in advance of a Syrian–Israeli settlement. To prevent this, he held regular consultations with Arafat and Arab foreign ministers (al-Assad 1993). Assad also felt entitled to privileged support from the United States in exchange for his support of the US-led coalition in the war against Iraq. When, contrary to his expectations, Israel opted to make progress on talks with parties who had been "on the wrong side" during the Gulf War, Assad was enraged. Then, to add insult to injury, the Palestinians and then the Jordanians solidified their agreements with Israel, flying in the face of Syria's "Arab unity" strategy and its demands for a comprehensive peace (Hinnebusch 1996, p. 48).

Damascus's influence in the region was evidently in decline, and it could ill afford to be obstructionist. Assad quickly revised his position on Palestinian matters, indicating that he would accept any solution that was acceptable to the Palestinians. At the same time, he increased support to anti-Arafat movements that opposed the Oslo Accord. At Clinton's request, he sent the Syrian ambassador to the United States, Walid al-Mouallim, to attend the Oslo signing ceremony on the White House lawn. It was clear, however, that he was not comfortable with the proceedings (Savir 1998, p. 86). The provisions of the Palestinian–Israeli Declaration of Principles lagged far behind Assad's expectations. Never a friend of Kissinger's "step-by-step" approach, the Syrian president deemed it necessary to be certain about the final outcome of negotiations before entering into the details. From his perspective, it made no sense to deal with minor issues if there was no meeting of minds on the difficult points. Assad was thus unimpressed both by the deal and by its form, and took the situation as a sign that his concerns about Palestinian reliability had been fully justified.

Damascus was also smarting from the feeling of having been "played" by Rabin. Just prior to the breakthrough with the Palestinians, Rabin had conveyed a message to Assad through US intermediaries offering "full withdrawal for full peace" in the form of a "hypothetical question." Though the list of Israeli demands for a full withdrawal was long, Assad did not immediately reject the proposal and was willing to negotiate. This exchange raised expectations in Syria that an agreement was possible, but the announcement of the Palestinian deal led Damascus to suspect that Rabin's offer was insincere.

From then on Syrian authorities took every opportunity to depict the "hypothetical question" as an Israeli commitment to complete withdrawal. Progress on other tracks of the peace process immobilized the Syrian track, with Rabin explaining that the Israeli public first had to digest the agreement with the Palestinians. In January 1994, President Clinton and President Assad met to discuss the possibility of progress on the Syrian–Israeli track. On this occasion, Hafez al-Assad confirmed to Clinton his commitment to peace as a strategic choice that would end occupation and allow for a life of security and dignity: "In honor we fought, in honor we negotiate, and in honor we shall make peace" (NYT, 17 January 1994).

Despite Clinton's undertaking to promote the Syrian track, Damascus's plans were once again overtaken by events. Negotiations between Israel and Jordan's King Hussein were in full swing, and a day after the Oslo ceremony the two agreed on an agenda for peace. The signing of the Jordan–Israel peace treaty a year later was viewed by Syria as another affront to its interests. In this case, the disillusionment was possibly even greater than it had earlier been with the Palestinians. The Americans, who themselves had not been fully aware of how far the discussions had progressed in Oslo, were, in this instance, directly involved in the negotiations between Israel and Jordan; yet none of the parties informed the Syrians of the agreement in advance.

According to Patrick Seale's account, at this stage Assad asked the United States for clarification from the Israeli government of its intentions regarding Rabin's hypothetical question:

Ross said that Rabin's commitment had been given not to Syria but to the United States. It was a "deposit in the American pocket." After more such hair-splitting, Assad said he did not need a letter. It would not add anything to the commitments he had already been given—by Secretary Christopher, by Ross, and by President Clinton himself. "It is recorded in your minutes and ours. It is on paper. It is not a non-paper," Assad had said. "It is in the files of the National Security Council. If all this does not constitute a commitment, nothing else will. If we did not consider this a commitment, we would not have embarked on the peace negotiations." (Seale 2000, pp. 72ff.)

In January 1994 Rabin announced that a popular referendum would be held if an agreement were reached on the return of the Golan Heights, a position he later reiterated on several occasions.[16] Syrian Foreign Minister Farouq al-Sharaa immediately declared that Israel had no right to make the occupied territory subject to a referendum (NYT, 19 January 1994).

Between 1993 and 1996, Major General Uzi Dayan served as head of the Planning Branch of the IDF General Staff, and in this position he headed the Israeli security committee at the peace negotiations with the Jordanians, Palestinians, and Syrians. In his view, the difficulties in the negotiations started with semantics but lay mainly in a difference in culture and thinking:

Negotiations with Syria were simple but tough. The Israeli side used to think and speak about "interests" and "needs" whereas the Syrians were talking about "values" and "principles". When I asked al-Mouallim what the Syrian values were, he responded: "Dignity." I asked what he thought about "sense of security" as a value. Mouallim answered: But General Dayan, how can you compare Syrian dignity with your "sense of security" which is not even objective?[17]

Meanwhile, Hafez al-Assad slowly began to prepare the public for the prospect of peace. The regime modified the language used in the official media with the aim of assuring the public that peace was a strategic choice to advance Syrian interests. Syrians were told that Assad would seek a "peace of the brave," as honorably achieved as a victory on the battlefield (Kedar 2005). The regime chose not to elaborate on what normalization with Israel might entail, noting that the situation would develop over time (Rabinovich 2004, p. 293).

Assad was conscious that a deal that could not be characterized as a victory would be worse than no agreement at all. His interest in achieving peace was balanced by the challenges that normalization and other concessions would doubtless pose for Syria (Savir 1998, p. 272). For this reason Assad was in no real hurry for the situation to change—but at the same time, he was concerned that Rabin was deliberately wasting time.[18] As noted by an Israeli negotiator: "For Hafez al-Assad, making peace was a possibility, not an obsession."[19] The situation grew particularly tense in mid-1995 when Rabin, convinced that Assad was being too demanding, complained, "Assad wants everything handed to him and he wants to do nothing for it" (Ross 2004, p. 91).

In September 1995, Israel and the Palestinian Authority signed the Interim Agreement, and the Syrian track was put on hold. This development brought with it a change in tone, and Rabin began to accuse Syria of sponsoring terrorism. By the time of Rabin's assassination, two months later, relations were so strained that Hafez al-Assad refused, even privately, to express his condolences (Ross 2004, p. 219).

The Interim Peres, 1995–1996

In the view of Itamar Rabinovich, Israel's chief negotiator with Syria, up to 1995 Hafez al-Assad "had conducted himself as if time were no constraint" (Rabinovich 1998, p. 9). Shimon Peres' term as prime minister demonstrated that changes of any kind could redefine the entire situation. Peres had been deputy prime minister under Rabin and had been jointly awarded the Nobel Prize for Peace with Arafat following their successful negotiations. However, personal differences between Rabin and Peres produced a less than harmonious relationship, and following Rabin's assassination it became clear that the prime minister had not fully informed his deputy about the state of the peace process.[20] As deputy prime minister, Peres had been party to the negotiations, but he did not enjoy the same level of public support and confidence as Rabin. Many Israelis were concerned that he would be too soft a negotiator. Peres thus sought to bolster his security credentials by taking harsh measures to combat terrorism. This strategy failed, as evidenced by the wave of violence that preceded the 1996 elections, which, in turn, provoked even more militancy among rejectionist groups.

Peres' negotiating style was entirely different from Rabin's, which posed a challenge for a Syrian regime now used to Rabin's slow and steady approach with a focus on foundation-building. Peres preferred the more dynamic image of "flying high and fast." Syrian Ambassador al-Mouallim critically remarked:

[H]e was in a hurry—he wanted to enter the elections with the Syrian–Israeli agreement in his hand. He wanted to "fly high and fast," as he used to say. I used to say to the Israeli counterpart that it is important to fly but it is also very important to know when and where to land—you can't continue to fly high and fast. We have our public opinion and we need to sell the agreement to them to get them to accept it. But he couldn't wait. (al-Mouallim 1997, p. 85)

Hafez al-Assad was concerned that by moving too quickly he might inadvertently fall into a trap. He was not prepared to adapt to a new pace just because his adversary sought to push him. Peres was aware that Syria was moving at another pace and compared it to the Syrian way of conducting "a military campaign—slowly, patiently, directed by strategic and tactical considerations" (Hinnebusch 1996, p. 44). Peres also made clear what he ultimately envisaged from a peace deal with Syria: a new regional system of cooperation and economic development in which Syria would be a key party (Savir 1998, p. 268). To Hafez al-Assad—for whom economic issues had never been a priority and who had done his best to isolate Syria from the global economy—these ideas were highly disconcerting, and he took Peres' expectation as yet another sign that Israel was bent on establishing regional hegemony. When, in February 2006, Israel concluded an agreement with Turkey on military cooperation, relations with Syria soured even further, with Damascus taking the agreement as indicating the formation of a Turkish–Israeli alliance against it and its regional interests.

At the beginning of his term, Peres claimed that he was eager to proceed quickly on all peace tracks and that, had he been in Rabin's shoes, he would already have concluded an agreement with Syria (Seale 2000, p. 75). Yet instead, his manner of conducting negotiations prevented progress on the Syrian track. His domestic security strategy failed; an upsurge in terrorist attacks left the Israeli population with an increased sense of insecurity, and on 29 May 1996 Peres lost the election to Benjamin Netanyahu.

The Netanyahu years, 1996–1999

The election of Benjamin Netanyahu signaled a definitive change in the tide of the peace process. Netanyahu's outright rejection of the previously agreed upon principle of "land for peace" seemed to make any progress during his tenure unlikely. Mistrust was at an all-time high. In the autumn of 1996, in reaction to reports of Syrian troop movements on the Golan, Israel mobilized its troops, and the two countries came to the brink of war (*Jerusalem Post,* 28 October 1996). It later came to light that the reports had been fabricated by a Mossad agent in an attempt to undermine Syrian–Israeli negotiations. The agent was later charged with treason.[21]

On another occasion, Hafez al-Assad allegedly sent a message to Netanyahu to assure him that Syria had no intention of attacking Israel. According to the Israeli newspaper *Ma'ariv* this message fanned the flames of concern for Israel because, as it turned out, the United States had tampered with the text of the message and added the thinly veiled threat that if "no progress were made in the peace process and the negotiations remained frozen, Assad would feel free to use every option and act."[22] This incident tarnished Syrian–American relations and cast serious doubts on the reliability of the American channel in the peace process.[23]

The Syrian government, always critical of the perceived bias of the US administration towards Israel now learned that US influence in Jerusalem was more limited than it had assumed. An Israeli political analyst commented after the 1996 London meeting between Clinton and Netanyahu that America's lack of influence on Israel was particularly harmful for Syria, observing that the United States could pressure Israel to a limited degree on the Palestinian track but that it did not have the leverage to do so on the Syrian track since it was virtually dead already.[24]

Throughout Netanyahu's presidency, relations between the United States and Israel remained tense. Less than a month after taking office Netanyahu declared that he would seek to reduce Israeli dependence on US economic assistance.[25] While pledging adherence to previous agreements with the Palestinians, Netanyahu left no doubt that the Interim Agreement should not be seen as the basis for a two-state solution. The Israeli Cabinet approved the extension of settlements in the West Bank, and negotiations with the Palestinians were not restarted. In September, the unannounced opening of the Western Wall tunnel caused a wave of violence. The domestic and regional climate had become poisoned within a few months of Netanyahu taking office, and Assad was disappointed by Israel's reluctance to acknowledge what from a Syrian perspective had already been achieved. In an interview with CNN in September 1996, Assad declared:

Within the framework of those commitments, agreement was reached between Syria and Israel on the Israeli withdrawal from the Golan up to the 4 June 1967 lines. ... This has taken place under the supervision and with the knowledge of the United States. It goes without saying that the present Israeli government has to abide by an agreement reached by the former Israeli government, which was a legitimate government, and so according to our considerations, it represented Israel. (al-Assad 1996)

Given the Clinton administration's commitment to the peace process, Netanyahu's policy of dismantling the existing achievements dealt a heavy blow to Israeli–American relations.[26] This also had a detrimental effect on US–Syrian relations because, as the peace process slowed down, the US administration reduced the extent of its engagement with Syria.

Despite the overt animosity and mistrust, secret negotiations were ongoing between the Netanyahu government and Syria. In a parallel channel, the former US ambassador to Syria, Ed Djerejian, and George Nader, an American journalist of Lebanese origin who had good access to a senior Netanyahu advisor, tried to advance negotiations.[27] In a 1999 report, Daniel Pipes shed more light on this parallel track, explaining that, notwithstanding his hardline image, Netanyahu was more willing than either of his predecessors to make serious concessions on territory and security in order to achieve a deal with Syria.

Yet, faced with Assad's steadfast rejection of these terms, he [Netanyahu, B. S.] capitulated and, in a stunning reversal, agreed that Israel would, indeed, return to the 1967 lines. Second, having initially demanded that the Israeli withdrawal take place over a ten- to 15-year period, he ultimately settled on 16 to 24 months. (Pipes 1999)

According to Pipes, Netanyahu's willingness to compromise on long-standing Israeli positions was rooted in a fear that, in the absence of progress on any track, the United States would force him to accept an accord with the Palestinians to which he was opposed. He was also aware that a breakthrough on the Syrian–Lebanese track would bolster his standing with the public in advance of the upcoming elections. In the end, the agreement did not materialize, as Netanyahu failed to win the necessary political support for his plan. Pipes' account was subsequently contested by Danny Naveh, a member of Israel's secret negotiation team, who rejected the idea that Netanyahu was even remotely conciliatory in his dealings with Syria.[28]

Revival of the peace process under Barak, 1999–2000

Ehud Barak became prime minister of Israel in the elections of 17 May 1999. Hafez al-Assad "welcomed" Ehud Barak to office in an unprecedented manner. In an interview with Patrick Seale, Hafez al-Assad spoke of Barak as a "brave and honest man" who had sufficient support and the right style to bring the Syrian–Israeli negotiations to a successful conclusion (*al-Hayat*, 23 June 1999). For Assad to communicate via the international media in such a way was exceptional, much as it was for him to refer to an Israeli counterpart in such positive terms. Syrian officials were familiar with Ehud Barak. Between 1991 and 1995, as the Israeli Defense Forces' chief of staff, Barak had been meeting Syrian military officials to discuss security issues related to prospective agreements.

Barak attempted to restart the Middle East peace process and revive the hitherto frozen tracks. December 1999 marked the first direct encounter between Syrian and Israeli officials in four years, as Syrian Foreign Minister Sharaa met with Prime Minister Barak in the presence of President Clinton and Secretary of State Madeleine Albright. The talks were marked by discord; Clinton's efforts to encourage both sides to conclude a deal were all in vain. The summaries prepared at the end of the talks on 8 January 2000 revealed the insurmountable differences between the parties. While Syria acknowledged that the 4 June line was not a border and agreed to the appointment of a border demarcation committee, it insisted that "withdrawal" from the Golan should extend both to the military and to civilians. For its part, Israel refused to commit to the evacuation of settlements.[29] Subsequent US efforts to bring the parties together also ended in failure. While Assad was apparently willing to make concessions regarding security arrangements (i.e. accepting an early warning station manned by American and French technicians on the Golan Heights), he remained adamant on the extent of the withdrawal.

This failure was followed by another bitter pill for Syria. In May 2000, Barak finalized Israel's unilateral withdrawal from South Lebanon, in one move depriving the Syrian government of its primary justification for maintaining military contingents in Lebanon, and Hezbollah of its *raison d'être* of liberating Lebanese territory.[30] Yet another card Syria held in the struggle against Israel had thus been rendered useless, and when Hafez al-Assad died just a few months later it became clear that the peace process would now take a backseat to the new Syrian president's efforts to consolidate his power domestically.

Despite the Syrian regime's initially positive response to Barak's election, the next round of Syrian–Israeli talks failed, as did the Palestinian–Israeli negotiations in Camp David in the summer of 2000. Barak was consumed with domestic problems and the breakdown of the Palestinian–Israeli track, which, together with Ariel Sharon's visit to the Temple Mount, sparked the second intifada and placed Barak's government under severe pressure. Barak called for early elections, which he lost to Sharon on 7 March 2001.

Barak's term highlighted just how difficult it had become to achieve a parliamentary majority that would back the continuation of negotiations. His government was weak from the beginning, and the chaos, pressure, and demands for immediate security measures left no room for serious progress on talks. For Syria, the end of negotiations also had implications for its relations with the United States. As pundit Flynt Leverett writes: "In March 2000, two months before Hafiz al-Assad's death, the Syrian track of the peace process effectively collapsed at the Clinton–Assad summit in Geneva, removing the principal framework for structuring Syria's relations with Israel and the United States" (Leverett 2005, p. 101).

Sharon's Approach to the Peace Negotiations, 2001–5

It was clear from the outset that Sharon would be less conciliatory than his predecessors, and it was also evident that he had no intention of making any concessions to Syria. At the 2002 Arab League summit in Beirut, member states made Israel a far-reaching offer of peace that included full normalization with all Arab countries in exchange for full withdrawal.[31] Since the content of the offer reflected long-standing demands, Bashar al-Assad backed the initiative (Jouejati 2003a). The Sharon government did not react to the proposal. Similar Syrian signals indicating a willingness to negotiate received a similar non-response or were explicitly dismissed as attempts to lure Israel into fruitless negotiations.

It was debatable how fruitful future negotiations would be under Bashar al-Assad. He could hardly have settled for less than his father would have accepted. At the same time, regaining the Golan Heights for Syria and delivering something his father could not might have boosted his domestic standing.

SYRIA, ISRAEL, AND PALESTINE

From 2006 to the present

While at the official level there was evidently little room for Syria and Israel to come to an understanding, an additional informal channel was established with Turkish assistance and Swiss support in 2006. Ibrahim Suleiman, an American businessman of Syrian origin, and Alon Liel, a former member of the Israeli foreign office, proposed transforming the Golan Heights into a park, which would remain under Syrian sovereignty but which would be accessible to the citizens of both countries.[32] Neither government ever overtly supported this "private" initiative, although the parties involved enjoyed the confidence of high-ranking officials on both sides (*Ha'aretz*, 16 January 2007).

Since 2006, there have been several calls from Israeli activists and intellectuals to test Bashar's readiness, and there have been other back channels through which Syria and Israel have been communicating.[33] However, a number of subsequent developments served to create new problems, the 2006 war in Lebanon being one of them. After Hezbollah had kidnapped two Israeli soldiers on the Lebanese–Israeli border, Israel launched a war to force their release. Only a year earlier, Syria had withdrawn its troops from Lebanon under international pressure. Now Syria threatened to intervene in favor of Hezbollah. On 6 September 2007, Israel bombarded a site in the north-eastern area of Syria close to Deir ez-Zor, which it suspected was being used as a prospective nuclear arms factory. Syria denied these charges, but the IAEA later concluded that the structure was that of a North Korean nuclear facility. A year later, on 1 August 2008, General Mohammad Suleiman, special presidential advisor for arms procurement and strategic weapons to Bashar al-Assad, was assassinated at his home on the beach in Tartous, allegedly by a sniper from an Israeli yacht (*Der Spiegel*, 2 November 2009).

Interestingly, this massive Israeli intervention into Syria did not lead to an interruption in the communication that Syria and Israel had pursued since April 2007 through a Turkish channel. Turkey, interested in raising its profile in the Middle East, held a series of meetings in which Syria and Israel could communicate indirectly. Whereas US negotiators had complained about Hafez al-Assad's "bladder diplomacy," imposing the most uncomfortable conditions on everybody involved in the talks, the atmosphere in this round was completely different.[34] One round of talks was held in 2008 during a "family vacation" of Bashar al-Assad in the Turkish coastal town of Bodrum, with Erdoğan and his family warmly receiving the president and his wife in the sea resort. The Gaza war in the winter of 2008, however, brought an end to the process.

In the fall of 2010, when Israeli talks with the Palestinians had stalled, Israeli Prime Minister Benjamin Netanyahu engaged in secret peace discussions with Syria, a process that was interrupted by the Syrian revolution. Since the Syrian regime's position towards Israel was widely shared by the opposition, it is unlikely that concluding a peace deal with any future government will be easier.

9/11 and the War on Terror

Soon after 9/11 the Israeli government began to draw parallels between the tragedy and the terrorist acts perpetrated by Palestinian militants and Hezbollah against Israel. By equating Hamas and Hezbollah with al-Qaeda, Israel sought to garner international support to deal with its own terrorist problem as part and parcel of the global war on terrorism. As one Israeli general stated: "We have to make Hezbollah the al-Qaeda of the region."[35]

For Damascus, it was important to differentiate between the 9/11 al-Qaeda attacks, which, in its view, constituted an act of terrorism, and the "legitimate resistance" of Palestinian and Lebanese groups against Israeli occupation. However, taking note of Israel's strategy, the Syrian regime recognized that at least a temporary change of policy would be necessary. Syria conducted itself with more caution than usual in this situation, and Foreign Minister Sharaa said on al-Jazeera that at times it was "necessary for a resistance movement to take a break."[36]

Cooperating with the United States to combat al-Qaeda did not exempt Syria from international scrutiny. Washington still sought to pressure Damascus to abandon its support for militant movements in the region once and for all. When US Secretary of State Colin Powell was dispatched to Syria in May 2003 to demand that the Syrian regime close the offices of Palestinian rejectionist groups, Damascus responded in classic fashion—complying in substance while refusing to give in at an official level.

The United States took no action against Syria at the time, but when Israel took matters into its own hands on 5 October 2003, carrying out a raid in Syrian airspace and bombing a deserted Palestinian training camp, the United States stood by and watched. It was alleged that

Islamic Jihad fighters had trained in the camp, run by PFLP–GC, and that the raid was a response to Islamic Jihad attacks on Haifa the day before. Syria, which at that time held a seat on the UN Security Council, asked the members to condemn Israel's actions, but in the face of US opposition the request got nowhere.[37] In his letter to the Security Council, Foreign Minister Sharaa highlighted Syria's restraint and warned that Israeli behavior could plunge the region into a crisis:

Syria is not incapable of establishing a balance of resistance and deterrence that would oblige Israel to revise its approach. Syria has demonstrated extreme restraint fully aware that Israel is attempting to fabricate all kinds of pretexts, gleaned from different quarters, to export its internal crisis to the region as a whole and to expose the region to a new escalation and a new conflagration.[38]

In 2004 there were two separate attacks on Hamas members in Damascus. Syria blamed Israel for both, and the Israeli government neither confirmed nor denied responsibility. In Syria the targeted killings were taken as a message that Israeli intelligence was not only aware of what was going on in Syria but that it was also able and willing to carry out precisely planned attacks.

Syrian–Palestinian Relations

The founding of the state of Israel had led to the flight of approximately 300,000 Palestinians to Syria. The Syrian government did not protest Israel's policy outright or resist the influx of refugees. The Syrian economy was strong at the time, and the demand for labor was high. President Husni al-Zaim indicated that Syria would be willing to resettle 300,000 Palestinian refugees permanently, on the condition that the international community provided financial support.[39]

Over the years, the "right of return" has become a constant theme in the Syrian government's policy and rhetoric. On the ground, Syrian policy appears to have been focused mainly on integrating Palestinians into Syrian society, and it did not experience the refugee issue in quite the same way as Jordan and Lebanon, both of which accepted many more Palestinian refugees relative to their populations than Syria.

While Damascus did not grant Palestinians Syrian citizenship, in many respects they were treated as citizens. They could attend school and university and have careers in the military and in government. Palestinians required special permits to purchase property, but they were not restricted to settling in particular areas or camps. Areas that began as Palestinian camps were steadily integrated into urban centers. Palestinian neighborhoods in Damascus today are hardly distinguishable from predominantly Syrian areas. Palestine Street in Yarmouk camp, for example, has become a popular shopping area for clothing and food, including the famous Bayt al-Kunafa. However, in some instances, predominantly Palestinian neighborhoods and the Neirab camp outside Aleppo lacked core infrastructure such as sewage systems. This was part of a deliberate political strategy on the part of the Syrian authorities to underscore that the Palestinian presence in Syria was temporary, and that someday the refugees would return home.

It seemed that the Syrian government had finally accepted that most of the Palestinians who came to Syria would remain in the country, having built new homes and new lives, even if a peace agreement were eventually reached. Some small but noteworthy steps have been taken in recognition of this reality. Development aid earmarked for Syria was invested in projects to improve the condition of Palestinian areas, and increased efforts were made to ensure that camps are better integrated with their surrounding environments.[40] As time goes on, it appears less and less likely that a right of return, even if granted, would be viable in practice. Syrian efforts to integrate the Palestinian community into the country's social fabric should not be underrated since they offer relief despite the failure to resolve what may be the most challenging issue in the Middle East conflict.

Assad and the PLO

Syrian efforts to manage its Palestinian population extended beyond their integration into existing institutions. A Palestinian wing of the army was created, as well as a special category in the Ba'th party. Hafez al-Assad paid great attention to both, not so much out of solidarity, but because he was acutely aware of the problems Palestinian movements with too much autonomy could create—as was the case in Jordan in 1970 and in Lebanon in the mid-1970s. Assad was eager to prevent any kind of Palestinian militant action against Israel being launched from Syrian territory, and by pursuing this integrative approach he sought to exert control over Palestinian activism. As a non-state actor, the PLO found itself in a dilemma. Forced to remain in exile, efforts to consolidate the movement were likely to interfere with the domestic policies of other states, and as a result the movement risked sparking conflict with host governments (Brand 1990, p. 25). The PLO's main aim was to secure Palestinian independence and the liberation of Palestinian lands, but the PLO's strategy required greater independence and freedom of action than Syria and other host states were prepared to allow.

Assad's relationship with PLO leader Yasser Arafat was characterized by animosity. The ill feeling dated back to 1970 when Damascus intervened in Jordan's crisis against the Palestinians.[41] Just a few years later, when Syria became embroiled in the Lebanese civil war, its troops once again clashed with the PLO. And when the PLO took on Israel, Syria did not lend its support.

The Syrian president never treated Arafat as an equal. In Assad's worldview, he was the one with the lead role in the relationship. He knew that an independent Palestinian entity would make its own decisions and that these would not necessarily coincide with Syrian interests. As a means of exerting pressure on Israel, Damascus welcomed the PLO to Syria, but not as an autonomous actor. Assad wanted to make decisions for the Palestinians, or, as his biographer Patrick Seale has put it: "In Assad's scheme of things, the Palestine problem was too important to be left to the Palestinians" (Seale 1988, p. 348). The Syrian regime under Hafez al-Assad appropriated the Palestinian cause in order to boost its own regional and domestic credentials. As an idea, as the ultimate cause to defend, the issue of Palestine remains an important element in Syrian policy. And yet, by and large, Assad did not trust the Palestinians. Arafat's support for Michel Aoun's government in Lebanon and for Iraq during the Gulf Crisis provided stark reminders of Palestinian decision-making that confirmed Assad's distrust of Arafat as they headed into the Madrid Conference.

Interestingly, Hafez al-Assad's death did not lead Damascus to reconcile with Arafat. In a lengthy interview in 2001, Bashar al-Assad explained that Syria would not oppose any deal that was accepted by the Palestinians but made clear that Arafat was not welcome in Damascus unless he adopted the Syrian approach toward peace negotiations (al-Assad 2001a).

Syrian–Palestinian relations after the 1993 Oslo Accords

Assad recognized that the Declaration of Principles concluded between the PLO and Israel would have an impact on the Syrian–Israeli track of the peace process. He was keen not to leave this solo act on the part of the Palestinians unanswered. It was a complex dilemma, since Syria could not afford to alienate Israel while negotiations continued between the two, or risk losing the recently won support of the United States and the international community. With this in mind, Hafez al-Assad was careful not to condemn the move too strongly, but he meanwhile quietly acquiesced to the establishment by ten Palestinian anti-Arafat groups based in Damascus of a new version of the National Salvation Front (NSF).[42] These Syrian-backed opponents of the Oslo Declaration were not known to be shy in expressing their views, and Assad calculated that this "Alliance of Palestinian Forces" (APF) could serve a convenient purpose in being more vocal than the Syrian government itself on issues to do with the peace process (Lesch 1995, p. 117).

In a way, the structure of the APF resembled the Progressive National Front in Syria, with its broad range of interests subsumed under one umbrella. The Syrian government permitted members of the APF to publish in Syria, and they even had their own radio station, al-Quds, which operated from southern Syria and was run by the PFLP–GC. All of the APF members were united in opposing Arafat and rejecting the Oslo agreement. While the NSF had previously consisted of only leftist and nationalist groups, in its new incarnation it included two parties with religious programs: Hamas and Palestinian Islamic Jihad (PIJ). These additions, while serving to expand the AFP's potential base of support, also limited the extent of any common ground within the group to a single point: rejecting a settlement as envisaged by Arafat.

The leftist organizations regarded the Islamic groups with growing concern because of their increasingly successful performance within the occupied territories. In contrast, the traditional rejectionist groups' standing had steadily declined over the years. The aging leaders could not mobilize the masses; there was little room for ideological innovation; and they failed to recruit a younger cadre of leaders. Popular confidence in their ability to introduce political change gradually faded. When, in the latter half of the 1990s, the situation in the occupied territories deteriorated massively and public disappointment with the peace process skyrocketed, the Palestinian population became polarized between the "old-school" leaders and the Islamist-oriented groups. Their hardline anti-Israel stance, militancy, and confessional dimension made Hamas and PIJ eligible for the kind of external financial sponsorship that was less accessible to the other Palestinian groups.

Syrian support for the Palestinian rejectionist groups was important from a logistics point of view. The ability to act in Syria and Lebanon was a geostrategic advantage, especially for the transfer of money and weapons. It was also easier for the groups to function in an environment where they had fewer concerns about American presence and involvement than in countries like Jordan or Egypt. Islamic Jihad was backed primarily by Iran; Hamas depended mainly on Saudi financing (Mishal/Sela 2000; Hatina 2001). Inside the territories, this money was used for social projects that had the desired result of enhancing public support for both parties. Even in less conservative circles, people appreciated Hamas's socio-economic engagement, which further broadened the group's support base. Unable to compete with this popularity, the other groups preferred to work within the group rather than have Hamas and PIJ as rivals; and cooperation with the leftists enhanced the nationalist credentials of the two Islamist-oriented groups.[43]

Hamas and PIJ were the last groups to establish a presence in Syria, and they did so only reluctantly. They were not keen to be too strongly identified with Syria (Hatina 2001, pp. 41ff.). PIJ, in particular, was concerned about being portrayed as an outside movement by Hamas and the PLO. Representative Fathi al-Shiqaqi always stressed that his organization's primary base was the occupied territories, and that having a base in Lebanon was necessary only because the PIJ leadership had been expelled from Israel in 1987. However, the move to Lebanon enabled the group to enhance its ties with Hezbollah and Iran. It focused its activities more on the Palestinian camps in Lebanon than in Syria, which would not have tolerated active recruitment and incitement on its own territory.[44]

While the value of the APF for Syria was more in the symbolic act of its foundation, its presence has been a central part of Damascus's two-fold strategy of negotiating while keeping other options open. Through these groups it has been able to demonstrate its commitment to the Palestinian cause and its continued opposition to Israel. As one US analyst put it: "While Israel has the Golan with which to negotiate a peace deal with Syria, Syria has no bargaining chips other than the Lebanese and Palestinian resistance groups" (Salhani 2003, p. 141). With respect to Hamas in particular, Syria was happy to provide an external base to an organization that could challenge the Palestinian Authority and keep it weak, rather than having the PA replaced by a confident and autonomous actor. However, if in backing the rejectionist groups Syria hoped it would at some point be asked for help in dealing with them and enjoy heightened regional and international influence as a result, the strategy has failed. Efforts to mediate between the Palestinian Authority and rejectionist groups have mostly been undertaken in Cairo and by the Egyptians—not only because of the good relations between the Egyptian, Israeli, and American governments, but also because of Egypt's relations with these groups (Kumaraswamy 2005). Rather than being positively credited for its potential influence on the groups, Syria has more often shared the blame for attacks perpetrated by the rejectionist groups.

The global post-9/11 focus on terrorism made the situation for the Palestinian groups and for Damascus more difficult. The international community had never accepted the Syrian argument that the Palestinian groups were part of a legitimate resistance against occupation. During the peace process, Israel had repeatedly demanded that the Syrian regime condemn attacks executed by Palestinian groups, and in 1994 Hafez al-Assad's reluctance to do so during a joint press conference with President Clinton led to a diplomatic crisis. Washington ramped up the pressure on Syria to oust the groups and close their offices, and five of the ten Damascus-based factions were listed as terrorist groups by the United States and Europe.[45]

After keeping a low profile for several months in order to take the pressure off Damascus, the Palestinian groups began to show their faces again; Hamas leader Khaled Mesha'al publicly praised the Syrian refusal to give in to US demands. He conceded that the relationship between Damascus and Washington was inherently problematic, with or without the issue of Palestinian groups in Syria: "Even if Syria changed its position because of those pressures, the situation will not change and Syria will remain the accused" (*Ha'aretz*, 18 May 2004). While it is hard to determine what role the outside groups play in the occupied territories, Damascus has, particularly in times when it has felt marginalized, seen a considerable symbolic value in hosting them. A consistent feature of Syria's foreign policy strategy has been that of positioning itself to "play the spoiler" when necessary, in order to influence outcomes to its advantage. Unfortunately for Syria, this policy has actually proven to be something of an obstacle in furthering its national interests, and with respect to Hamas in particular, the stronger the group becomes the less likely it is that Syria will have any influence on its leadership.

The election victory of Hamas in 2006 was not widely celebrated in Syria. Having assumed a strong position in Gaza, it was clear that this would give the Palestinian organization more leverage and independence from Syria. Right after the elections, Hamas-leader Khaled Mesha'al travelled to Tehran, thus enhancing his relationship with Iran, a move that resulted in generous Iranian funding for Hamas. Syria, eager to be in control over the movement, watched these developments skeptically. Hamas maintained the Damascus office, but its relations with the Syrian state remained lukewarm.

For Hamas, the more people were killed by the Syrian government during 2011, the more difficult it became to justify its relations with Damascus. Some of the demands of the Syrian protesters were aiming at a reform process similar to that Hamas had envisaged for Palestine, and President Assad's rejection did not fit with Hamas' policy. In November 2011, Hamas began to relocate away from the Syrian capital, mostly to Egypt. It did not openly break with the Syrian regime and sought to downplay the prospects of this happening in its official statements (*The National*, 25 November 2011). Reportedly, Mesha'al made an offer to mediate between the government and the protesters, and when Assad was not interested, relations cooled further (*The National*, 26 December 2011). Of the Palestinian movements, only Ahmad Jibril's PFLP–GC decided to side and fight with the Syrian government in the revolution.

Conclusion

Between 1990 and 2011, the question of peace negotiations has gone through several different stages. The conference of Madrid meant a new opportunity in a changed political landscape. The ensuing peace process did not achieve progress on the Syrian–Israeli side, although there have been different channels through which both sides have been communicating.

On the surface, the Syrian–Israeli conflict looks as though it should be relatively simple to resolve, given that it is mostly a territorial conflict. Yet the practice on both sides of making satisfaction of their most extreme demands a precondition for negotiation has meant that the process has effectively led nowhere. Hafez al-Assad finally learned that time was not on his side in the peace process. It was difficult for him to adapt to the different approaches of the changing Israeli prime ministers and to understand the constraints that small majorities and coalitions imposed on successive Israeli governments. When Bashar came to power, he needed to bolster his domestic position, for which negotiations with Israel were not a priority. On the contrary, they could have had a negative impact.

The preferred Syrian strategy of keeping all options open—entering into negotiations and consistently reiterating interest in a peace deal while backing Palestinian opponents to the Oslo Accords—has in effect come home to roost. It has made it easy for Syria's adversaries in Israel to cast doubts on Syria's credibility, and extremely difficult for the peace camp in Israel to lobby for a continuation of negotiations. It has also had a profoundly negative effect on Syrian–US relations, especially after 9/11 when Israeli "hawks" reached an understanding with the US neo-conservative establishment whereby fighting international terrorism must also include the regional terrorism faced by Israel.

A peace agreement would provide the conditions for developing relations in other fields. However, it is difficult to envisage whether there will be any progress on this issue in the near future. The "traditional" Syrian opposition, from which many members of the National Coalition stem, did not differ from the government with regard to Israel or the Golan. Among the "new" players that have emerged on the ground, there are some radical Islamist groups for whom peace with Israel will not be a priority, and from which Israel fears a new military threat. The Israeli government has therefore been hesitant to speak out in favor of the revolution. However, there was no "ideal" way to approach the issue from an Israeli angle: had the Israeli government embraced the Syrian revolution, this would have further nurtured the rumors about a foreign conspiracy behind the revolution.

4

BACK TO SQUARE ONE

SYRIA AND TURKEY

For a brief period, 1998 until 2011, Syria's connection with Turkey was something of a positive anomaly in Syria's foreign relations. Having been mired in crisis in the late 1990s, Syria's relations with Turkey were anomalous in that they improved significantly. After 1998, Damascus and Ankara had overcome serious bilateral irritants, including a territorial dispute over the Turkish province of Hatay,[1] the question of water distribution in the border region, and the issue of Syrian support for the Kurdish Workers' Party (PKK), to arrive at a high-level of cooperation over the following years.

The case of Syrian–Turkish relations is fascinating: Turkey is the only country with which Syria has been brought to the brink of war during the period discussed in this book. Turkey did not leave any doubt about its readiness to intervene militarily and was, back then, supported by Israel: a massive threat that led Syria to accede to Turkish demands. This deep crisis was the catharsis for an unprecedented blossoming of relations, boosting trade and tourism, but also security cooperation and support for the Syrian regime in crises. When Syria was under massive international pressure in 2005, its relations with Turkey were unaffected. In 2007/8, the Turkish government even hosted a series of indirect Syrian–Israeli peace talks. The strain placed on Syrian–Turkish relations during the Syrian revolution, however, was simply too great. After initial calls for President al-Assad to change course, the Turkish government altered its position and began to offer full support to the opposition, before asking Assad to step down in the summer of 2011.

In this chapter I examine the different periods of Turkish–Syrian relations—conflict until 1998, the development close relations between 1998 and 2011, and the collapse of the relationship due to the Syrian regime's handling of the uprising. Given the particular importance of the PKK, both in the 1990s and today, I also discuss their role in the broader context of Syrian–Turkish relations.

Regional developments in the early 1990s

The Madrid peace process, which began in the early 1990s, opened the door to Turkish–Israeli cooperation. Israel had long expressed an interest in improved ties with Ankara, but the latter had been hesitant, always concerned about its relations with Arab states. Israel was interested in Turkey because of its geostrategic position bordering Syria, Iraq, and Iran. And it was exactly this that made Syria suspicious of and nervous about a rapprochement between the two countries, but which finally moved Syria to pursue cooperation with Turkey.

This chapter examines the vicissitudes of Syrian–Turkish bilateral engagement since 1990, with particular emphasis on the period between 1990 and 1991, when the Madrid process and Turkish–Israeli rapprochement began; the period between 1995 and 1996, when tensions between Syria and Turkey rose in response to military cooperation agreements signed with other parties; and the period between 1998 and 1999, when the Turkish–Syrian crisis culminated in the Adana Agreement which set the stage for future engagement between the two countries. Examination of the relationship between Syria and Turkey shows that major developments were prompted in large part by changes in Turkey's dealings with Israel. It also demonstrates that Damascus's shift to a broader view of its interests enabled it to pursue a successful and strategic partnership with its influential neighbor—until the harmonious relationship collapsed in light of the current situation.

BACK TO SQUARE ONE: SYRIA AND TURKEY

Sticking points: the Hatay dispute

The territorial dispute between Syria and Turkey centered on the Syrian district of al-Iskanderun (now referred to by its present-day name 'Hatay') and has been a major sticking point in Syrian–Turkish relations. In 1939, the French mandate authority ceded the province of al-Iskanderun to Turkey with the aim of enlisting Ankara's support in the Second World War. For many years Syria refused to acknowledge that the province was Turkish. On official maps the international border was indicated by a dotted line, implying that Damascus still regarded the province as part of its own territory, though it never attempted to retake it militarily. However, when the PKK launched its first attack in Hatay in July 1995, Syria's instigation was suspected. By 2001 the picture was quite different. Syrian Foreign Minister Farouq al-Sharaa said that the territorial dispute was no longer a priority, but rather an issue that could be addressed in the future:

Issues that seem sensitive today could be easily resolved in the future when the bilateral climate reaches a level at which they will not pose difficulties. It is wrong to give priorities to such issues now because this could harm cooperation in other fields ... In the end they will be resolved but we should not push more than we do.[2]

Over the years, Syria seemed to have quietly accepted the status quo and did not publicly renew the claim to Hatay after Bashar al-Assad came to power. Maps in post-2003 Syrian textbooks showed the internationally recognized border, and posters depicting Syria at government-sponsored protests no longer included Hatay.[3] In its formal dealings with Turkey, Syria did not drop the matter officially but agreed to postpone the discussion. For its part, Ankara no longer sees the issue as problematic. When in 2005 Turkish Foreign Minister Abdullah Gül was asked about Syrian recognition of Turkish sovereignty over Hatay, he said there was "no territorial disagreement between Turkey and Syria."[4]

The challenge of managing water

Water management and distribution has long been a contentious topic in Syrian–Turkish relations, particularly with respect to the Euphrates River, which flows from Turkey into Syria and Iraq. In a region with increasing scarcity, water has become a security issue in its own right. As downstream neighbors, Syria and Iraq are concerned about the impact of reduced water flow on agriculture and their respective economies. Damascus has regularly and vehemently opposed Turkey's extensive dam projects, complaining that the downstream flow permitted by Turkey is insufficient for Syria's needs. Aware of the potential for conflict, Ankara employed a carrot-and-stick strategy: threatening Syria with water shortages when it was uncooperative, while at the same time promising access to water to develop closer ties with Syria, the Gulf States, and Israel.

For many years, regional dynamics prevented Syria and Iraq from developing a united front against Turkey on water issues. In 1984, Syria began supporting PKK incursions into Turkey as a means of pressuring its northern neighbor, thereby adding a security dimension to the disagreements over water (Williams 2001, p. 29). Angered by Syria's decision to side with Tehran during the Iran–Iraq War, Iraqi President Saddam Hussein began cooperating with Ankara against the PKK. The same year, Iraq and Turkey signed a "Hot Pursuit" agreement allowing Turkey to launch incursions into northern Iraq in pursuit of PKK fighters (Sayari 1997, p. 47). When Ankara and Damascus signed a security protocol in 1987, the Turks offered a guaranteed amount of water in exchange for Syrian cooperation in security matters. Damascus signed the agreement but was unhappy with the Turkish offer.

In an effort to drum up support for its cause, the Syrian government increasingly sought to transform the issue from a bilateral matter to one involving Turkey and the rest of the Arab world (Bengio 2004, p. 132). In addition, Syria continued backing PKK activities, particularly in areas earmarked by the Turks for dam construction. The PKK had its own motivations for trying to sabotage Turkish plans, viewing them as tantamount to the theft of Kurdish waters. For many years, Ankara denied the existence of a direct link between water issues and terrorist activity, as this would have entailed implicitly acknowledging that Syria had a concrete objective in encouraging PKK activity. Only in the mid-1990s did Turkish officials finally state publicly that Syria was using the PKK to achieve concessions from Turkey regarding water flow, and their message was quite clear: Turkey would not be bullied, and would never agree to the provision of "more water for no terrorism" (Williams 2001, p. 31). Though Syria never managed to obtain the desired amount of water from Turkey, it was successful in transforming the bilateral issue into one of regional importance.

BACK TO SQUARE ONE: SYRIA AND TURKEY

In the early 1990s Turkey decided to use its water resources as a means of improving its position in regional politics. The Madrid peace process included a working group on water in which Turkey participated, putting forth the notion that Turkish water could play a vital role in the settlement of the Middle East conflict. Based on the suggestion of an Israeli diplomat in the course of bilateral consultations, Ankara offered to sell water to Syria, Jordan, and the six Gulf States (excluding Iraq), all of which were increasingly concerned about water scarcity. Far from seeing the so-called "Peace Pipeline" as potentially complementary to the Middle East peace process, Arab countries received the proposal with skepticism. Apart from the considerable costs involved, they saw a danger in becoming too dependent on Turkish water, and the idea was summarily rejected (Rubin/Kirisci 2001, p. 100).

In the wake of this decision, Ankara began to monitor developments on the Syrian–Israeli track closely, fearing that success on that front would come at Turkey's expense if Hafez al-Assad were to persuade Israel and the United States to pressure Turkey into releasing more water downstream (Kohen 1996, p. 1). Noting regional dynamics, Turkey decided to try a different strategy—still portraying itself as a water-rich country with resources that could be used as political incentives—but this time proposing to transport water to Israel (Williams 2001, p. 27).

Not surprisingly, Damascus reacted strongly, complaining to the European Union and the Arab League about Turkey's unilateral water policy. Syria convened a conference of Arab foreign ministers in Damascus, with the final declaration calling for a "just and acceptable" sharing of waters between Turkey and Syria and criticizing the lack of consultation on water issues and the detrimental effects of dam construction.[5] This was the first time that such a range of states, including even Egypt and Saudi Arabia, had openly criticized Turkish water policy. Turkish officials quickly responded, suggesting that "Syria needed more water because they have to wash their hands from the blood of terrorism" (Robins 2003, p. 176). The water issue was consequently taken off the table, and water sharing always remained a bone of contention between Turkey and Syria.

Syria and the PKK

Unable to change Ankara's position on water sharing by diplomatic means, Syria attempted to pressure its northern neighbor by supporting non-state actors that could conduct operations in Turkish territory. Initially, Damascus worked through the Armenian Secret Army for the Liberation of Armenia (ASALA). Armenians fleeing persecution in Turkey had found refuge in Syria, forming a sizeable community there. Noting ASALA's cooperation with the PLO in Lebanon, in 1983 Damascus invited ASALA to move its headquarters to Syria, and permitted it to establish training camps (Pipes 1996, p. 58). The relationship with ASALA had little to do with the group itself, but more with the Syrian regime's rather indiscriminate policy of support to terrorist groups in order to pressure Turkey.[6] By the late 1980s ASALA had all but vanished, but the Kurdish Workers' Party (PKK) had meanwhile successfully expanded.[7] In shifting its support to the PKK, Syria employed its age-old strategy of using proxies to influence problematic relationships with other regional states, though this was by no means intended to imply that it now supported the establishment of an independent Kurdistan (Knudsen 2003, p. 206).

Political pressure on the PKK and leftist groups in Turkey increased in 1980 when the military took power in Ankara. Syria welcomed this opportunity to offer its services to these groups and, in turn, use them as tools in its own political wrangling with Turkey. The founder of the PKK, Abdullah Öcalan, fled first to Syria, then on to Lebanon.[8] The support he found in Syria and the training facilities at his disposal in Lebanon's Bekaa Valley enabled him to build the PKK into a fighting force that was able to declare an armed struggle against Turkey in 1984.[9] Öcalan maintained a house and an office in Damascus, training was conducted mainly in Lebanon, and cross-border PKK operations against Turkey were staged from northern Iraq, as opposed to Syria.

Öcalan did himself and the Syrian government a great favor in the mid-1990s when he stated publicly that a large number of the Kurds in Syria were not Syrian but were actually of Turkish origin (MacDowall 1998, p. 66). This was precisely the argument used by the Syrian regime to justify its refusal to extend Syrian citizenship to Kurds rendered stateless after the census of 1962. Öcalan played on the situation and successfully convinced thousands of frustrated and politically active Syrian Kurds to join the PKK struggle, simultaneously strengthening his own movement and channeling the anger of the Kurds toward Turkey and away from his Syrian sponsors.[10] The Syrian regime not only tolerated PKK activism in its territory but also recruited members in the Syrian

Kurdish community. As Omar Sheikhmous, a researcher and long-time observer of Syrian policy vis-à-vis the Kurds, recounts:

They [the PKK in Syria] had very good recruiters, especially among students and women. They were clever in recruiting youngsters, who were sent to Lebanon first and then to Turkey. For Syrian Kurds, the PKK was very attractive because the Syrian Kurdish community was corrupt and factionalized, and Syrian security had infiltrated it … About 30–35% were recruited by government organs. It was mainly "amn ad-dawle" (state security) that worked as an initiator and organizer. They had a number of contacts in the Kurdish community, mainly in Ifrin, Damascus, Qamishli and Aleppo. There was a clear agreement: "You'll be sent to fight in Turkey and therefore you'll not be asked for military service, and after several years you can come back." This worked through professional people who were influential in the Kurdish community, e.g. doctors. When the recruits left Syria, security kept their identity cards. There were two considerations behind this: First of all, they could not easily return but needed permission of security to do so. Second, if they were killed or tracked in Turkey, there would be no reflection on Syria.[11]

This strategy worked well for the Syrian regime: it provided a useful means for getting rid of Kurdish activists, while indirectly fighting Turkey. The Syrian army could not possibly have stood up to Turkish forces in a military confrontation, and thus the PKK's guerrilla strategies and constant low-level warfare served as a much more effective instrument to weaken and pressure the Turkish government. As in the case of Palestinian groups and Hezbollah, Syria was evidently involved in some way, but it was difficult to identify exactly how. At the same time Syria was keen to make the most of its leverage in negotiations with Turkey. Damascus and Ankara signed a security protocol in the mid-1990s, resulting in a strained relationship with the PKK. Syrian officials began to refer to the PKK as a "terrorist group," though the regime did not outlaw the organization or take measures to curb its activities. In fact, the offices of the now renamed PKK still remained active in northern Syria. Their relationship with the Syrian government and security apparatus has been ambiguous, and while local leaders were willing to meet with foreign diplomats and journalists, they were quick to state that they were no longer involved in training, recruitment, or military operations.[12]

Turkish journalist Ismet G. Imset provides what may be the most illustrative account of Syrian relations with the PKK up to 1992. In 1991 he visited a PKK training camp, "PKK Mahsun Korkmaz Academy," in the Bekaa Valley, where he also met Abdullah Öcalan.[13] He encountered unexpected openness and was even permitted to take photographs. PKK activists wanted to make clear that they considered themselves soldiers, not terrorists, saying: "There is no need to worry. We are an army and these people will all be part of a war. We have nothing to hide" (Imset 1992, p. 349).

Soon afterwards, Ismet travelled to Zakho in northern Iraq, where in 1991 he interviewed Nizamettin Taş (also known as "Botan"), a member of the PKK central committee and commander of all PKK guerrillas throughout the 1990s. Taş depicted the relationship with Syria, in which the PKK was an independent party, as based on mutual tolerance, shared values (an anti-imperialist orientation), and common interest. In his words, the PKK was only "exploiting the balance between the forces in the region and exploiting their contradictions. That is all" (Imset 1992, p. 358). But there were still challenges for the PKK in its dealings with Damascus. The Syrian government had never formally recognized the PKK or given it official permission to operate in the country, and on occasion Syrian authorities arrested PKK members or obstructed their passage through the country. Taş made it clear that while Syrian sponsorship had been crucial in enabling the PKK to grow and develop, it no longer needed this support:

Or else, we have no certain alliance with Syria and we have not entered any relationship. Had this been the case, it would have supported us, it would not have arrested us and it would not have blocked our way. There are problems of this kind and they will continue in the future. As far as a disagreement with Syria, we have no agreement in the first place. So, it cannot be severed. We have always had problems but according to our mutual interests, we have walked together. (Imset 1992, p. 358)

However, he also stressed that the PKK would "not allow anything that could create problems" for Syria, a statement that reflects some degree of self-awareness on the part of the PKK (Imset 1992, p. 358).

Early Turkish–Syrian security protocols, 1987–1993

Recognizing that Syrian support for terrorist activities would continue until bilateral relations improved, in 1987 Turkey launched its first initiative on security cooperation, offering guarantees on water distribution in exchange for an end to Syria's support of the PKK. The two neighbors signed a bilateral protocol in July of 1987 in which both agreed to prevent the illegal crossing of persons or goods into each other's territory, and to obstruct the activities of organizations, groups, or individuals "aimed at threatening or undermining the security and stability of the other party."[14] The protocol made no specific mention of terrorism or the PKK, but left no doubt that both were uppermost in the minds of those who had drafted it. Ankara evidently attached some importance to the protocol, to the extent of sending the prime minister to Damascus to sign it. For its part, the Syrian regime demonstrated its good will by signing the agreement, but this did not extend to admitting to Öcalan's presence in Syria; instead the regime allegedly sent him to Lebanon for an extended period (Olson 1997, p. 170). For some time after the protocol came into effect, the PKK was noticeably less active, but it was not long before it once again stepped up its activities in Syria.

The protocol was only the first of a series of Turkish initiatives to obtain Syrian commitments on security matters. For many years, the Turkish side had been reluctant to accuse Syria directly of support for the PKK, attempting to handle the matter more diplomatically. Whenever the situation was hinted at, Damascus steadfastly denied any links with the PKK, noting that the Bekaa Valley was not fully under its control and therefore Syria could not be blamed for activities taking place there. In March 1992, Turkish Prime Minster Demirel publicly denounced Syrian behavior as "unacceptable," claiming that PKK members crossed Syria with heavy weaponry and then entered from Iraq (Imset 1992, pp. 175ff.). In April 1992, Turkey's interior minister visited Syria, where he was received by President Hafez al-Assad and allegedly confronted Syrian officials with videotapes showing PKK-leader Öcalan going in and out of official buildings in Damascus. It was clear to the Syrian side that the Turks were taking the matter very seriously, and in the face of such evidence Syria could no longer deny its involvement with the PKK.

Anticipating a Turkish military attack on Syrian bases in Lebanon or a diplomatic intervention to sour relations with the United States, in April 1992 Damascus signed a security protocol with Turkey and for the first time officially acknowledged the PKK presence in its territory. Though the Turkish interior minister was convinced that Syria would abide by the security protocol, others in Turkey were more skeptical, bearing in mind the failure of earlier agreements. The latter view was also reflected in discussions with Iraqi Kurdish leaders, who noted Syria's interest in "keeping the PKK as a spare part. Something to be used when the time arises" (Imset 1992, p. 179).

By late 1993, Turkey had decided that it was now time to get tough with Syria on security matters. The Turkish prime minister traveled to Damascus in November to present Hafez al-Assad with an ultimatum. The visit resulted in the signing of the "Minutes on a Security Matter," in which Syria and Turkey condemned terrorism and agreed to prevent terrorists taking shelter in each other's territory. The agreement further stated: "If one party declares an organization as outlaw, the other Party would also prohibit the same organization. The apprehended members of outlawed organization [sic] would be extradited to the other Party" (Robins 2003, p. 175). In contrast to the previous bilateral security agreements, the "Minutes" made specific reference to the PKK. Damascus accordingly declared the PKK a terrorist organization and agreed to extradite its members to Turkey in the event of arrest. Syrian officials continued to make public statements denouncing the PKK, but refrained from expelling Öcalan or forcing the PKK to cease its activities in Syria, which, following a brief lull, noticeably increased. After some time, frustrated with Damascus's inaction and failure to make good on its promises, the Turkish military began to pursue PKK fighters across the Syrian border (Robins 2003, pp. 175–6).

Turkish–Israeli relations and the issue of the PKK

Turkish–Israeli cooperation progressed rapidly in a variety of areas. On the issue of terrorism, however, Israel was reluctant to take any step that might imply opposition to Kurdish activism. Until 1996, Israel's way of dealing with this was to treat the PKK issue as an internal Turkish matter. This approach changed once Benjamin Netanyahu took office. Rabin's assassination and increased terrorist activity during Peres' interim government had moved the issue to the forefront of the Israeli agenda. In a statement on Turkish television, Netanyahu announced his opposition to the notion of a Kurdish state and condemned PKK activities, characterizing Turkey and Israel as being similarly afflicted in dealing with terrorist threats: "Turkey has suffered from terrorist attacks from the PKK and we see no difference between the terrorism of the PKK and that which Israel suffers."[15] This change of policy produced a marked anxiety in Damascus, where the regime grew increasingly concerned about becoming the target of a coordinated attack from both the north and the south.

Although it is mountainous northern Iraq which serves as a safe haven for PKK fighters, rather than Syria, Damascus still retains a significant amount of influence over the organization. Syria initially abided by the Adana Agreement and refrained from any action related to the PKK—but this was to change in 2011. When Ankara slowly stepped up its criticism of the Syrian regime in the summer of 2011, the PKK launched a new series of attacks in which more than fifty Turkish soldiers died between July and November 2011. For a short time, the Turkish government seemed to be less outspoken on the Syrian crisis, presumably because of this development. Domestically, hardly any issue creates more pressure for Ankara than Kurdish attacks. However, in November and December, Turkey embarked on a stricter course, both in its military action against the PKK and in asking the Syrian government to end the violence and for President Assad to step down (*Die Zeit*, 17 August 2011). For Ankara, it has become increasingly difficult to handle the effects of the Syrian crisis. Turkey has received hundreds of thousands of refugees in the border area and also allows the Syrian opposition to reside and be active in Turkey. However, the Kurdish issue remains extremely sensitive, and the social situation in the border areas and particularly in Hatay has also produced social tension and a fear of a spill-over of the conflict. There have been some instances with the potential for escalation. In June 2012, for example, the Syrian Air Force shot down a Turkish fighter jet in international airspace—rumor had it they believed it to be a Syrian plane with a defecting pilot—and there have also been other violent events, such as a cross-border shooting and the explosion of a minibus in a border crossing where representatives of the National Coalition were supposed to pass into Syria. Yet aside from retaliatory strikes in October 2012, after five inhabitants of a Turkish border town died due to Syrian shelling, Ankara has so far avoided becoming directly involved in a military conflict.

Stepping up to the plate: Turkey's Middle East engagement

For many years, Ankara's relations with Arab states were characterized by awkwardness and mistrust, a holdover from the Ottoman period that neither side was fully able to bridge. By contrast, Turkey's connection with Israel began on a positive footing. Turkey was the first predominantly Muslim state to recognize the state of Israel officially and to establish diplomatic relations in 1949. While this move was not welcomed by the Arab states, it failed to result in their severing of relations with Ankara. From 1967 on, Turkey began to take an increasingly pro-Palestinian stance on regional issues, a move designed to satisfy the domestic demands of a population sympathetic to the Palestinian cause. Despite striving for balance in its Middle East dealings, Turkey has historically been hesitant to offend its Arab trading partners who also happen to be its main suppliers of oil, and this affected the extent to which Ankara engaged with certain states. Turkey's relations with Egypt, for example, expanded considerably once Arab states came to terms with Camp David and re-admitted Cairo to the Arab League (Rubin/Kirisci 2001, p. 102).

Until 1990, Turkey tried to avoid getting drawn into regional disputes, seeking instead to maintain good relations with all states in the region—Iran and Israel included. Syria was the only exception.[16] The Hatay dispute cast a shadow over the relationship, as did issues of water distribution and Syria's backing of the PKK. Damascus was uncomfortable with Turkey's NATO membership and close relations with Western powers, while Turkey was equally suspicious of Syrian–Soviet cooperation. Turkey made a point of siding with Iraq in almost all disputes involving Damascus and Baghdad. Syria in turn fostered closer relations with Greece and supported its position on Cyprus against the Turks (Alaçam 1994/5, p. 4). But the two countries eventually found themselves on the same side when, motivated by the promise of improved relations with Washington, they joined the international coalition against Iraq in the First Gulf War (Makovsky 1999, p. 92). As one of Iraq's key trading partners, Turkey's economy was hit hard during this period. The UN embargo limited Turkish–Iraqi trade, and Turkey also agreed to close the Turkish–Iraqi oil pipeline. At the same time, the rise in Turkish–Arab trade that Ankara had expected ultimately failed to materialize (Sayari 1997, p. 46). This state of affairs prompted Turkish officials to develop new partnerships with the aim of bolstering the country's flagging economy, underscored by a new approach to foreign policy (Aydin 2005, p. 3).

In the words of Turkish President Turgut Özal, Turkey would no longer be "passive and hesitant" but a more "active" player in foreign affairs (Robins 1992, p. 70). Nowhere was this change more obvious than in the Middle East. Turkey not only diversified its relationships but adopted an assertive position, making clear that it was prepared to use (as in the case of its incursions in northern Iraq), or to threaten to use, military force to defend itself. The signing of a 1996 military cooperation agreement with Israel and participation in joint exercises with Israel and the United States in the late 1990s also served to underscore this message and enhance Turkey's more assertive image.

Some observers described the changes in Turkish foreign policy as a necessary adaptation in the face of changing circumstances, rather than a spontaneous choice (Kut 2001, p. 10). Yet whether by choice or necessity, it is clear that Turkey had to deal with new sources of instability and conflict in its neighborhood. The demise of the Soviet Union led to the emergence of a host of new states with unsettled domestic dynamics, increasing the potential for regional insecurity. Throughout the 1990s the Turkish military became steadily more involved in foreign policy, with the Foreign Ministry playing only a "subordinate role" (Aras 2000, p. 161). According to the Turkish constitution, the military chief of staff carries almost the same rank as a minister, and due to the chief of staff's role in the National Security Council the holder of this position is generally deferred to on security-related matters. A prominent Turkish analyst describes the situation as follows:

[T]he most important change in shaping foreign and security policy during the 1990s was the increased role of the Turkish military. ... The active involvement of some neighbouring countries in support of separatist and religious fundamentalist groups threatened Turkey's stability. These developments pushed the military to the forefront of decision making, often in a manner that undermined the authority of civilian institutions. (Özcan 2001, p. 13)

Turkish and Israeli interests coincided politically in some areas, but bilateral rapprochement was mainly driven by the desire for increased military cooperation between the two. Therefore, most analysts see the military as the driving force behind this relationship. That Turkey had eleven different foreign ministers during the 1990s, while the position of chief of staff had only four incumbents in the same period, may also have helped the military solidify its grip on foreign policy (Bengio 2004, p. 81). This issue is particularly interesting in the context of Syrian–Turkish relations.

Historically, the extent of any diplomatic and political cooperation between Ankara and Damascus was limited by unresolved bilateral disputes. Until the late 1990s, security agreements were dealt with through these somewhat strained diplomatic channels, which may account for these arrangements producing few tangible results. The signing of the Adana Agreement in 1998 and its strong focus on bilateral security cooperation opened the door for the Turkish military and security establishment to take on a greater role in this relationship and perhaps prompted the Syrians to take security cooperation more seriously than in the past.

Moving beyond sensitivities: The Peace Process and Turkish–Israeli rapprochement

The Madrid Conference in 1991 created an opportunity for Turkey to pursue rapprochement with Jerusalem. Arab states had implicitly accepted the existence of the state of Israel by participating in the Madrid process, and thus were not in a position to oppose this development. For Turkey this was a welcome turn of events. It could now respond to Israeli overtures without having to worry about Arab sensibilities:

With the opening of peace talks between Israel and the Arabs in 1991, Turkey found the opportunity to get rid of walking on the tight rope in dealing with the two sides. It hoped that it would not have to be apologetic about its relations with Israel any longer as the Arabs themselves got involved in direct talks with Israel. (Sever 1996/7, p. 121)

Turkey, having adopted a more independent stance in its foreign policy, was confident in furthering cooperation with Israel. Finding the right pace took some time, however, and developments between Israel and the Arab states continued to influence the Turkish–Israeli relationship.

In general, Turkey had mixed feelings about the peace process. Ankara by and large supported negotiations and recognized that a solution to the Arab–Israeli conflict would be beneficial for the entire region. With this in mind, Turkey participated in all related multilateral working groups.[17] In May 1993 Turkey was asked to lead the workshop on "Military Exchanges of Information and Pre-Notification of Certain Military Activities," indicating Turkey's increasingly elevated status in the eyes of regional states (Rubin/Kirisci 2001, pp. 101–2). At the same time Ankara feared losing out if Syrian–Israeli relations improved. In particular, Turkey was anxious that it might be pressured to cooperate on water issues in order to facilitate a Syrian–Israeli deal, or that a change in the status quo would prompt Damascus to review its strategic military arrangements and redeploy its military capacity from southern Syria to the northern border.[18]

A deal between Israel and Syria would also have raised Hafez al-Assad's standing in Washington while reducing his concerns about Turkish–Israeli cooperation, neither of which was in Turkey's interest; matters like the Hatay dispute, for many years relegated to the back burner, could also move to the top of Damascus's agenda (Inbar 2001, pp. 117–18). Consequently, Ankara regarded developments on the Syrian–Israeli track of the peace process with some caution, aware of how much influence they might have on its relationship with Israel. Israel, meanwhile, was keen to ensure that rapprochement with Turkey would not adversely affect the prospects for negotiations with Syria.

After much internal discussion, the Rabin government decided to continue its efforts on both fronts (Bengio 2004, pp. 91f.). Turkey's last-minute cancellation of its foreign minister's visit to Israel in July 1993 in light of Israel's military operation in Lebanon is illustrative of bilateral relations taking a back seat to regional affairs: "The visit would have been the first of its kind; but in spite of imminent progress in the Palestinian–Israeli secret peace negotiations, Turkish policy appeared to slip back to being a hostage to old concerns and fears of offending the Arab world."[19] Instead, the visit took place in November 1993 once the situation had calmed and the Middle East peace process appeared to be yielding results with the signature of the Oslo Accords. Neighboring states—and Syria in particular—watched this development with trepidation. Syria's two most powerful neighbors, and the countries with which it had the most strained relationships, were coming together, leaving Syria fearing that it was about to be caught in a pincer movement (Bengio 2004, p. 147).

Heating things up: the military cooperation agreements of 1995/6

By 1996 Turkey had lost patience with Syria's lack of action in dealing with the PKK and decided to send Damascus a powerful message by putting military cooperation with Israel on a more formal footing.[20] The Syrian–Israeli negotiations held in December 1995 and January 1996 in Wye, Maryland, which were described by the head of the Syrian delegation as the most fruitful peace talks in years, caused anxiety in Ankara and were another factor prompting it to seek its own agreements with Israel:

THE WISDOM OF SYRIA'S WAITING GAME

Although in the final analysis nothing came of these discussions, the perception at the time that a breakthrough was about to happen must have propelled Turkey into concluding an agreement with Israel soon afterward, in February 1996, and to send President Süleyman Demirel to Israel the following month on an official visit—another first. ... Ankara feared that an agreement between Syria and Israel might cause it to lose strategic cards vis-à-vis Damascus. Ironically, this made Israel even more attractive to Turkey, as Ankara sought to counterbalance a Syrian–Israel agreement with a deal of its own. Turkey's alarm about the Israel–Syria talks was displayed during a visit to Israel in January 1996 by Deputy Foreign Minister Onur Öymen. He was quoted as saying: "How come you talk to these bastards? We beg you officially to stop the talks with Syria." (Bengio 2004, p. 80)

Turkey had also become aware of Syrian attempts to form a "counter-axis" with the aim of balancing growing Turkish–Israeli cooperation. This included signing a defense agreement with Greece in June 1995.[21] The text of the agreement was not published, giving rise to much speculation about its content (Robins 2003, p. 171). Whether or not the agreement posed an actual threat to Turkish interests, Ankara considered it worrisome and yet another reason to find multiple ways to enhance its security (Rubin/Kirisci 2001, p. 96). In September 1995, Turkey and Israel signed an agreement on military cooperation that envisaged, among other activities, air force exercises over each other's territory. On 23 January 1996, Ankara delivered a note to Hafez al-Assad, stating that it retained the right to act in self-defense should Syria not halt PKK activities immediately (Özcan 2004, p. 3).

In the following year Turkey and Israel concluded another two military cooperation agreements. Though the content was never officially disclosed, leaks indicated that the agreements provided for joint military exercises, upgraded military technology for Turkey, and intelligence cooperation on Syria, Iran, and Iraq. Chief of Staff Çevik Bir signed the first agreement on behalf of the Turkish government—a clear signal that the military considered cooperation with Israel to be its domain. The military concluded the second agreement with Israel in August 1996 without even informing the rest of the government (Staudigl 2004, pp. 155ff.).

For Syria, the Israeli–Turkish agreements were a most unwelcome development, and, to add insult to injury, they came into effect during a particularly tense period in Arab–Israeli relations following the election of Benjamin Netanyahu. Despite public declarations from both

Israel and Turkey confirming that the cooperation agreements were not directed at any particular parties, the Arab states were convinced of a hostile agenda, their suspicion due in some measure to the contradictory statements of Turkish officials.[22] Speaking to the Washington Research Institute, for example, General Çevik Bir, who had played a pivotal role in furthering Turkish–Israeli cooperation, stated that Israel had requested Turkey's assistance in collecting intelligence on Syria and Iran.[23] A May 1997 visit to the Golan Heights by the Turkish defense minister only served to exacerbate Syria's worries. In an attempt to discredit the cooperation accord, Syria and Iran denounced it as "anti-Muslim," since Turkey, in signing the accord, was the first predominantly Muslim state to ally itself openly with Israel.[24]

Attempts by Syria, Egypt, and Saudi Arabia to convince Turkey to reconsider its relations with Israel and to refrain from any activity that could harm its relations with Arab states proved fruitless, as did Syrian accusations suggesting that, by signing the agreements with Turkey, Netanyahu had undermined the Syrian track of the peace process (Sever 1996/7, p. 125). For Turkey and Israel, the cooperation agreements were too advantageous to give up, and Syria's protests fell on deaf ears. In the end, Damascus failed to mobilize widespread Arab opposition to Turkey's position, and Ankara was spared the setback it had feared in its relations with other Arab states.

The 1996 agreements became a cornerstone of Turkish–Israeli cooperation and appear to have been particularly useful in enhancing Turkey's capacity to deal with the PKK. Although never confirmed officially by either country, Turkey's markedly improved performance in fighting the PKK from 1996 onwards is likely attributable to the training provided by Israel under the agreement.[25] Indeed, the Turkish military became so effective in combating the PKK that Öcalan, after he was finally captured, conceded that the PKK had been defeated from a military standpoint as early as 1997 (Lüders 1999).

Tightening the noose: the crisis of 1998

The first joint Turkish–Israeli naval exercise took place in January 1998. The United States participated in the exercise, and Jordan, which had also been invited, sent an observer. Damascus was extremely troubled by this development; not only did it demonstrate American support for

Turkish–Israeli cooperation, but it also indicated that Ankara was attempting to improve its relations with Washington via Jerusalem. The joint exercise, known as "Reliant Mermaid," took on a symbolic significance in the region. With the Madrid process all but dead, the Arab states saw it as an outright provocation, especially given US participation in the exercise, and it caused a storm of protest. Syria felt surrounded—caught in a steadily tightening noose.[26] Of all the Arab states, only Jordan viewed Turkish–Israeli cooperation as an opportunity. Ever suspicious of Syria's intentions, Jordan hoped that the Israeli–Turkish axis would be a bulwark to enhance Jordanian security, yet it still remained cautious about becoming too involved with these partners:

Jordan, which sees Syria as a threat, clearly feels an affinity with the Turkish–Israeli partnership. Yet, despite its peace treaty with Israel, Jordan's Hashemite monarchy will feel constrained from overtly joining a trilateral security relationship with those two states until there is clear progress toward a final Israeli–Palestinian peace; roughly two-thirds of Jordan's population is Palestinian. (Makovsky 1999, p. 102)

Hafez al-Assad continued to lobby Arab governments for an official condemnation of Turkish cooperation with Israel. A conference of Arab League foreign ministers was convened, with the final statement calling on Turkey to end military cooperation with Israel and describing it as "an act threatening the security of Arab countries" (Makovsky 1999, p. 102).

Turkey's "Undeclared War" on Syria

Tensions between Ankara and Syria escalated in early October 1998 when Turkey massed its troops along the border and announced an "undeclared war" in a bid to force Damascus to expel Abdullah Öcalan. There is no single explanation why Turkey chose to act at precisely this point in time. The decision could have been linked to increased PKK activity in Hatay province,[27] whereas some have suggested that Ankara had earlier refrained from acting on the issue so as not to disturb the Syrian–Israeli peace negotiations. Turkey might also have had doubts regarding the effectiveness of military action in changing Syrian policy (Olson 2001, pp. 105–6). Other analysts point to the increased self-confidence of the Turkish military as a determining factor, and the appointment of a hardliner chief of staff with years of experience in fighting the PKK.

It took the Syrian regime some time to react. Initial plans to send troops to the north in a symbolic show of force had to be abandoned due to the sorry state of Syrian military equipment.[28] Aware that a military encounter with Turkey would result in certain defeat and unwilling to risk coming under pressure simultaneously from both north and south, Hafez al-Assad soon backed down. Egyptian President Hosni Mubarak offered his services to help resolve the situation, in consultation with Saudi Arabia and Iran, and the crisis officially came to an end with the signing of the Adana Agreement on 20 October 1998.

Under the agreement, Damascus committed itself to cease all support for the PKK, to declare it an illegal terrorist organization, and to close the organization's training camps in Syria and Lebanon. It further declared: "As of now, Öcalan is not in Syria and he definitely will not be allowed to enter Syria."[29] Öcalan, seeing the writing on the wall, fled Syria as negotiations were ongoing. The two countries set up an elaborate framework to ensure compliance with the agreement, which also extended to Lebanon, thereby creating a far more expansive structure for cooperation than the protocols signed in 1987 and 1993.[30] Syria also pledged that it would not attempt to incite Arab League countries against Turkey. Inured by years of non-performance on security cooperation, Ankara remained skeptical as to whether the Adana Agreement would produce any fundamental changes in Damascus. Even so, the agreement was very much seen as a victory for Turkey.

Öcalan himself was finally arrested on 15 February 1999 at the Greek embassy in Kenya, before being brought to Turkey. When it became publicly known that Israel had assisted in Öcalan's capture, Kurdish groups staged protests at several Israeli embassies.[31] In Berlin, three protesters were killed as they attempted to storm the Israeli consulate.[32] Weakened by the loss of its leader, the PKK declared a unilateral ceasefire. Many of its fighters found refuge in northern Iraq. In 2002, the PKK officially stopped its activities and changed its name to "Kadek," which was changed again in the following year to "Kongra-Gel."[33]

Israel's assistance in apprehending Öcalan demonstrated in concrete terms the extent of Turkish–Israeli cooperation on security matters. It was not lost on Ankara that Israel risked coming under attack by Kurdish groups as a result of its involvement.[34] But this was more than just a "favor to a friend." Ankara understood that Israel expected something substantial in return, likely in the form of intelligence on Syria, Iraq, and Iran.[35] The United States also played a role in Öcalan's capture, though not so overtly.[36] In these circumstances it made sense for Hafez al-Assad to mend fences with Ankara in order to protect Syria from joint Turkish–Israeli pressure tactics; but he was also realistic enough to start looking for support elsewhere in the region.

After the conflict: Syrian–Turkish cooperation post-Adana

Aware of Turkey's increasingly cozy relationship with Israel, Damascus began to push for a speedy rapprochement with Ankara. While the Hatay dispute remained unresolved, in most other areas it seemed that the Adana Agreement had provided an important catalyst for bilateral cooperation (Knudsen 2003, p. 211). Economic and trade relations between the two countries improved rapidly, including the revival of a Joint Economic Commission, joint ventures by Turkish and Syrian companies, and cooperation in the oil and gas sector (Aydin 2005, p. 9). In 2002, Damascus and Ankara concluded a milestone agreement on military training and cooperation, with both countries committing to an ambitious program that implied a high degree of mutual trust. For Damascus, the agreement was a marked contrast to Adana, which had been a humiliating experience for the Syrian side. This time, Syria felt itself an equal partner, and having such an agreement with Ankara considerably allayed its fears of a joint Turkish–Israeli attack. Despite initial complaints from Ankara about the slow pace of cooperation under the agreement, both sides soon began to express satisfaction with the results.[37]

Eager to play a stronger role in the region, Turkey had also offered to mediate between Syria and Israel. In 2008, four rounds of talks were held. This did not lead anywhere, however, because Turkish–Israeli relations had soured due to Israel's policy on Gaza. In 2009, the Syrian government once again suggested that it was willing to enter negotiations and underlined that it still trusted Turkey with the role of the mediator. Yet Israel was no longer willing to accept Turkey as a mediator, and criticized the Syrians for not seeking a direct channel.

Syria, Turkey, and the Iraq crises of 1991 and 2003

Turkish–Israeli cooperation has been a determining factor in the evolution of the relationship between Damascus and Ankara. The Iraq crises of 1991 and 2003 also played an important role. The establishment of a Kurdish autonomous region in northern Iraq following the First Gulf War caused great concern in Damascus and Ankara. Despite tense bilateral relations at that time, Syria and Turkey entered a period of intense security cooperation, united by what they perceived to be a common threat. Iran joined them in trilateral meetings that underscored the importance of preserving Iraq's territorial integrity by all possible means (Staudigl 2004). This close coordination ended in 1995 when the three countries judged that a prolonged period of violent infighting between the two main Kurdish forces in Iraq had significantly reduced the threat.

Ankara's challenging decision as to whether to participate in the 2003 US-led war in Iraq presented an altogether different problem. Turkish public opinion was vehemently against Turkey joining the war, and Ankara was concerned that relations with important members of the EU might be strained if it did so, presenting a potential obstacle to EU accession. Turkey was also loath to complicate its dealings with Syria and Iran, both of which were adamantly opposed to the war. After carefully weighing the options, the Turkish government, with some hesitation, opted for war. As one analyst explains:

If Turkey lacked the power to prevent the war, it was thought, it was better to support the USA and remain a good ally than to disappoint the USA and lose the ability to have a say in Iraq's post-war reconfiguration. After intensive negotiations, the USA had also agreed to offer a generous package of financial compensation for the economic losses that Turkey's fragile economy would incur as a result of the war. The more problematic reason ... was the belief that joining the coalition was the only way in which Turkey could minimize the potential negative consequences for Turkey's domestic Kurdish conflict. (Somer 2005, p. 112)

Ankara had assumed that the parliament would endorse its proposal, but parliament refused, earning Turkey much respect in the Arab world. Syrian–Turkish relations continued to improve—conveniently ignoring the fact that the Turkish government had initially been willing to support the US effort in exchange for financial compensation.

The post-war situation, however, gave Damascus and Ankara new cause for alarm, each fearing that its territorial integrity might be compromised if the Kurdish populations in Syria and Turkey attempted to join an autonomous Kurdish state. Ankara was also concerned for the well-being of the Turcoman population in northern Iraq in what would be a Kurdish-dominated region, and that the area would provide a new safe haven for the PKK from which it could resume its cross-border attacks. The PKK had enjoyed the support of the Kurdish Democratic Party (KDP) and its rival, the Patriotic Union of Kurdistan (PUK), at different times throughout the 1980s and 1990s.[38] Relations had eventually soured, but the PKK successfully re-established ties with both, and in August 2004 officially ended its almost five-year ceasefire. Turkey was determined to curb the steadily increasing frequency of operations launched from across the border and considered a military intervention into northern Iraq, even at the risk of antagonizing the United States. Damascus was more anxious about the spillover effect that the collapse of central authority in Iraq might have at home, and the possibility that Kurds in Syria would move to join ranks with Iraqi Kurds.

Soon after the war ended, rumors began to spread that Israeli intelligence was active in northern Iraq. While many Turkish Kurds were still angry about the Mossad's alleged involvement in apprehending Öcalan, Iraqi Kurds had for many years been on good terms with Israel. It was not surprising, therefore, that the Israelis would indicate an interest in further cooperation.[39] Kurdish sources, however, were at pains to deny the link, dismissing the rumors as part of a Turkish smear campaign to tarnish their image (Abdel-Latif 2004). The situation highlighted not only the deep internal cleavages dividing the Kurds, but also the continued willingness of regional states to employ cooperation with Kurdish factions as a tool to undermine or confront other states—and sometimes other Kurdish groups.

Ankara regarded cooperation between Israel and the Kurds of northern Iraq as a harmful betrayal of Turkish interests. Still under attack from across the border, Ankara demanded that the United States take steps to prevent these actions, but saw little in terms of actual results. For Turkey, this meant that two of its key partners were not only tolerating but also facilitating a breach of Turkish security, and it was this realization which led Ankara to revive cooperation with Syria and Iran.

Israeli–Turkish relations reached a new low in November 2003 when Israeli Prime Minister Ariel Sharon passed through Ankara and requested a meeting with Prime Minister Erdoğan, which the latter rejected (NZZ, 7 January 2004). The bilateral connection continued to deteriorate as a result of Israel's increasingly bold moves vis-à-vis the Palestinians.[40] Ankara canceled a planned visit of its foreign minister to

Israel and recalled its ambassador for consultations. It condemned the "targeted assassination" of Sheikh Ahmad Yassin, the spiritual leader of Hamas, in March 2004, and the killing of his successor by the Israeli army in April of the same year. Prime Minister Erdoğan also publicly criticized Israel's massive military intervention in Gaza, noting the untold destruction and suffering that it had caused. Israel fought back, declaring that it expected more understanding from a country so familiar with terrorist threats (Singh 2004). Erdoğan did not back down in his statements and instead likened Israel's behavior to terrorism. In July, Deputy Prime Minister Olmert paid a special visit to Ankara to smooth things over between the two countries. Both sides reaffirmed their commitment to the relationship but were hard pressed to hide their differences (Scham 2004).

Turkey, interested in assuming a greater regional role, offered its services in indirect negotiations to the Syrian and the Israeli government and hosted a series of meetings for that purpose until the winter 2008 Gaza war brought things to a halt. The most telling incident here is the widely reported summer vacation of the Assad family in Bodrum in August 2008, when the Turkish prime minister with his wife and daughter came to the sea resort's airport to receive Bashar al-Assad and his wife, demonstrating that the ties with neighboring Syria went way beyond the official to a much more familiar, personal level.

U-turn: Turkey and the Syrian revolution

Three years later, in the summer of 2011, Prime Minister Erdoğan called upon Assad to step down. As suddenly as relations had changed to the positive in 1998, they now turned into the opposite when the Syrian revolution started. The Syrian government's violent response to the protests that had started in March 2011 poisoned the relationship. Bashar al-Assad reactivated the Syrian government's relations with the PKK—which in turn led to a flare-up of PKK activity. Ankara opened its doors to refugees and to the political opposition and hosted the opposition's first larger movement, the Syrian National Council (SNC), which was established in August 2011.

Before the uprising, Syria had been an important trade partner. Up to 2011, the annual volume of trade between Turkey and Syria was worth more than $US 2 billion a year. Nonetheless, Turkey decided to join the

117

Arab League's sanctions on the neighboring country in November 2011. "Every bullet fired, every bombed mosque has eliminated the legitimacy of the Syrian leadership and has widened the gap between us," Turkish Foreign Minister Ahmet Davutoğlu said at a press conference (*Huffington Post*, 30 November 2011). Apart from its bilateral implications, the conflict with Syria has the potential to tarnish Turkey's relation with another important regional player, Iran, which has thus far continued to offer its support to the Syrian regime.

Ankara's ambitions to use the Syrian crisis to raise its international profile were not entirely successful, however. In November 2012, the National Coalition of Syria incorporated the SNC into a larger framework. This was announced in Doha, with the leadership declaring it would move to Egypt. Ankara also came under international scrutiny due to its support of the opposition. It was argued that Turkey was so preoccupied with keeping Kurdish Syrian groups from growing more powerful that it did not mind engaging any actor, including Islamists, as long as they opposed Kurdish aspirations. In the second half of 2012 the United States consequently started to enhance its work with the armed opposition through Jordan, which it considered to be more steadfast than Turkey in its opposition to Islamist actors.

While Qatar and Turkey in general have the same position towards the Syrian revolution, the unexpected and quick shift of US engagement for the National Coalition's establishment in Doha in autumn 2012, which led to a decline in the significance of the Istanbul-based SNC, cast a shadow on Turkey's ambitions for a greater role in Middle Eastern affairs. This situation was further compounded by US policy from the end of 2012, when Washington began to provide support for high-ranking defectors from the Syrian army in Jordan, thereby creating additional friction in Turkish–US relations. Videos from southern Syria have also shown the proliferation of much more sophisticated military equipment through the Jordanian border, while some advanced equipment in Turkey—due to US pressure—has not yet been delivered to the rebels. Especially after the onset of clashes between Kurdish and Islamist fighters in Ras al-Ayn at the Turkish border in November 2012, it seemed that Ankara prioritizes supporting those groups pitted against Kurdish militias. The United States, itself on good terms with a number of Kurdish actors, considers radical Islamists more problematic, and therefore seems to have enhanced its cooperation with Jordan, which shares this view. Thus although it is important that Turkey is involved in the present and future situation in Syria, the extent of Ankara's involvement, and the success of its policy towards the revolution, will likely be limited if this disparity in US and Turkish interests with regard to Islamism and the Kurds persists. As one Jordanian source was quoted as saying in *The Guardian*: "The Americans now trust us more than the Turks, because with the Turks everything is about gaining leverage for action against the Kurds" (*The Guardian*, 8 March 2013).

Conclusion: focusing on the bigger picture

Syria's relations with Turkey between 1990 and 2011 demonstrate that, by focusing on the broader picture instead of being reactive and seeking short-term gains, Damascus had the capacity to develop and sustain a constructive bilateral engagement that proved beneficial for both sides. While issues of water distribution and the "return" of Hatay province remained unresolved, these were far outweighed by the benefits of trade, as well as cultural, and, most particularly, military, cooperation between Syria and Turkey.

Damascus had to reach the brink of war and experience the humiliation of the Adana process before it would move away from the arguably unhelpful strategy of using terrorist groups to exert pressure on Turkey. In the end, it had little choice but to cooperate—on Ankara's terms— even as Turkey was busy expanding its ties with Israel. And herein lies the key: the realization of just how far Israel was willing to go in furthering cooperation with Turkey forced Hafez al-Assad to redefine his priorities and re-evaluate his strategy, moving from playing the "spoiler" and focusing on the single issue of water distribution, to adopting a broader and more active approach which he hoped would pre-empt a possible Turkish–Israeli move against Syria. Though not usually known for taking the long-term view in his dealings with neighboring states, Assad saw that diversifying cooperation with Turkey would be far more effective in guaranteeing Syria's security than continuing with a limited bilateral agenda; this was an exceptional and prescient move on his part.

But it must be emphasized that this was Hafez al-Assad's move. He combined political maneuvers from opposite ends of the spectrum: radical reversals of policy as well as patient perseverance, until the conditions had changed. This clearly needs to be mentioned in light of the current policy of his son and successor, who during the whole process of the uprising and even before did not show the slightest interest in changing course: be it his declaration in the light of the Egyptian and Tunisian revolution that Syria is "immune" from such moves, his quipping first speech in parliament weeks after the security forces had already killed more than 100 protesters in the southern city of Daraa, or his continuous escalation of the violence ever since. Particularly in view of his father's radical shifts in his Turkish policy or, as mentioned before, in siding with the United States on Iraq in the First Gulf War, it seems that Bashar al-Assad inherited only one option from the spectrum: the waiting-game.

Between 1998 and 2011, relations between Syria and Turkey remained stable with regular high-level visits, tourism, trade, and cooperation on cultural projects between the two countries. Ankara stood by Damascus—against Washington's advice—even when traditionally friendly states like Egypt and Saudi Arabia gave Syria the cold shoulder following the assassination of former Lebanese Prime Minister Hariri. In so doing, Ankara threw Damascus a lifeline during what has to be one of the most politically challenging periods for Syria in recent memory. The difference in the current situation is that Turkey is concerned with the Syrian government's behavior towards its own people and the effects this has already had on Turkey. The Turkish opposition's siding with the Syrian regime, the growing divide between Sunna and Shia, and the enhanced importance of the Kurdish question are three issues of major domestic concern for the Turkish government. The ethnic and religious conflicts that are increasing in Syria during the current crisis are confronting the Turkish government with problems that it might find itself facing in the near future—particularly if events spiral out of control in Syria. But Turkey's solidarity with Syria even after the Hariri assassination shows how far Ankara was willing to go to maintain good relations with Damascus—and how deep the current shift has been to motivate it to break completely with the regime.

5

LOVE THY NEIGHBOR

SYRIA AND LEBANON

Lebanon has been a central pillar of Syria's regional policy for decades. Syria secured a foothold in Lebanon in the early 1990s under the guise of bringing stability to the war-torn country, before subsequently expanding its political and economic influence despite vehement opposition from regional and international actors. Rising discontent with Syrian hegemony in Lebanon, coupled with Damascus's deteriorating relations with Europe and the United States, eventually culminated in a crisis. When former Lebanese Prime Minister Rafiq al-Hariri was assassinated in Beirut in February 2005, all fingers immediately pointed to the Syrian regime. Despite Syria's seemingly entrenched position in Lebanon, international pressure left it with no choice but to beat a hasty retreat.

Hafez al-Assad regarded control over Lebanon as a key element of his policy vis-à-vis Israel. The Syrian president wanted to prevent his country from coming under Israeli control and regarded Lebanon's Beqa'a Valley as a weak spot in Syria's line of defense. He worried that Israel would take advantage of the post-civil war vulnerability in Lebanon to attack Syria. In an elaborate effort to prevent this, Damascus turned Lebanon into its fiefdom, obstructing the development of independent foreign relations and using the country as a pawn in its own international dealings. For Syria, Lebanon served as both buffer zone and battle ground in a proxy war with Israel. Damascus did its best to capitalize on close ties with Lebanese Hezbollah and Palestinian groups inside Lebanon in order to enhance its bargaining position with third parties and to underscore its position as a key actor in the Middle East that should not be ignored. At the same time, Lebanon was also a "playground" for Syria's business interests.

Following Israel's withdrawal from South Lebanon in 2000, it became more difficult for Syria to justify its continued military presence there. Bashar al-Assad, charged by his father with responsibility for Lebanese affairs in 1998, tried to create the impression that he was adopting a more conciliatory course, but in reality he showed no serious intention of withdrawing from Lebanon. Bashar kept to the same course after becoming president, unwilling to cut back the privileges of high-ranking members of the political and military establishment in Lebanon because they were useful for consolidating his power base at home. Lebanese discontent with Syria's iron grip continued to grow, but Damascus failed to read the signs both domestically in Lebanon and on the international stage, thereby missing the opportunity to change its strategy before it was finally forced to do so.

While less visible, the Syrian government remained a powerful actor in Lebanon even after its withdrawal in 2005. This is why the Syrian domestic conflict evolving from the revolution is an ultimate threat to Lebanon, already at the time of writing affecting the country considerably. This chapter explores the motivations for Syrian engagement in Lebanon, the manner in which Damascus engaged with or established control over various Lebanese actors, and the reasons behind Syria's failure in Lebanon. It also looks at the impact of the Syrian crisis on Lebanon.

The foundations of Syrian dominance in Lebanon

The outbreak of civil war in Lebanon in 1975 caused Syria much anxiety. Firstly, Damascus worried that fighting between Lebanese and Palestinian factions, and the PLO's strong and autonomous position in Lebanon, would destabilize the country. Of even more concern was the prospect of other actors, namely Israel, taking advantage of this weakness to bring Lebanon under their control. The Syrian regime also feared the domestic spillover effect of conflict in Lebanon given the close family and community ties between the two countries and the similarly diverse makeup of Lebanese and Syrian society. With all this in mind, Damascus did not hesitate to intervene in Lebanon when asked to do so in 1976 by Christian groups requesting assistance.

Arab states criticized Syrian involvement in Lebanon but grudgingly sanctioned the deployment of an Arab peace-keeping force.[1] Israel, primarily interested in stability and concerned about the PLO's role in the fighting, did not oppose Syria taking a firm hand in Lebanon as long as it respected certain unwritten "red lines." However, after the 1982 Israeli intervention in Lebanon, the country turned into a proxy-battleground for Syria and Israel.

The Syrian government seemed to expect that Lebanon and the Arab world would consider it a savior and be grateful for Syria's sacrifice in confronting Israel and saving Lebanon from Israeli domination. Yet in fact, the Arab League regarded Damascus more as part of the problem than the solution given Syria's obvious desire to maintain a form of influence in Lebanon that necessitated keeping all parties in a perpetual "balance of weakness" in which no single Lebanese actor could gain the upper hand.

For its part, the Arab League showed itself woefully unable to deal with the Lebanon crisis, in large measure due to its policy of non-interference in the internal affairs of member states. This changed when General Michel Aoun declared war on Syrian troops in March 1989, and the Arab League decided to set up a "Higher Tripartite Committee" (HTC) to encourage the re-establishment of political order in Lebanon, to explore possibilities for constitutional reform, and to assist in the election of a new president, all with the aim of achieving a comprehensive and durable peace. The HTC was essentially an attempt to circumvent Syria, but after so many years of engagement in Lebanon, Hafez al-Assad was unwilling to leave the field to others and refused to cooperate with the HTC, which was forced to suspend its work after only three months. The Syrian government was still holding on tight to Lebanon and its strong position there made any progress impossible without its consent. The HTC issued a complaint, and finally, after consultations with the Algerian president, Hafez al-Assad agreed to a debate on Syria's presence in Lebanon—provided that it (Syria) was involved in the process. Notwithstanding regional and international discontent with Syrian tactics, it was clear that there was no other way to achieve a settlement.

THE WISDOM OF SYRIA'S WAITING GAME

Syria and the Palestinian dimension in Lebanon

Syria's decision to intervene in Lebanon was closely connected to the Palestinian issue. The Palestinian community in Lebanon was much larger proportionately than its counterpart in Syria, and it also acted much more independently, with the result that Palestinians were very much a political force in Lebanon. Hafez al-Assad, who sought to control the Palestinian movement and who was convinced that he knew far better how to deal with Israel, had not welcomed the Palestinian aspirations to take their fate into their own hands. In 1969, the Arab League decreed that Palestinians had the right to defend their cause from foreign soil. Militant Palestinians claimed autonomy in the refugee camps in Lebanon and led their military attacks against Israel from Lebanese territory. These actions had brought the whole Lebanese state under strain, and while this was not—as is often claimed—the reason for the outbreak of the civil war, the various Palestinian factions did become parties to the internecine conflict. When called upon for help by Christian Palestinian factions in Lebanon in 1976, Syria first sent Palestinian troops to deal with the problem before arriving with the rest of its army.

A major aim of the intervention—and a point on which Syria and Israel agreed—was to oust Arafat's PLO from Lebanon. Under siege in Beirut, the PLO leadership evacuated to Tunis. The PLO was defeated in Lebanon, and Syrian proxies like Sa'iqa and Fatah al-Intifada took control of the northern camp of Nahr al-Bared. Unlike other refugee camps that were outside the strictly Syrian-controlled area during the civil war, in Nahr al-Bared no internal security council was established, and the camp remained under indirect Syrian control.

Hafez al-Assad recognized the explosive potential of the situation in the Palestinian camps. From the outset, Palestinian refugees in Syria were far better integrated than in Lebanon. While Lebanese refugee camps even to this day are crowded ghettos with people living in inhumane conditions, the Syrian camps were barely distinguishable from poorer Syrian neighborhoods. In Lebanon, Palestinian refugees are excluded from higher education and from professional and skilled technical employment.[2] In Syria, Palestinians have mostly been treated like Syrian citizens (until the uprising began), and careers in the army, administration, and even in the higher echelons of the military and Syrian ministries were not rare. UNRWA schools for Palestinians in Syria consistently produced the students with the highest marks, and while Palestinians in Syria encountered challenges, the difficulties are not comparable to those faced by Palestinians in Lebanon.

The structure created for Palestinian refugees in Lebanon was quite deliberately intended to maintain the pressure on the international community to recognize the Palestinian right of return. Syria, however, took a somewhat more pragmatic position with respect to Palestinians in its territory. Based on its own security interests, Damascus did not tolerate camp autonomy, and Palestinian groups in Syria were forbidden from carrying arms unless expressly permitted or armed by the Syrian government. Syria has always recognized the potential of Palestinian factions in Lebanon to create unrest, and at times Palestinian groups have acted as the "long arm" of the Syrian regime, but only as long as they did not create problems for Syria. The Palestinian groups in Lebanon have to some degree fulfilled Syria's desire to have a counterweight to Hezbollah.

The Ta'if Agreement and Syria's role in ending the civil war

The Ta'if Agreement formally ended the civil war in September 1989 and was approved by the Lebanese parliament in November the same year. One chapter of the agreement dealt with the reorganization of domestic affairs, focusing on issues that had contributed to the outbreak of civil war, while the others addressed challenges arising from the war including the restoration of Lebanese sovereignty over the entire territory of Lebanon, the liberation of South Lebanon from Israeli occupation, and the establishment of a privileged relationship between Syria and Lebanon.

For Lebanon, the agreement proved problematic from the outset. It altered certain elements of the country's institutional setup but failed to remove provisions that were among the root causes of civil war. The result was a weak government with sectarianism entrenched in Lebanon's political system, leaving it vulnerable both to domestic infighting and to external influence. For Damascus, however, the agreement was a great success, as it essentially gave Syria carte blanche to establish hegemony over Lebanon. Though it was obvious to many that Syria's involvement in Lebanon had actually served to prolong the war rather than provide a solution to the conflict, the Ta'if Agreement attributed to Damascus a tangible role in ending the conflict and for all intents and purposes gave written, internationally recognized approval for its engagement in Lebanon. Ta'if envisioned a role for Syria in a variety of ways, from assisting with the disbanding and disarmament of the various militias present in Lebanon, to close coordination on political, military, and other matters owing to the "special relationship" between the two neighbors.

The Accord underscored the need for Damascus's consent in decision-making, which had the effect of leaving even domestic Lebanese matters to be determined by Syrian interests. For Damascus, one of the most important aspects of Ta'if and the restrictions it imposed on Lebanese foreign relations was that it virtually ruled out the possibility of Lebanon and Israel concluding an independent peace deal.

Ta'if represented a clear triumph for Syria over Israel. The Accord recognized the right to resist Israel's occupation of Southern Lebanon. Given the excellent relations between Syria and Lebanese Hezbollah, it in effect allowed Damascus to support an armed confrontation with Tel Aviv without becoming directly involved. Moreover, the withdrawal of Israeli troops from Southern Lebanon was explicitly mandated in the Accord, while provisions related to Syrian troops were far less specific. This lack of detail gave the Syrian regime the space to "reinterpret" Ta'if, and for most of the 1990s the number of Syrian troops in Lebanon remained unchanged (Perthes 1997, p. 18). Following Israel's withdrawal from Southern Lebanon, Syria did redeploy some of its troops but left between 10,000 and 14,000 soldiers and an unknown number of intelligence agents in the country, thus falling somewhat short of a complete withdrawal. When asked in 2001 about the pace of Syria's withdrawal from Lebanon, Bashar al-Assad declared:

Did Syria say or did any Syrian official or any Syrian party say, since the entrance of Syrian forces to Lebanon in 1976 that the Syrian presence in Lebanon is permanent? No one has ever said this. On the contrary, the Syrian view says that the Syrian forces have entered to help Lebanon, and when the requirements of the presence of these forces are no longer existent in Lebanon these forces shall go back to Syria. (al-Assad 2001a)

From the beginning, the powerful position granted to Syria under Ta'if met with criticism inside Lebanon. Years of civil war had weakened the country, and it was clearly in no position to negotiate with a bigger, more domineering neighbor that could easily impose its will and vision for a future relationship.[3] Critics were quick to point out that while Ta'if had been touted as an all-Arab solution, its ultimate beneficiary was Syria (Maila 1994, p. 34).

Implementing Ta'if proved to be a challenge, not least because of questions over the legitimacy of political office-holders in Lebanon. The interim government appointed by outgoing Lebanese President Pierre Gemayel in September 1989, comprising a council of three Muslims and three Christians headed by Lebanese army commander General Michel 'Aoun, lacked credibility from the outset. The problem was compounded when the Muslim appointees refused to participate. At that point, two rival governments emerged: East Beirut was under the control of the military government of 'Aoun, supported by Iraq; and in West Beirut, backed by Syria, former Prime Minister Selim al-Hoss proclaimed himself the rightful leader of Lebanon. 'Aoun steadfastly refused to participate in the Ta'if negotiations and continued to reject the agreement even after it was passed by the Lebanese parliament on 21 August 1990. 'Aoun's intractable position, coupled with his extensive influence in Lebanon, created a major obstacle to the implementation of Ta'if.

Ironically, it was the Iraqi invasion of Kuwait that provided a way out of the deadlock. Syria's decision to join the international coalition against Saddam Hussein gave it new leverage in dealing with the United States, and Damascus used this opportunity to exert pressure on 'Aoun:

It was widely believed that in return for Syria's participation in the US-led multinational force, Washington had agreed to facilitate total Syrian hegemony over Lebanon by exerting pressure on Israel not to intervene. Having received this assurance, Syria on 13 October 1990 launched an armed assault on the presidential palace in Ba'abda, the seat of General 'Awn, who was heading the opposition against the Ta'if agreement. (Nasrallah 1994, p. 135).

Israel did not react to the incident, which contributed to the idea that Syria had acted with Washington's blessing (Nasrallah 1994, p. 136). With this operation, the last obstacles on the road to the implementation of Ta'if and establishment of Syrian hegemony over Lebanon were eliminated.

Syrian–Lebanese relations after 1989

Syria's leading role in negotiating the Ta'if Agreement laid the foundations for its hegemony in Lebanon. A series of post-Ta'if treaties purported to give the Syrian presence some legitimacy while Lebanon went through a period of internal stabilization, but it soon became evident that the Syrian regime had no plans to leave, or any intention of supporting the Lebanese in re-establishing their autonomy.

For years, the presence of Syrian troops in Lebanon was the most visible sign of Damascus's hegemony, but the two states were also linked in myriad other ways. The Syrian regime made it a priority to establish political control over the Lebanese government, and Syrian intelligence penetrated Lebanese society and institutions. Large numbers of Syrians sought work in Lebanon, mainly in construction and agriculture, sending back significant remittances to their families in Syria. Even as Damascus tightened its grip on Lebanese institutions and grew increasingly involved in business dealings there, it maintained close ties with Hezbollah, which, with its extensive support base and capacity for independent action, consistently challenged both the sovereignty and authority of the Lebanese government. For Damascus, this two-pronged and seemingly contradictory strategy appeared to suit its objectives perfectly—enabling it to establish de facto control in Lebanon without taking on a formal role that could be contested both in Lebanon and in the wider region. Despite Hafez al-Assad's constant references to the relationship of "brotherhood" between the two countries, the imbalance of power in the dynamic was all too evident; as Augustus Richard Norton and Jillian Schwedler note: "Indeed, Syria is playing the role of a bullying big brother, although most Lebanese would chose a more colorful term" (Norton/Schwedler 1994, p. 48).

Constructing legitimacy: Syrian–Lebanese bilateral treaties

Damascus was keen to situate its involvement in Lebanon within a formal framework. The "special relationship" between Syria and Lebanon referred to in the Ta'if Accord set the stage for this, and resulted in the "Treaty of Brotherhood, Cooperation and Coordination" which was signed on 20 May 1991. The agreement set up a structure for bilateral engagement between the neighbors and also made reference to the withdrawal of Syrian troops from Lebanon, noting that this would be the subject of discussion between Damascus and Beirut once Ta'if expired. The Treaty of Brotherhood was followed closely by a defense and security pact, then a series of agreements on economic and social issues, and, finally, in 1994, an arrangement for sharing Orontes river water (Harris 2005). The water agreement was undoubtedly for Syria's benefit, whereas both countries stood to gain from those dealing with economic and business matters and guaranteeing the free movement of goods between the two countries. Syria expert Volker Perthes notes, however, that it was not so much the treaties themselves as their selective implementation that reflected a pro-Syrian bias and the imbalance of power in the relationship (Perthes 1996, p. 32).

Building on the provisions of Ta'if, Damascus's main impetus in signing the Treaty of Brotherhood was to prevent Lebanon from reaching an independent peace deal with Israel. Against the backdrop of the Madrid peace process, Hafez al-Assad was concerned that Syria's politically vulnerable neighbor might be an easy target for Israel, calling into question his ideal of a united Arab front. Damascus, with its sights set on a comprehensive peace deal, viewed partial solutions to the conflict as advantageous to Israel and detrimental to Arab interests. While Assad did not have sufficient clout to stop Jordan's King Hussein or Yasser Arafat from concluding separate deals with Israel, his firm grip on Lebanon guaranteed that at least one other Arab state would remain without a peace deal until negotiations with Syria were finalized.[4]

The Treaty of Brotherhood prohibited Beirut from negotiating independently with Israel[5] and stipulated that it could only proceed with talks in conjunction with Syria. Since Syria did not participate in the multilateral talks, neither did Lebanon. Damascus and Beirut regarded UNSCR 425 as the basis for any negotiations involving Lebanon, but since this resolution stipulated a full Israeli withdrawal from Lebanon, the Lebanese government insisted that negotiations could only begin after Israel implemented the resolution. Israel meanwhile insisted on obtaining security guarantees as a precursor to serious negotiations. Not surprisingly, under the circumstances, the negotiations went nowhere. Israel's withdrawal from Lebanon in 2000 gave rise to questions about Syria's continued presence there, but for the next few years Damascus was able to maintain its position with only a few minor modifications.

Motivations for Syrian involvement in Lebanon

The "special relationship" between Syria and Lebanon effectively enabled Damascus to have its cake and eat it too. Syria was in a position to impose its will on Lebanon without having to take actual responsibility for the country or the activities of non-state actors with connections to

THE WISDOM OF SYRIA'S WAITING GAME

Damascus. Officially present as a stabilizing force to prevent the resumption of conflict, the Syrian government felt no obligation to assist Lebanon in becoming more autonomous and self-sufficient. Yet officially, Damascus rejected the notion that it dominated or even influenced Lebanese politics:

The Americans spoke of Syrian hegemony over Lebanon. When a country wants to create hegemony it should have hidden or declared goals. Did we in Syria aspire for money? Are there natural resources in Lebanon for us to seek? Is there oil in Lebanon that we want to appropriate? Did we take Lebanese electricity, Lebanese water? No. We took nothing from Lebanon, but we gave blood. Had we wanted hegemony over Lebanon, we would have withdrawn our forces in stages from Lebanon in the last five years up to the last withdrawal.[6]

So what was Syria's interest in maintaining influence in Lebanon? Had it been solely to do with preventing a peace deal between Israel and Lebanon, the Syrian government would have been able to withdraw well before 2005, when it was eventually forced out. So, given that Syria did not withdraw, perhaps this begs the question of Lebanon's position within the framework of Syrian foreign relations.

In the Syrian worldview Lebanon was more object than subject, with matters involving Lebanon being handled as domestic affairs. The civil war had prevented Lebanon from developing its own foreign policy—something that Damascus was not eager to see change. So, while the conclusion of bilateral treaties between the neighbors appeared to signal recognition of Lebanon as a sovereign state, the actual structure of Syrian–Lebanese relations told a different tale.[7] Lebanon fulfilled certain functions for its larger neighbor, relieving it of the need to use its own territory at times when it would have been, at best, inconvenient, and, at worst, dangerous; it was consequently imperative for Damascus to hold on to its Lebanese outlet.

Syria's "Hong Kong"

Lebanon became a preferred place for Syrians to do business. While the Syrian economy was largely sealed off from world markets, the Lebanese system was much less restricted. Thus the Syrian business community began to take advantage of opportunities in Lebanon. Members of the Syrian political and security elite welcomed the chance to set up profitable businesses in Lebanon and abused their official roles by taking a cut on deals. Cross-border smuggling of electronics and other items that could not legally be imported to Syria was another big moneymaker. I recall the year I first arrived in Damascus, when Coke and Pepsi were not officially available in Syria. Every so often, news would spread around the diplomatic community that a stock of one or the other had arrived at the "Kodak" store, where many expatriates shopped, and within a few short hours every last can would be gone, despite the significant price mark-up. The Lebanese border villages of Chtoura and Zahle, less than an hour's drive from Damascus, flourished thanks to the numerous banks that gave Syrians access to the outside world, as did shops that benefited from a steady stream of Syrian and expatriate border traffic.[8]

While this system is sometimes described as exploitative, the term does not entirely reflect the reality of the situation, as Syrian profits were often shared with segments of the Lebanese business community or political establishment that were part of the process. In this way, corruption and smuggling created patronage networks that in turn helped Syria maintain its hold on Lebanon. Meanwhile, Syria offered its troops and security services based in Lebanon an "unmatched opportunity to supplement their meager incomes through drug smuggling, rackets or other activities," thereby ensuring that actors at all levels of the Syrian system had an interest in remaining in Lebanon (Rabil 2001, p. 30). This was also true of the increasing number of Syrians working in Lebanon, who, by the late 1990s, were collectively sending home almost $US4 billion a year in remittances, not to mention easing tension in a Syrian labor market characterized by high unemployment (Blanford 2006, p. 57).

According to some observers, by the time of Syria's withdrawal in 2005, private business interests had replaced politics as Damascus's principal motivation for wanting to maintain its position in Lebanon. For many, business continued after the withdrawal, but the unfettered access of the Syrian political elite came to an end.

Syria's pressure relief valve

Despite Syrian dominance in Lebanon, freedom of speech was much less restricted than in Syria itself. Lebanon has always had a tradition of high-quality journalism featuring diverse voices, quite unlike the media landscape in Syria. Damascus did not overtly repress the Lebanese media, but rather made its "red lines" well known. The media in turn generally refrained from direct criticism of Syria and Syrian politics, but this still left considerable freedom to report on Syrian and regional affairs and to offer different points of view. On more than one occasion, high-ranking Syrian officials have mentioned their lack of confidence in the Syrian press, noting that if they wanted to know what was happening, they would rather look at a Lebanese newspaper than a Syrian one.[9] On certain occasions, the Lebanese press actually proved useful for the Syrian regime because it was able to offer more in-depth explanations on certain issues.[10]

But it was not only the Syrian regime that made use of the Lebanese media to serve its interests. From 2000 on, Syrian writers increasingly availed themselves of the opportunity for publication in Lebanese newspapers. For Syrian intellectuals, the Lebanese press provided an outlet and a forum for views for which there was no room in Syrian newspapers. Lebanon also became a place for Syrian intellectuals to meet and exchange views with a measure of anonymity not available at home. Syrian researcher Wael Sawah explains:

All regretted losing Lebanon: The Syrian workers because they lost their labor market, the Syrian bourgeoisie because they lost their shopping opportunities, the Syrian smugglers … and the Syrian opposition because it lost its lungs for respiration.[11]

In this way, Lebanon was actually a very useful pressure relief valve for Syria. Damascus used Lebanon to make up for certain weaknesses in the Syrian system—easing domestic pressure through the import of material and immaterial goods that citizens longed for. In refusing officially to admit a lack of goods in Syria, and failing to officially permit demand being satisfied via Lebanon, the regime effectively killed two birds with one stone: it could, as it saw fit, prosecute individuals benefiting from illicit trade, or silence critics who used the Lebanese media as an outlet, all the while monitoring the pulse of public discontent.[12]

The murder of Rafiq Hariri served as the catalyst for a significant change in the tone and content of Lebanese journalism. For many critics of Syria, this brutal act was a sign that the time had come to reject Syrian dominance in Lebanon once and for all. Following a series of assassinations and attempted assassinations directed at journalists, criticism of Syria and its involvement in Lebanon became more pronounced than ever.

LOVE THY NEIGHBOR: SYRIA AND LEBANON

Managing Lebanon

The Syrian regime must have come to the realization fairly early on that maintaining control over Lebanon would not be easy. It required constant attention and tactical maneuvering by seasoned Syrian diplomats and experienced members of Syrian intelligence. Damascus systematically brought all elements of the Lebanese political system under its control—from the president, the prime minister, and the Cabinet, to the parliament, as well as Hezbollah, which was gradually transforming itself into a political force to be reckoned with in Lebanon.

Despite years of referring to the "special" relationship between Syria and Lebanon, Hafez al-Assad never once visited Beirut. It took Bashar al-Assad a full two years after coming to office to make an appearance in the Lebanese capital in March 2002, immediately prior to the Arab League summit.[13] The established practice was for Lebanese officials to travel to Damascus seeking approval of their position by the Syrian president—or to be summoned. It was a humiliating procedure, instituted to provide a constant reminder of the imbalance of power between the two neighbors. This dynamic certainly contributed to the degree of anger that many Lebanese felt toward Syria as their leaders "routinely trod the path to Damascus like petulant children to be scolded, have their wrists slapped and be told to behave by the Syrian parent" (Blanford 2006, p. 50).

Syria's management of Lebanon, apart from constantly highlighting the inequality in the relationship, was intimately linked to who was in charge. This being the case, Damascus was determined to ensure its dominant role in the selection and election of the Lebanese president. Article 49 of the Lebanese constitution limits the presidential term of office to six years. Thus in 1995, when Hafez al-Assad decided he wanted to keep President Elias Hrawi in office, the constitution had to be amended. As a result, shortly before President Hrawi's term in office was due to end, Major General Ghazi Kana'an, Syria's head of military intelligence and the most senior figure in Lebanon, simply announced that the constitution had to be amended, and rather than voting on the amendment through secret ballot, the parliamentarians would vote through a show of hands. As described in *al-Hayat*:

Kana'an then raised his hand, saying that the vote would take place by a raising of hands and would not be secret ... Karami stood and his color changed ... Everyone looked as if they had just been through a cold shower ... The party broke up early. Presidential hopefuls departed with their wives, one complaining of tiredness, another saying he had a headache. (*al-Hayat*, 2 October 1995)

This announcement was part of a Syrian "strategy of calculated insults,"[14] the sole purpose of which was to demonstrate that Damascus had the power to humiliate even the most high-ranking politicians in Lebanon. By publicly forcing Lebanese politicians to adhere to Syrian rules, this effect was reinforced, as it was during the heated debate over extending the term of President Emile Lahoud, Hrawi's successor. Damascus was bent on Lahoud remaining in his position despite the need to again amend the Lebanese constitution. Hafez al-Assad made his contempt for Lebanese sovereignty crystal clear when he noted in an interview, "I don't see altering one or two clauses as being of such great importance as to justify debate" (Harris 1997, p. 296). And so, in 2004, the Lebanese parliament duly voted to grant Lahoud a three-year extension of his mandate—compromising the constitution yet again. This latest example of Syria's blatant meddling in Lebanese affairs met with severe criticism from the international community; the UN passed UNSCR 1559, which called for a withdrawal of Syrian troops from Lebanon, yet Damascus continued to defend its position.

Speaking at a conference of Syrian expatriates in October 2004, Bashar al-Assad outlined his objections to UN Resolution 1559. The "whole world changes constitutions," he said, and it was legitimate for the Lebanese to do the same. Bashar questioned the motives of those international actors who had criticized the extension of Lahoud's term:

If they are against the extension in principle, why did these countries and the same people agree to the 1995 extension, [yet] oppose it in 2004—even though the section [of the constitution] is exactly the same section? That means that the problem is not with the principle. If it were the principle, the position would not have changed in nine years. (al-Ba'th, 9 October 2004)

While technically correct, this assessment stopped short of recognizing that the international community had never intended for Syria to have a permanent presence in Lebanon, or any involvement in Lebanese internal politics. On the contrary, the international community, and particularly the states involved in setting up Ta'if, had—however mistakenly—expected Syria to assist Lebanon in regaining sufficient stability to be able to function with autonomy. Confronted with a reality that differed so markedly from what had been envisaged, the international community increasingly began to view Syria's blunt interference in Lebanese affairs as a provocation. Damascus's unapologetic use of force and repression had won it few friends, and international pressure to decouple Syrian and Lebanese affairs was greeted warmly by large segments of Lebanon's political establishment as well as the general population.

Balancing and weakening Lebanese political forces

In addition to bringing Lebanese institutions under its control, Syria's management strategy for Lebanon involved weakening and undermining the Lebanese opposition and preventing potential rivals from gaining ground. To this end, the Syrian government engaged in political manipulation, pushed for changes to Lebanese legislation, and did not hesitate to assassinate opponents. Syria, for example, forced former Prime Minster General Michel Aoun to leave Lebanon so that Samir Geagea would remain the only influential Christian leader in the country. Geagea, however, did not want to be part of a Syrian dominated Cabinet (NYT, 25 October 1990). So, instead, the Syrian regime directed its efforts at splintering his movement into smaller factions (NYT, 16 January 1993). Pressure on Geagea mounted, and in 1994 he was arrested and condemned on dubious charges.[15] The day of his arrest, the Lebanese government gave orders to dissolve his Lebanese forces. Likewise, Syria tried to play off different forces within the Druze community against each other, backing Talal Arslan against its then ally, the Druze leader Walid Jumblatt, before facilitating reconciliation between the two.[16] Damascus regularly employed the same divisive strategies to stifle anything and anyone that might upset its dominant role in Lebanon.[17]

Losing Lebanon—the full implementation of Ta'if

The Israeli withdrawal from South Lebanon in 2000 brought Syria's role in the country sharply into focus, both within Lebanon itself and internationally. Meanwhile, Bashar al-Assad's ascension to the Syrian presidency following the death of his father seemed to offer some hope that it might bring with it the promise of change in the bilateral power dynamics of Syrian–Lebanese relations. Inside Lebanon, voices calling for a redefinition of the Syrian role grew much louder. Christian opposition, spearheaded by Cardinal Sfeir, became increasingly pronounced, and Druze leader Walid Jumblatt publicly demanded more independence for Lebanon. It became clear to the Syrian regime that it was time to act, and so it responded by redeploying troops and reducing its overall military presence in Lebanon. Yet it was evident that these measures were only symbolic and were aimed more at enabling Syria's continued presence in Lebanon than as a step toward its independence.

With the renewed focus on Syria's involvement in Lebanon came a gradual but marked shift in Washington's position on the matter. The administration's tacit understanding of Syria's "stabilizing role" in Lebanon was suddenly of less importance, as was the successful US partnership with Damascus on counterterrorism and intelligence sharing. Both fell victim to strong domestic pressure in the United States from pro-Israel groups to extend the scope of counterterrorism activities to target Hezbollah and Palestinian rejectionist groups. Deputy Secretary of State Richard Armitage began referring to Hezbollah as the "A Team" of terrorists—a threat to be eliminated—quite clearly ignoring the fact that Hezbollah was not operating outside the Lebanese–Israeli scene.[18] Thus in the final calculation, Syria's leverage over Hezbollah did not turn out to be the "bargaining chip" it had hoped for in its dealings with Washington. On the contrary, evidence of the close relationship was used to isolate Damascus and label the Syrian regime a sponsor of international terrorism.

In April 2003, the US Congress passed the "Syria Accountability and Restoration of Lebanese Sovereignty Act" (SALSA), which aimed, among other things, at forcing Damascus to withdraw its troops. The Act enjoyed the support of the Lebanese and Israeli lobby and was signed on 11 May 2004 by President Bush. Although the measures taken within the Act's framework were somewhat symbolic, it was a clear signal that Syrian–US relations were changing.

Not long afterwards, Syria's previously successful policy of dividing and managing political forces in Lebanon began to falter as Prime Minister Rafiq Hariri and Jumblatt grew increasingly frustrated with Lahoud's obstructive pro-Syrian policy. To alleviate the burden of Lebanon's suffocating public debt, Hariri convened international donor conferences, the last in 2002 in Paris.[19] "Paris II" was very successful, generating more than $US10 billion for Lebanon in grants and loans. Hariri also tried to attract foreign investment, assuring potential investors throughout the conference that their money would be safe and that there would not be an outbreak of hostilities between Israel and Lebanon. But forces at home were already working against him.[20] The following day, Hezbollah launched a missile attack on Israel. This was only the beginning of the attempts to undermine Hariri's standing. The credit and loans obtained for Lebanon at Paris II were conditional on a series of tough reforms. President Lahoud, however, with Syrian backing, successfully blocked most of Hariri's reform initiatives (Leverett 2005, p. 110).

France, traditionally sympathetic to the interests of both Lebanon and Syria, was eager to see Paris II succeed. Yet in view of Damascus's attempts to block necessary reforms in Lebanon and its overt interference in Lebanese internal politics, the patience of the French administration started to wear thin. Relations between Paris and Damascus grew increasingly tense when, in the spring of 2004, an oil exploration contract awarded by the Syrian government to a French company was revoked and given to another consortium. French frustration with Syria mounted further over the course of the year amid questions over the future of the Lebanese presidency. It was anticipated that Syria would push for an extension of Lahoud's mandate, something that France vehemently opposed. Syrian officials denied that Syrian–French relations were in any way strained. But President Bush's visit to Normandy in early June sent a different message, and it soon became obvious that the rapprochement between France and the United States was linked to regional affairs. At a joint press conference, Chirac stated: "[O]n the subject of Lebanon, precisely, we have expressed renewed conviction and belief that Lebanon has to be ensured that its independence and sovereignty are guaranteed."[21] This development laid the groundwork for UN Resolution 1559, adopted on 2 September 2004.

UN Resolution 1559 did not mention Syria directly—a fact the Syrians depicted as a "victory"—but there could be no doubt about the country to which the resolution referred. It was a clearly and strongly worded resolution, announced only a few short hours before the decision on the extension of President Lahoud's term as president was due. The Syrian government had received warnings from various quarters not to interfere, and while it was assumed that Damascus wanted Lahoud to stay in office, it was also evident that this would provoke a harsh international reaction. Thus it came as something of a surprise when the Lebanese parliament confirmed Lahoud's extension on 3 September. In the international community this was viewed as a deliberate act of provocation by the Syrian regime. One can only speculate about what, in the end, convinced the Syrian president to opt for the highly contested amendment of the Lebanese constitution; but, without a doubt, the decision was based on a severe miscalculation of the degree of opposition it would generate both in Lebanon and internationally, and in turn, the dire consequences it would have for Syrian foreign policy. Immediately after Lahoud's extension was confirmed, four Lebanese ministers resigned in protest, and Hariri indicated that he intended to do the same. On 1 October there was an assassination attempt on one of the former ministers.[22] Three days later, Hariri resigned.

Starting in October 2004, the UN began reporting on the implementation of UNSCR 1559. But before the next six-month report could be issued, another dramatic event occurred, adding even more urgency to the situation—on 14 February 2005, Rafiq al-Hariri was assassinated in a massive explosion that targeted his convoy as it drove along the Beirut seafront. Damascus was immediately blamed for the technically sophisticated attack. Unusually quick to respond, Syrian officials made public statements denying any involvement in the attack. Yet the nature of the operation—and the degree of planning and attention to detail it involved—made it seem unlikely that it could have been planned and carried out without the knowledge of Syrian and Lebanese intelligence. Hours after the attack, the United Nations convened an extraordinary session in which it asked for immediate implementation of UNSCR 1559. On 15 February, the American ambassador to Syria, Margaret Scobey, was recalled to Washington, leaving the US ambassador's post vacant until 2010, and on 1 March France and the United States issued a joint statement calling for the immediate withdrawal of all Syrian military and intelligence personnel from Lebanon.

Daily protests began in Beirut, with hundreds of thousands of people gathering in the streets demanding "*al-Haqiqa*"—"the truth." These were soon countered by pro-Syrian demonstrations. With Lebanon in turmoil, the United Nations mandated the establishment of a fact-finding commission that began its work on 25 February, followed by the creation of a UN investigative committee under the leadership of Detlev Mehlis.[23]

The Syrian side was in disarray over how to respond, but it soon became clear that the pressure would be too much for Damascus to resist. Two weeks after Hariri's assassination, it seemed that Syria still hoped to be spared from full compliance with 1559. In an interview on 28 February, Bashar al-Assad spoke of a withdrawal by the end of the year as being "technically possible," but qualified it as being contingent on obtaining Israeli guarantees in return.[24] This issue was immediately dropped, however, and bowing to international and regional pressure, including from Saudi Arabia and Egypt, Bashar grudgingly committed to Syria's withdrawal from Lebanon within the timeframe set by the UN.[25]

On 26 April 2005 the last Syrian troops left Lebanon. Damascus went into "spin mode," portraying the withdrawal as a voluntary end to a successful mission, and describing the Lebanese army as having been "rebuilt on solid national foundations" and capable of protecting the state.[26] The Syrian government maintained that it had not been involved in Hariri's murder and set up its own investigative committee. Yet despite Syria's comprehensive intelligence network in Lebanon, no evidence was produced to substantiate Syrian claims that external forces were responsible for the attack. As Mehlis recalls:

A Syrian cabinet minister once wrote in a newspaper article that there was proof that Israel was behind the assassination. We immediately sent a letter of request, saying that we would be utmost grateful if we could obtain this proof to close the case as soon as possible. The answer we got were a few lines saying that the Minister had relied on newspaper articles.[27]

Meanwhile, Syria's ambassador to the United States, Imad Moustapha, did his best to reframe the situation, noting that, with Lebanon no longer an issue, President Bush could "focus his attention on the really terrible occupation of the Palestinian territories and the occupation of Syrian territories by Israel" (CNN, 8 March 2005).

The investigation into the assassination took different dynamics under the different heads of the investigation committee. Senior Public Prosecutor Detlev Mehlis, who had in earlier years proven the involvement of Syria in terrorist attacks in the 1980s in Europe, seemed eager to find evidence against Syria. The investigation reports presented to the United Nations in October and December 2005 presented a number of facts pointing to Syrian involvement but they were highly controversial because of their reliance on false witness statements. His successor, Serge Brammertz, was much less controversial, but he did not finalize the investigations before resigning in 2008.

139

The Lebanese government requested that the United Nations Security Council establish a Special Tribunal for Lebanon (STL), which was subsequently created in 2007. With evidence mounting that members of Hezbollah played a major role in the assassination, the issue became more and more problematic for Lebanon, until, in January 2011, the Lebanese government collapsed when Hezbollah and its allies resigned from the Cabinet in a dispute with Western-backed factions over upcoming indictments in the 2005 assassination of Hariri. Syria and Saudi Arabia had reportedly tried to mediate in this issue before, but had been unsuccessful.

Hassan Nasrallah repeatedly declared that he rejected the tribunal and the Lebanese funding of it, amounting to 49 per cent of the STL's overall budget. In an unexpected move, in October 2011 Syria declared it did not oppose the funding of STL (*Daily Star*, 27 October 2011). Instead of siding with its traditional ally Hezbollah, Syria supported the interests of Prime Minister Najib Mikati, and Walid Jumblatt, the leader of the Progressive Social Party who holds three posts in the Cabinet. This was due to the critical situation in which Syria found itself at that time: Lebanon was one of the two Arab countries still abstaining from implementing the sanctions the Arab League had imposed on Syria. Syria was not interested in losing this tacit backing, and its strongest concern was the continuity of the government and its stability.

Rumor had it that Bashar al-Assad had personally intervened in favor of the funding, which was supported by the fact that despite acting against Hezbollah's interests, on 11 December 2011, Hassan Nasrallah pledged to "stand by the (Assad) regime of resistance" (Karam 2011).

Syria, Amal, and the Lebanese Hezbollah

In dealing with Lebanon, Syria was always careful not to put all of its eggs in one basket. While at one level Syrian hegemony was well entrenched, Hafez al-Assad had pursued engagement with Hezbollah with the aim of gaining leverage in Arab–Israeli affairs (Harris 1997, p. 284). Syrian involvement with Hezbollah began during the civil war, with Hezbollah emerging as a Shi'a militia following the Israeli invasion of Lebanon in 1978. At that time the Syrian government was a supporter of a rival Shi'a militia, Amal, but once it became evident that Hezbollah was developing into a key player on the Lebanese scene,

Damascus began to pay it more attention—on one hand wanting to balance Iran's strong influence on the organization and, on the other, determined to ensure that Hezbollah would not grow sufficiently autonomous to challenge Damascus's hold over Lebanon. In 1988, when armed clashes between Amal and Hezbollah prompted Syrian forces to intervene, the Hezbollah leadership requested a meeting with Hafez al-Assad. It is thought that this discussion may have laid the foundation for a closer relationship between Hezbollah and the Syrian government.[28] By the end of the civil war, Hezbollah had established itself, and it was clear that the organization would continue to play a significant role in Lebanon's future. The extent of Syria's influence on the group was never entirely clear. It certainly did have some influence, but Hezbollah was always keen to underscore its independence.

This dynamic was particularly evident during the Lebanon hostage crisis in the 1980s, when more than a dozen Western citizens were kidnapped in Beirut and held for years. Syria tried to use the incident to improve its relationship with the United States and Britain by offering to help broker a solution. Hezbollah spokesman Na'im Qassem asserted that the group "has never been involved in or responsible for any of these incidents" but at the same time referred to them as "a form of objection ... and pressure used to persuade the targeted side to offer concessions or to give in to demands" (Qassem 2005, p. 232). To UN chief negotiator Giandomenico Picco it was clear that Hezbollah, if not fully responsible for the kidnappings, was at the very least involved in the choreography of releasing the hostages, thereby demonstrating some measure of independence from Syria. As he recalls: "The relationship between Hizbollah and the Syrians who controlled Lebanon was peculiar and at times unstable. The kidnappers, who prided themselves on being Lebanese, were always looking for ways to show their independence of action" (Picco 1999, p. 221).

Despite questions regarding the extent of Syria's control over Hezbollah, in the end a deal only became possible by engaging with Damascus. It was arranged that the hostages would be transferred to Damascus, where Syrian officials would release them to their respective embassies. In one case, the kidnappers tried to circumvent the Syrians by handing a hostage over to Picco directly, putting him in a rather difficult situation. "This arrangement was obviously part of a political message being sent by Hizbollah to the Syrians, and I was not pleased to be the messenger."[29]

The transformation and diversification of Hezbollah—from militia to political actor

The Ta'if accord, which provided for the disbanding of all "Lebanese and non-Lebanese militias," would, in normal circumstances, also have included Hezbollah; but Syrian backing for the group, as well as widespread popular support, spared it from having to disarm.[30] Hezbollah launched a successful public relations campaign, including the release of a political program, with the result that the Lebanese government characterized Hezbollah's military wing as a "resistance movement"—not a militia—and allowed Hezbollah to retain its arms because of its role in resisting Israeli occupation (Alagha 2006, p. 150). Hezbollah's strength lay in combining continuity in its core resistance activities with a more mainstream program, participating in the political process through elections, and adapting to changing circumstances by broadening its support base through the provision of a wide range of services and creative public relations, all while maintaining close ties to two states as different as Syria and Iran.

Hezbollah's efforts to secure domestic support were aided significantly by the financial resources at its disposal. Generous funding, mainly from Iran, allowed it to offer benefits to its supporters that other actors on the Lebanese scene could not afford. While there is no conclusive data, estimates indicate that Hezbollah receives $US1 billion annually from Iran that is channeled solely to the organization's social development activities.[31] Hezbollah filled a gap and became active in areas in which the state was either too weak or lacked the means to satisfy its citizens' needs, particularly in the provision of social services. Lebanon's mounting foreign debt, coupled with the ever-increasing socio-economic divide between the small, wealthy elite and the growing number of families living in or threatened by poverty, underlined the need for such extra-governmental services.

Syria, Iran, and Hezbollah were united by their common opposition to Israel, yet they had vastly differing visions for Lebanon's political future. Initially, Hezbollah was focused on a religious and ideological program that brought it close to the Iranian government. Over time, however, Hezbollah acquired more independence from the Iranian religious authorities and transformed into a more open, pragmatic, and political entity. The aim of establishing an Islamic state in Lebanon was dropped in favor of a form of government acceptable to all parties and factions within Lebanon. This brought Hezbollah closer to the secular Syrian regime. The object of Hezbollah's initial activity—fighting the Israeli invasion—remained unchanged, but Hezbollah nonetheless recognized that its survival and influence were contingent on working out a more nationalist, down-to-earth approach to other matters of importance to Lebanon (Alagha 2006, pp. 149ff.).

This was especially the case following the Israeli withdrawal from Lebanon, which gave rise to an identity crisis for Hezbollah and with it the need for a reorientation. While the UN verified the completion of the Israeli withdrawal in June 2000, Syria and Lebanon insisted that the Shabaa farms, a part of Lebanon, were still under occupation. This 25-square kilometer strip of territory provided Hezbollah with a pretext to continue its armed struggle. This was important for Damascus, as it wanted to retain Hezbollah as an effective means of pressuring Israel.[32] While in public the Syrian regime supported Lebanon's claim to the territory, the issue was not actually settled between the two countries. According to Assad, the final demarcation should only be made after an Israeli withdrawal. For years, in official communication between the two countries, Damascus made no explicit reference to the Shabaa farms, something which did not escape the attention of influential Lebanese figures like the writer Gibran Tuéni who, in a December 2005 article, criticized Syria's habit of insisting on the farms being Lebanese without ever giving written confirmation of this to Lebanon (Tuéni 2005). Just over a week later, on 12 December 2005, Tuéni was killed by a car bomb in Beirut, one of a series of assassinations of Lebanese politicians and intellectuals who had dared to criticize Syria's role in Lebanon.[33]

The Syrian government dealt with the Lebanese government and Hezbollah as two different entities, both enjoying Syria's full and equal support. Inevitably though, the different roles and interests of the two created challenges. On several occasions, militant Hezbollah activity provoked massive retaliatory action from Israel, bringing the Lebanese government under pressure and at the same time rendering it impotent in resolving the situation. That Hezbollah's activities were often more closely coordinated with the Syrians than with the Lebanese government exacerbated the difficulties (Palmer Harik 2005, p. 113). Over time, Hezbollah managed to establish itself as a kind of state within a state in Southern Lebanon, not only limiting Lebanese government sovereignty in domestic affairs but also in its relations with external actors like Israel, Syria, and Iran.

Especially after the withdrawal, the Israeli–Hezbollah confrontation became more symbolic and the "rules" of engagement more obvious. Hezbollah and Israel threatened each other—Israel with its supersonic over flights along the length of the Lebanese coast—Hezbollah responding with anti-aircraft fire. It was obvious to UN observers that Hezbollah was deliberately firing low on these occasions to avoid running any risk of damaging an Israeli airplane, well aware of the heavy-handed reaction that would inevitably result.[34] Until the Israel–Hezbollah confrontation in the summer of 2006, both sides seemed to be aware of the rules and in general adhered to them, thus avoiding further confrontation.[35]

That said, on several occasions Israel engaged in confrontations with Hezbollah with Syria as its actual target. The best examples of this are the military assaults Israel launched in 1993 and 1996, "Operation Accountability" and "Operation Grapes of Wrath." The official reason given for both operations was retaliatory and preventative action for Hezbollah's shelling of northern Israel.[36] Both operations caused casualties and resulted in extensive damage to Lebanese civilian infrastructure, but they failed to subdue Hezbollah. On the contrary, they enabled the organization to portray itself as the military victor and further improve its standing with the Lebanese population, in large part because of the efficient relief and reconstruction efforts of the companies and agencies at Hezbollah's disposal.

In conducting the two operations, Israel had hoped to force the Lebanese government to take action against Hezbollah, thereby driving a wedge between Syria and Lebanon. Speaking on Israeli Radio, Shimon Peres described the objectives of the 1993 attack:

The Lebanese government has to decide whether Hezbollah represents it or not. If it does, then the whole of Lebanon is at a state of war with Israel and this also means that Hezbollah seeks the destruction of all of Lebanon. The Lebanese government will then have to cooperate with us in silencing Hezbollah and ending its activities. (Palmer Harik 2005, p. 115)

Three years later, during the 1996 "Operation Grapes of Wrath," Israel's ambassador to the United States, Itamar Rabinovich, declared in a radio interview: "I think that the effective address is Syria" (Seale/Butler 1996, p. 21), adding that Israel's aim was to negotiate with Syria in working out a ceasefire. Rabinovich viewed Syrian policy as the real threat in Southern Lebanon—thus identifying the need to engage with Syria directly in order to deal with Hezbollah. From his perspective,

Syria had the power to restrain Hezbollah, and Iranian influence on the organization was contingent on Syria's willingness to allow it to do so (Seale/Butler 1996, p. 21). The timing of the operation was crucial. With elections on the horizon, Peres wanted to make a show of strength in confronting terrorism and changing the power balance with Damascus. But the Israeli strategy did not produce the desired result. Hezbollah emerged from the operation stronger than ever, and the election victory went to Netanyahu.

The Syrian regime was unwilling to give up on Hezbollah as a vehicle for military action against Israel, but, somewhat predictably, it began to grow concerned at the idea of Hezbollah gaining too much independence. Looking for ways to limit the organization's autonomy and fearing that the upcoming parliamentary elections would provide a platform for Hezbollah to expand its position in the Lebanese parliament, Damascus forced Hezbollah and Amal to form one bloc (Usher 1997). With this issue apparently taken care of, the Syrian regime continued to benefit from the status quo—having Hezbollah take action that was in Syria's interest but for which Damascus could not actually be blamed.

In 2002 Israel signaled that it was no longer willing to accept this state of affairs and retaliated against Syria by attacking positions in the Beqa'a Valley, not far from the Syrian–Lebanese border. Israeli Prime Minister Ariel Sharon, who had come into office in February 2002, was trying a new strategy. In mid-April he ordered Israeli fighter planes to target a Syrian radar installation. Several Syrian soldiers died in the operation, and the incident raised international concerns about an escalation of tensions between the two states.[37]

On 2 July 2002, two days after Hezbollah launched attacks on Israeli troops in the Shabaa farms, Israeli missiles destroyed a Syrian radar station in the Beqa'a. Hezbollah responded immediately, and Syrian Foreign Minister Farouq al-Sharaa and his Lebanese counterpart Mahmoud Hammoud released a joint statement underscoring the close foreign policy coordination between the two countries and warning that the incident threatened to destabilize the region (Palmer Harik 2005, p. 157). Evidently, Damascus's strategy of supporting Hezbollah against Israel and trying to dodge accountability was no longer working as effectively as it had in the past.

THE WISDOM OF SYRIA'S WAITING GAME

Hezbollah after the Syrian withdrawal

If the Israeli withdrawal in 2000 extended the geographic space in which Hezbollah operated, then Syria's withdrawal in 2005 opened the way for it to take on a greater role in the Lebanese political arena. Following Bashar al-Assad's 5 March 2005 announcement that Syria would comply with UNSCR 1559, Hezbollah decided to join the Lebanese Cabinet. As long as Syria was present in Lebanon, Hezbollah had been under its political protection and had thus made the "irrevocable decision" not to join the Cabinet. But with this marked change in the situation, Hezbollah now felt obliged to take on the responsibility of protecting Lebanon from Western influence (Alagha 2006, p. 173). The matter was portrayed in such a way as to make it appear that Hezbollah's previous decision not to participate in government was directly attributable to its confidence in Syria's ability to guarantee protection for Hezbollah and its interests. Regardless of the propaganda, however, it was clear that Hezbollah had experienced a surge in its power and autonomy following the Syrian withdrawal.

By this point in time, the Syrian regime had no real objections to Hezbollah's participation in the Lebanese elections. The political framework it had tried to establish had failed, and its central concern now was to complicate matters for Lebanon and for those in the international community who had insisted on Syria's withdrawal.

In 2006, Hezbollah kidnapped two Israeli soldiers on the Lebanese–Israeli border. Israel responded with massive force, killing over 1,000 people and severely damaging Lebanon's infrastructure. The war ended with a UN-brokered ceasefire in August 2006. Nasrallah in hindsight said if he had known the magnitude of Israel's retaliation, he would not have approved the kidnappings, which were interpreted by analysts as a sign of Hezbollah's more autonomous role after the Syrian withdrawal.

2011: Crumbling control in Syria and its effect on Lebanon

The ongoing conflict in Syria in many respects imposes a burden on Lebanon. Pre-revolutionary Syria was Lebanon's main partner in imports and exports; agricultural products were packed in Syria and transported through Syria to third countries. This is no longer possible. The Lebanese can no longer buy cheap clothes, household items, or high-quality medication at reasonable prices from Syria. The upmarket cafés, restaurants, and shops in Beirut are deserted because the developments have scared away rich Gulf tourists who used to pass their vacations here and were a major source of income for Lebanon. Around 1 million Syrian refugees are already estimated to have arrived in Lebanon, and there is hardly any international support for them.

Most worrisome, however, are the developments at the political level. The conflict in Syria with its increasingly sectarian dimension has had repercussions in Lebanon. Whether pro- or anti-regime, there is no interest in Lebanon for importing the conflict into its own territory. Lebanese political leaders have been eager, therefore, to keep the situation calm and have largely been muted in terms of their rhetoric.

Hezbollah is very interested in keeping the Assad regime in place, but the uprising in Syria fundamentally changed the role of Hezbollah, which had never before been involved in military affairs inside Syria. The organization somehow got trapped in its early, clear positioning. It has been losing popularity, and there is now a need to think about its post-Assad strategies. As Lebanon expert Doreen Khoury explained in June 2012:

Given Nasrallah's eminent pragmatism and Hezbollah's constant long-term planning, it is very unlikely that he will allow anything detrimental to happen to his party to safeguard the Assad family, from whose increasingly weakened position he derives less and less benefit. Hezbollah's survival in Lebanon depends on a post-Assad strategy, which could translate into deeper entrenchment in the Lebanese state and which already began after the withdrawal of Syrian troops in Lebanon in 2005, and more control over the various security agencies.[38]

Tensions are tangible, however, and with the growing involvement of Hezbollah, as well as pro-revolution groups in the border areas, the situation is becoming more volatile. Eight months later, the tone of Nasrallah's 20 April speech did not show much pragmatism. Contrary to the common understanding of sectarianism as a taboo he referred to rebel groups in Syria as "takfiris"—extremists, or literally Muslims who denounce other Muslims for not following Islamic law in a strict sense.[39]

The crisis has highlighted the weakness of the Lebanese government. Its inability to negotiate the return of Lebanese hostages kidnapped in Syria in May 2012 has demonstrated that—other than the Iranian government, which managed to have forty-eight Iranian hostages in Syria released in January 2013—Lebanon does not have enough leverage vis-à-vis the Syrian government. This does not mean that nothing in the Syrian–Lebanese equation has changed, however: in an unprecedented move on 9 August 2012, Michel Samaha, a high-ranking pro-Syrian politician, was arrested. Samaha was accused of a conspiracy with Syrian intelligence chief Ali Mamlouk to kill Christian religious leaders on a visit to the predominantly Sunni Akkar, in north Lebanon, in order to spread the Syrian conflict to Lebanon and enhance sectarian tensions. The Lebanese authorities, who had never before dared to raise allegations against Syrian officials, now indicted Mamlouk. In early February 2013, an arrest warrant against him was issued. This shows the degree to which Lebanon became more self-confident in the face of the once dominant neighbor.

Conclusion

Observers of Syrian politics often refer to Hafez al-Assad's handling of the "Lebanese file" as his most notable achievement, concurrently blaming Bashar's lack of judgment for the change in the status quo. This view, I believe, fails to recognize the inherent difficulties in the completely unbalanced bilateral relationship between the two countries, and it also discounts Lebanon and the Lebanese entirely, dismissing them as passive actors incapable of changing their situation. In fact, I would suggest that the groundwork for Syria's withdrawal from Lebanon was laid well before Bashar even came to power—most notably due to the disrespect, and even contempt—that Damascus had displayed in its relations with Lebanon.

It is obvious that Bashar tried to keep Lebanon under control using the same means as his father, but the "script" he inherited for handling foreign policy matters no longer fitted with the situation.[40] The Israeli withdrawal had changed the political landscape and challenged the legitimacy of Syria's role in Lebanon—just before Bashar's accession to the presidency. Meanwhile, the Syrian regime attempted to maintain control, as it did in other contexts, by allowing too many parties with too many differing interests to pursue their own contradictory aims.

The study of Lebanon shows several instances in which Hafez and Bashar got away with initially criticized policies. Syria's overture towards the United States and its support in the 1991 Gulf War was rewarded, among other things, by granting Syria a dominant role in Lebanon.

Then, when Israel withdrew in 2000, this put pressure on the Syrian government to follow suit. This, as well as the UN resolution calling for withdrawal, left the Syrian regime unimpressed, however, and only in 2005 did international threats became serious enough for Assad to give in—yet only formally, while maintaining Syrian influence and demonstrating through a series of assassinations that their interests could not be ignored.

The long history of the Syrian regime's behavior in these situations might have indicated to the international community that they would need to be prepared for a Syrian strategy of winning time while unaffectedly continuing to do what it wants. This does not mean that in the current situation Assad's combination of brutal violence with political persistence will enable the regime's survival—but it does indicate why Bashar al-Assad and the higher echelons of the Syrian leadership believe that it will.

In the current crisis, Lebanon does not need to be as afraid of Syrian control as of the Syrian government's loss of control, which might endanger Lebanese stability, creating a dangerous situation where thousands of Alawite members of the Shabiha, the army, and the security services will seek refuge in Lebanon, thereby shifting the confessional and political balance—which could easily escalate into a new civil war, given the high tension already existing in Lebanon between the mostly Sunni supporters of the revolution and the mainly Shiite supporters of the Syrian regime.

6

THE ODD COUPLE

SYRIA AND IRAN

Over time, Syria's unique relationship with Iran has proven to be one of the most durable alignments in a volatile Middle East. Hafez al-Assad's decision to forge ties with Tehran close on the heels of the Iranian Revolution clearly demonstrated that power politics were more important to him than ideology. In joining forces with Iran, he braved the outspoken criticism of other Arab states and his own public in order to enlist the support of one of the region's strongest powers. This close bilateral connection, conceived on the basis of perceived mutual interest, has not been devoid of tension. Damascus and Tehran have occasionally been at odds in their objectives, and the alliance remains unpopular with the public of both countries. However, it is the Syrian regime's only consistently cooperative relationship with a regional power, and even on the occasions when the two states have pursued differing or perhaps even contradictory interests, neither has openly considered withdrawing from the alliance.

For Iran, the alliance with Syria is a core element in its regional strategy. It is therefore determined to avoid a toppling of the regime—it is not likely to have a similar relationship with any future Syrian government, which would make it difficult to continue its strong support for Hezbollah. This chapter examines Syrian–Iranian relations in the period between 1990 and the present in order to understand the motivations of both parties in perpetuating this "special relationship" and to explore what this relationship means in practice in the current circumstances.

The early days of the relationship

Hafez al-Assad initiated cooperation between Damascus and Tehran during a time of sweeping change and upheaval in the region. Iran's revolution had produced a theocracy that openly advocated the "export" of a similar Islamic revolutionary model to Arab countries. The success of an Islamist movement in toppling a regime so strongly supported by the United States encouraged and emboldened Islamist movements in the entire region. It was thus highly conspicuous, not to mention some- what ironic, that Hafez al-Assad chose to deepen relations with Iran at the very time when he was violently crushing the Islamist-led uprising against his regime in Syria.[1] However, Assad needed an ally, and changes in the region's political landscape motivated him to act. Egypt was no longer an option, having been forced out of the Arab League after enter- ing into a peace agreement with Israel. Relations with Baghdad were strained following Hafez al-Assad's failed attempt at unification with Iraq, and because of ongoing Iraqi support for the Muslim Brother- hood's activities in Syria. Thus with the two strongest Arab states out of the running, and the Syrian regime growing ever more concerned about Israel's increasing strength, Iran was the logical choice. The rapproche- ment between the two countries bore fruit for the Syrian regime almost immediately: Tehran, while steadfastly proclaiming the need for Islamic revolution throughout the Muslim world, refused to permit persecuted members of the Syrian Muslim Brotherhood to take refuge in Iran and refrained from backing the political upheaval in Syria—a clear signal of support for its new ally (Goodarzi 2006, p. 9).

In the years following the Iranian Revolution, the US administration was consistently critical of Syrian–Iranian cooperation, yet it made a concerted effort to win over the Syrian regime in order to have Damas- cus act as a go-between in resolving its difficulties with Iran. In the 1980s, for example, the Syrian government assisted in securing the release of Americans abducted in Lebanon (Picco 1999). Damascus was, in effect, speculating on its relationship with Tehran: speculating that by offering a service to the United States that could not be obtained elsewhere, it would gain valuable leverage that would be of benefit in future.[2] However, the slow and sometimes unsuccessful negotiations demonstrated that Syria's influence on Iran, in reality, was quite limited (Picco 1999).

Hafez al-Assad and Iranian leader Ayatollah Ruhollah Khomeini shared two main objectives: each sought to assume a regional leadership role and to oppose external influence in the region's affairs. Both men were highly critical of American interference in the Middle East, vehemently anti-Israel, and fearful of Iraq's expansionist aspirations. However, the two leaders had quite different visions of how best to achieve their objectives and deal with their "enemies." Khomeini sought to broaden Tehran's sphere of influence by promoting and exporting a pan-Islamist revolutionary model, while Hafez al-Assad was primarily interested in bolstering his credentials as an Arab leader. From an ideological standpoint, the two states could not have been more different; yet the clear convergence of political and security interests prompted the Islamic Republic to cooperate with secular Syria, and Damascus to place pragmatism over pan-Arabism and align itself with the only regional actor that could provide a counterweight to Israel.

The underlying confessional dimension—Assad's regime being considered a Shiite offshoot—did not play any apparent role in those days, as Goodarzi argues: "Overall, the religious element has not been a determining factor and has had little, if any, salience" (Goodarzi 2013, p. 39). However, it eased the partnership as an implicit commodity, given the outrage in Saudi Arabia about Hafez al-Assad ordering the killing of thousands of Sunnis from the Muslim Brotherhood in Hama in 1982 and the deep Saudi–Iranian enmity at that time. Naturally, the Muslim Brotherhood's relations with Sunni regimes were closer than with the Shiites in Iran.

The benefits of the relationship were not one-sided. Tehran also needed a regional ally, especially in the wake of Iraq's invasion of Iran in September 1980. Syria was not in a position to offer military support, but the alliance had the potential to save Iran from facing a wider Arab coalition.[3] Well aware of Baghdad's military might, Syria had an interest in seeing Iraq weakened, but no appetite for becoming embroiled in the actual conflict. Siding with Iran in the conflict was thus a strategic choice that served Syria's national security interest as well as the desire to curb Iraq's regional ambitions.[4] On occasion—particularly in the late

1980s—the alliance with Iran served to increase Syria's relevance in the eyes of Western countries looking to Damascus to mediate in times of crisis. In these situations, Tehran became an asset or a card to be played, rather than a strategic partner.

Rivalry and cooperation in Lebanon

Syrian–Iranian relations have always been characterized by a degree of rivalry when it comes to Lebanon. Historically, both Damascus and Tehran have sought to increase their influence in the country by sponsoring Shia groups. Syria initially focused its efforts on supporting Amal as a way to bring balance to Lebanese power dynamics, and as Iran became more involved in Lebanese affairs, Damascus grew concerned that its "control" over this important segment of the Lebanese population would diminish. Iran played a fundamental role in establishing Hezbollah and contributing to all aspects of its development. Tehran financed and equipped Hezbollah and provided training for its recruits, creating a reliance on Iranian money and material support that continues to this day.

With Lebanon's demographic landscape changing rapidly as a result of its growing Shia population, Tehran hoped that in the event of civil war the region would see the birth of another Shia-Islamist dominated state. However, Iran's stated interest in supporting these movements was to be able to fight Israel on Lebanese territory, thereby bolstering its credentials with Arab governments and the street. Invoking "resistance" as the basis of its engagement in Lebanon made Iran's activities more palatable to both Lebanese and Syrian partners, despite the fact that the Syrians, especially, were in no hurry to see an Islamic state emerge right on their doorstep, in a country that they regarded as part of their own territory.[5]

The event that ultimately brought Iran's and Syria's Lebanon policy together was Saddam Hussein's decision to channel his support to Christian militias under the leadership of General Michel Aoun in an effort to challenge Syrian–Iranian influence and cooperation in Lebanon. Not to be out-maneuvered, in the late 1980s Tehran and Damascus mediated a cease-fire between Amal and Hezbollah and advocated closer policy coordination to ensure that their own interests would not fall victim to political infighting and fragmentation (Hamzeh 2004, p. 102).

However, Hafez al-Assad was uneasy about the power that Iran was able to wield through Hezbollah. Syria regularly monitored Iranian and Hezbollah activities in Lebanon through its extensive network of troops and intelligence operatives and on several occasions intervened, through its proxies or using its own military personnel, to curb Hezbollah activities.[6] The more Hezbollah grew in strength and influence, the more crucial it became for Syria to bring it under its control—at least to the same extent as Tehran was able to manage. Hezbollah expert Palmer Harik explains:

Although Damascus' past experiences with fundamentalism had been extremely negative, Assad expected to have as tight a grip on Hezbollah as he had on all the other parties under the Syrian politico-military umbrella. This expectation was tested in 1987, when Hezbollah partisans refused to remove a check point from the road before their West Beirut barracks on the orders of the Syrian troops that had arrived to control the area. The Syrian officer in charge simply arrested the two-dozen or so men involved, lined them up and shot each one through the head with his pistol. ... The tensions at times between Hezbollah and Syria and between Tehran and Damascus illustrated the fact that the three-sided relationship was obviously a marriage of convenience and only later became a closer one. (Palmer Harik 2005, p. 40)

Iran, Syria, and the 1991 Gulf War

The 1991 Gulf War was another fork in the road for Syrian–Iranian cooperation. While both countries had an interest in seeing Iraq weakened, and had advocated a diplomatic solution to the crisis, they ultimately chose very different paths in the lead-up to the war. Tehran, unlike Damascus, deemed joining the US-led coalition impossible and instead adopted for a neutral stance. It condemned Iraq's behavior, and openly proclaimed its support for Kuwaiti sovereignty and the emir of Kuwait as the legitimate ruler of the country. This position was particularly remarkable considering that not long before the Iranian leadership had encouraged Kuwaiti opposition forces to overthrow the Al Sabah family (Fürtig 2002, pp. 100f.).

When it finally became obvious to Saddam Hussein that he had grossly underestimated the international response to his assault on Kuwait, he attempted to "buy the tolerance of his former enemies" and convince Tehran to side with him (Fürtig 2002, p. 102). This concilia-tory approach was a complete failure. It did nothing to soften Iran's position, nor did it succeed in changing the Iranian leadership's fundamental mistrust of Saddam Hussein.

The First Gulf War brought the issue of regional security sharply into focus for Arab governments. Motivated by a strong desire to reduce the region's dependence on foreign actors and its own reliance on Iran in security matters, Syria explored options for restructuring the region's security framework. Its efforts culminated in a joint initiative with Egypt and the Gulf Cooperation Council (GCC) known as the "6 + 2" initiative and the so-called "Damascus Declaration"[7] signed on 6 March 1991. From Syria's perspective this was an important step in decreasing US military engagement in the region through the deployment of Syrian and Egyptian troops to Saudi Arabia. Tehran, which was excluded from the talks, made it clear that it found the whole initiative offensive.

For the Iranian leadership, the Damascus Declaration was a setback in its ongoing efforts to improve relations with GCC states, signaling as it did that the Gulf Arab states remained more willing to enter into security arrangements to contain Iran's regional influence and military might than to consider establishing a common security system that would include Iran. The Damascus Declaration created tension in Syrian–Iranian bilateral relations. As soon as the news broke, high-ranking Iranian officials traveled to Damascus to protest. Foreign Minister Ali Velayati and Vice President Hassan Habibi personally expressed Tehran's fears for the country's security and strategic interests, in addition to conveying their grave disappointment at the behavior of their Syrian ally, taking the opportunity to request that arrangements be modified to include both Iran and Iraq (Fürtig 2002, pp. 105ff.). In an effort to mend fences with Tehran, Hafez al-Assad suggested to the GCC states, as well as Egypt, that their reservations were baseless, and that the Iranians should be made part of the security agreement. The Syrian leader's efforts failed, but the gesture was successful in appeasing Tehran. As it turned out, despite having signed the Declaration, the Gulf States had no intention of discontinuing the US military presence in their countries and leaving their security in the hands of an Arab defense force. In the summer of 1991, Egyptian and Syrian troops left the Gulf. The military component of the Damascus Declaration was officially abandoned at the GCC summit in Dakar in December 1991. So ended the plan to establish an Arab regional security framework, and with it the controversy between Iran and Syria over this matter. Content now that the regional security framework was off the table, Tehran resumed its efforts to improve relations with all the Gulf States. Had the parties to the Damascus Declaration succeeded in laying the foundations for a viable regional security system, Syria might have reconsidered its alignment with Iran or even have been forced to abandon it. However, in the absence of other options, withdrawing from the alliance with Iran would have exposed Syria to additional insecurity and was thus not an option for Assad.

The Middle East peace process

The two countries' central objectives remained largely unchanged, but neither Syria nor Iran saw it necessary to deepen their ties. Cooperation continued over Lebanon and Hezbollah, but each state followed its own interests. Changing regional dynamics led Syria to explore different possibilities for bilateral cooperation, outside the framework of its bilateral relationship with Tehran, including with the United States.

A strain occurred, however, with regard to Syria's participation in the Middle East peace process. Once Syria had decided to engage in the peace process in 1991, Iran was left alone—the only state in the region to remain adamant in its rejection of negotiations with Israel. Tehran understood that militant activism against Israel was central to broadening its popular base in the region. The Iranian leadership consequently viewed a potential peace accord between Syria and Israel as counter to its own interest and ambitions; it thus went out of its way to denounce the Madrid Conference, and even held a parallel conference in Tehran at the very same time. While some 400 delegates from sixty countries attended the conference to support "the Islamic Revolution in Palestine," which aimed at creating an alternative to the PLO, the absence of key Palestinian players meant that the effort, unsurprisingly, ended in failure.[8]

Nonetheless, Iran was aware that its firm stance with regard to Israel created an opportunity to build up its credentials with the Arab street. Iran's long-standing support to Hezbollah and Palestinian movements making up the Arab "resistance" against Israel, as well as growing anti-Americanism and intransigence in its official rhetoric, earned the country respect in the Arab world—at least from those who were not directly or adversely affected by Iranian policy. Iran's stance, as International Crisis Group analyst Karim Sadjadpour explains:

makes Ahmadinejad's star shine in places such as Cairo, Amman, and Damascus. Currying favor on the Arab street is integral to Iran's goal of becoming the Middle East's dominant power and a bulwark against perceived U.S. imperialist ambitions in the region. … the Arab masses … praise the defiant political order from afar but do not wish it for themselves. (Sadjadpour 2006/7, p. 155)

There was appreciation in the Arab world for aspects of Iranian foreign policy: its confrontational approach towards Israel, including the material support to Hamas and Hezbollah, for which it was a much more important supporter than any Arab country. However, its religious orientation, and the fact that many states of the region are uncomfortable with Iranian power, meant that Iranian foreign policy continued to lack mass appeal.

When the Syrian–Israeli negotiations stalled in the late 1990s, the newly elected Iranian President Mohammad Khatami saw a chance to strengthen cooperation with Syria on the Palestinian groups. In May 1999, he became the first Iranian president to visit Syria, and in meetings with heads of Damascus-based Palestinian rejectionist groups he assured them of Iran's support.[9] In a joint statement Khatami and Assad called for an end to Israel's occupation of the Arab territories and recognition of the right of return. Khatami further stated that under these conditions Iran would support the peace process and refrain from imposing solutions on the Palestinian people. When Syria recommenced negotiations with Israel in 2000, Iran made clear its support, comfortable that discussions would not explicitly address the subject of Palestinian rights. In 2002, President Khatami adopted the position taken by Syria in the mid-1990s, stating that any solution acceptable to the Palestinians was also acceptable to his country, and that he officially welcomed all steps towards a just peace in the Middle East (Ahouie 2004, pp. 7ff.).

While the value of the Iranian–Syrian relationship from Damascus's point of view mainly consisted in the joint efforts against Israel, it has served more of a symbolic function rather than offering any form of practical protection. It did not deter Israel from launching military strikes on Syria in 2003, 2007 or 2013, for instance, and despite Iran's 2004 commitment to defend Syria in the event of an attack, no such protection has been forthcoming. On the contrary, both Iran and Syria have been careful not to respond to provocative Israeli acts with military force.[10]

THE ODD COUPLE: SYRIA AND IRAN

Syrian–Iranian relations under Bashar

Rather than considering these incidents a setback, Iran and Syria have instead focused on what they consider as their joint achievements in confronting Israel. Most important in this regard was the Israeli withdrawal from South Lebanon in 2000, which Hezbollah characterized as a direct result of its resistance efforts.[11] In fact, in his book, the deputy secretary general of Hezbollah, Na'im Qassem, includes a chapter on how to adapt Hezbollah's experience to other contexts, proudly discussing Israel's withdrawal from Lebanon and the parties that contributed to the organization's success:

When Hizbullah liberated South Lebanon and the Western Bekaa with the effective help of Iran, it achieved its declared goals for which martyrs contributed their sacrifices. Through this, Iran realized its vision of rejecting occupation and supporting mujahideen freedom fighters. These are recorded gains for both Hizbullah and Lebanon, as well as for Iran; they are also marked rewards for Syria, the Palestinian Intifadah and for every person who believes in resistance and liberation. (Qassem 2005, pp. 237, 224)

The image of Hezbollah as the only force in the Arab world able to pose a serious military challenge to the Israeli Defense Force made the organization something of a popular hero in the region. The 2006 war in Lebanon underscored this impression, with King Abdullah of Jordan, among others, roundly criticizing Israel for having elevated Hezbollah's status on the Arab street through its actions (BBC, 3 August 2006).

It was thought by the United States and others that UN Security Council Resolution 1559, which called for the withdrawal of all foreign troops from Lebanon as well as the disbanding and disarming of Hezbollah—coupled with the international pressure that had forced Syria to withdraw from Lebanon in 2005—would be the final step in ending Syria's long-standing influence on its neighbor. However, this plan has had only limited success. Hezbollah, neither disarmed nor disbanded, is now far stronger and more autonomous than before.

Syrian–Iranian relations and the 2003 war in Iraq

Damascus and Tehran present a study in contrasts with regard to how each chose to behave in the lead-up to and during the 2003 Iraq War. Both countries vehemently rejected American intervention in the region. Syria went on the attack, alienating regional allies like Egypt and

Jordan with its outspoken and populist positioning against the war.[12] As a consequence, Bashar al-Assad found himself friendless in the face of mounting American pressure. Having predicted that the quick US military victory in Iraq would give way to chaos, Syrian officials fully expected that the US administration would request assistance in getting out of the crisis.[13] But no such request was forthcoming, only renewed demands to stem the flow of foreign fighters into Iraq that had already earned Damascus the reputation of encouraging hostilities against US forces, and which had failed to result in any increased leverage in Iraq. Iran meanwhile remained less vocal, taking advantage of the turmoil in Iraq to extend its power and influence there through its already extensive and long-standing network of relationships.[14]

Both Syria and Iran had agreed to a rapprochement of sorts with Iraq in the late 1990s, each for its own strategic reasons. With the Syrian–Israeli peace track at a dead-end, and the prospects for a peace dividend looking increasingly remote, Syria sought a source of revenue that did not come with political conditions attached.[15] Hafez al-Assad was also motivated to mend fences with Iraq due to his concerns regarding an increase in Israeli–Turkish cooperation. Iran's interest in engaging with Iraq was security-related.[16] The two countries began discussions on contentious border issues and support for militant groups in each other's country. Iraq agreed to stop assisting the Mujahedin-e Khalq, and Tehran declared it would expel Iraqi dissidents from its territory, including Iraqi Shia leader Ayatollah Hakim, who was already preparing to move to Syria.[17]

In both cases, the relationship was based on pragmatism, without any particular loyalty to the regime of Saddam Hussein. In fact, for Damascus and Tehran, the situation was ideal: Saddam Hussein was weak enough not to be a threat to either and was desperate enough to approach both of his arch-enemies to improve relations and break Iraq's isolation. They were in control. Completely apart from the moral and legal considerations related to the 2003 intervention, neither Syria nor Iran was in any hurry to see the end of what was for them a highly advantageous situation. In an interview on 5 April 2003, Rafsanjani made a statement that essentially encompassed the position of both countries: "We won't be shedding many tears for the Iraqi Government. ... However, we say that the Security Council should come. The concern we have is that the Americans should [sic] take the place of Saddam in Iraq."[18]

THE ODD COUPLE: SYRIA AND IRAN

Competing for influence in the aftermath of the 2003 Iraq War

One of the unintended consequences of the 2003 Iraq War was a sudden boost in Iran's regional power. The fact that it had not only cultivated ties with like-minded Iraqi opposition groups during Saddam Hussein's time, but had turned them into an asset after the war had ended was the principal difference from Syria, which had also hosted Iraqi opposition groups but due to its obstructive policy during and after the war was unable to benefit from this.

Syria's involuntary withdrawal from Lebanon in 2005 left the regime in Damascus vulnerable and Tehran with fertile ground in which to extend its direct relations with Hezbollah and thereby its influence in Lebanon. The relationship has become increasingly asymmetric over time, in no small measure due to Iran's very open nuclear ambitions, which, though they may have hampered its relations with Western countries, have ensured that it is taken seriously as a regional power—far more so than Syria.

The speed with which allied forces toppled Saddam Hussein's regime enhanced fears in Syria and Iran that they would be next on the list of US targets. American officials became increasingly outspoken in their criticism of Syrian and Iranian policy in the region, and as the rhetoric continued, Damascus and Tehran felt that the threat of foreign intervention had become more and more palpable. Hence both states welcomed the difficulties that kept the international coalition busy in Iraq, hindering the country's transition to democracy. Had the process in Iraq gone smoothly, it might have encouraged Syrians and Iranians to question the legitimacy of their governments and mount an effective opposition to the status quo. Instead, Syrians and Iranians saw innumerable scenes of chaos and bloodshed, which they soon came to associate with democracy.

Once it became obvious to Iran and Syria that a US attack was not on the cards they became significantly more confident, secure in the knowledge that American military intervention in the region was on hold for the foreseeable future.[19] The 2003 war in Iraq effectively reshuffled the deck of regional influence between Syria and Iran, and Iran, for the most part, came out the winner. Over time, both countries have undergone an evolution in their Iraq policy. Where at one time Damascus and Tehran saw the benefit of protracted violence and unrest that would keep American forces occupied and focus attention away from their own countries, both now prioritized maintaining the territorial integrity of Iraq as a means of preventing separatist ambitions from crossing the border—notwithstanding Syria's discomfort with Iran's strengthened role.

Optics versus substance

Syria and Iran have signed agreements on security cooperation, and the scope of bilateral investments and joint ventures between the two countries has also increased. According to Asharq al-Awsat, by 2006 Iran was investing some $US400 million per year in Syria, making it the third-largest investor in the country (after Saudi Arabia and Turkey).[20] Syria welcomed this foreign investment, but there was growing uneasiness about dependencies, and about Tehran's motives, as Iran focused its investment on Syria's core industries (Naylor 2007). Bashar al-Assad visited Iran three times during his first eight years in office, and was the first foreign head of state to visit Iran after Ahmadinejad came to power.[21] There is no other country with which Syria exchanges the same number of high-level official visits, and this in itself is indicative of the efforts being made to maintain the relationship.

Perceiving an apparent lack of substance to Syrian–Iranian relations, analysts have suggested that over time the relationship had become more about appearances, with regular official visits between the two countries but little concrete cooperation. As analyst Sharam Chubin remarked in 2000: "Posturing is not policy and certainly not strategy. Rhetoric and vituperation, however satisfying, are not a substitute for a sustainable policy" (Chubin 2000, p. 22).

Already before the current war in Syria, there have been instances of external pressure drawing the two countries together. Decisions to increase the depth and scope of this special relationship were generally taken in response to regional developments, rather than a desire to strengthen the alliance itself. In the mid-1990s, for example, concern over growing cooperation between Israel and Turkey prompted Syria and Iran to enhance their relations, thereby forming a counter-alliance of sorts. In 1997, Tehran and Damascus agreed to expanded intelligence cooperation in third countries, as well as more regular exchanges between their armed forces.[22]

One example is Syria's reliance on Iran after the 2005 assassination of Lebanese Prime Minister Rafiq al-Hariri in Beirut. Damascus found itself increasingly isolated, blamed by many for Hariri's death. Iran stood firmly with Syria, and since that time the two countries have signed a variety of agreements to foster bilateral cooperation (Taheri 2006). The day after Hariri's murder, amid accusations that the Syrian regime was behind the assassination, Syrian Prime Minister Naji al-Otri visited Iran, declaring that Iran and Syria had to establish a "common front" (Lesch 2005, p. 133). Iranian Vice President Mohammad Reza Aref declared that his country was "ready to help Syria on all grounds to confront threats": "Our Syrian brothers are facing specific threats and we hope they can benefit from our experience. We are ready to give them any help necessary."[23] Meanwhile, Syria's ambassador to the United States, Imad Moustapha, stressed that Syrian–Iranian cooperation was not designed to target the United States:

Today we do not want to form a front against anybody, particularly not against the United States. Syria is trying to engage constructively with the United States ... We are not the enemies of the United States, and we do not want to be drawn into such an enmity.[24]

The American take on Syrian–Iranian relations

Under President Clinton, Syria's relations with Iran and the ensuing rapprochement with Iraq during the latter half of the 1990s were not well regarded by the United States; however, extensive cooperation from both Syria and Iran in the Bush administration's War on Terror did help to ease relations with Washington somewhat. Syria's main contribution was in the field of intelligence, while Iran's support was required in Afghanistan. The Iranian leadership had never been fond of the Taliban regime and consequently had no objection to cooperation with the United States on Afghanistan. Initially, the US administration welcomed Syrian and Iranian support in its counterterrorism efforts. Within a short time, however, Washington's fervor in addressing the broad spectrum of terrorist activities began to strain its cooperation with Tehran and Damascus, which was focused on combating al-Qaeda. Allegations surfaced that Iran was giving sanctuary to al-Qaeda fighters crossing the border from Afghanistan and that it was pursuing policies hostile to US interests in Afghanistan.[25] These allegations, coupled with Syria's and Iran's forceful opposition to the 2003 Iraq War and their support for militias and foreign fighters in Iraq, resulted in relations with the United

States taking a turn for the worse. Washington's tolerance for Syrian–Iranian cooperation vanished now that it was no longer of use to US interests, and the administration decided to step up the pressure on both governments.

Over the years, the United States and others have attempted to drive a wedge between Syria and Iran by putting pressure on Damascus, which they see as the weak link in the relationship. Clearly, these efforts have not had the desired effect. In fact, some observers maintain that Western policies have "pushed Syria into Iran's arms."[26] This is borne out by the signing in more recent years of unprecedented agreements between Damascus and Tehran on bilateral defense cooperation, including a "memorandum of understanding" on 26 February 2004, followed by agreements in 2005 and 2006 assuring that the parties will assist one another in the event of an attack, as well as a defense treaty in June 2006. These developments were a source of relief for Bashar al-Assad, who was keen for Damascus and Tehran to further security cooperation in the face of high international pressure and the continued presence of American troops in Iraq.

In 2008, Syria and Iran lobbied jointly for bringing Syria onto the board of the International Atomic Energy Agency, a move that met with fierce resistance: in 2007, Israel had bombarded an alleged nuclear site in Syria, al-Kibar, and the United States refused to allow Syria to join the board until the investigations of the site had been concluded. Syria finally withdrew its candidature (*Daily Star*, 4 October 2008).

The Arab perspective: treason or constructive alliance?

Over the years, Syrian cooperation with Iran has been the subject of stinging criticism from Arab states that viewed Damascus's decision to side with Tehran during the Iran–Iraq War as tantamount to treason. To them, Syria's alliance with Iran presented an obstacle to the development of a more unified Arab bloc. Syria defended its position, claiming that it was first and foremost interested in bringing about an end to the Iran–Iraq War because of its negative impact on Arab interests. In Hafez al-Assad's view, Iraq's military engagement with Iran was weakening the common Arab stand against Israel both psychologically and materially. As David Lesch explains, Syria had a dual interest in pursuing its alliance with Iran: "Assad believed that Hussein's follies were an untimely and misdirected application of vital Arab resources and assets away from the Arab–Israeli arena; but they also created an opportunity to weaken an inter-Arab rival, thus allowing Syria to play a leading role in the region and fill the shoes vacated by Egypt" (Lesch 2005, p. 41). Not all Arab states were convinced by Assad's rationale, but they grudgingly accepted the alliance, just as they also acquiesced to Syria's engagement in Lebanon.

The states of the region have been observing Syrian–Iranian cooperation with some suspicion. While often referred to as an "alliance," Damascus and Tehran prefer a different terminology. In 2006, for example, Syrian Foreign Minister Walid al-Mouallim, speaking on al-Jazeera, specified: "We have a special relationship with Iran, not an alliance."[27] In the 1980s, many observers considered it a temporary phenomenon that would end after the Iran–Iraq War. Baghdad's assertive regional policy was certainly a principal driving force for the rapprochement between the two, but other common interests undeniably emerged over time; and particularly for Syria it was preferable to cooperate with the only regional power that could act as a real counterweight to Israel. Opinion was also split about the effect of Syrian–Iranian cooperation on the rest of the region. Some analysts described it as a "force for regional stability," pointing to its continuity and durability (Ehteshami/Hinnebusch 1997, p. 4). Others, pointing to the potential of both powers to influence regional developments negatively, dubbed it an "axis of instability."[28]

Iran and the Syrian Revolution

When Arab rebellions started in Tunisia and Egypt, Iran praised the protests; it portrayed them as being directed against pro-Western regimes, whose toppling signaled the advent of a new era in the Middle East, in which Islamist movements would take the lead. Obviously, Iran had not calculated that the wind of change would affect Syria, where the prospect of a Sunni regime coming to power was an entirely different matter. Iran's close ties with the Assad regime were based on shared strategic objectives, not on the sectarian nature of the regime. However, Iran was aware that a Sunni and probably an Islamist government in Syria was more likely to cooperate with Saudi Arabia and the Gulf States than Iran, and this would clearly constitute a major setback for the

Iranian regime. Iran therefore chose to back Bashar al-Assad. Presumably, it underestimated the magnitude of the uprising and thought that with its support, the Syrian regime would easily crush the rebellion the same way as Iran had done when confronted with the "Green Revolution" of 2009/10. In the end, both regimes were simply different flavors of authoritarianism, so what had worked for Iran could also be applied in Syria. When this had not materialized by mid-summer 2011, Iran undertook efforts to get in touch with the Syrian opposition groups. These meetings do not seem to have borne fruit. In December 2011 Burhan Ghalioun, then leader of the Syrian National Council, left no doubt about his position on relations with Iran after regime change:

The current relationship between Syria and Iran is abnormal. It is unprecedented in Syria's foreign policy history. A new Syria will be an indispensable part of the Arab League and it will work on improving the role of the Arab League and the role of Arab states regionally, specifically because they took a historic and unprecedented decision to back the Syrian people. (Ghalioun 2011)

As a result, the Iranian regime decided to back the Syrian regime with any means needed. Whereas in the previous crises in Syria Iranian support had been stronger in words than in deeds, Iran now sent military equipment, advisors, and—allegedly—paid for Russian arms deliveries to Damascus.[29] Starting in August, a number of arms shipments from Iran addressed to Syria were intercepted (*Today's Zaman*, 5 August 2011), and in December 2011 Syrian rebels captured five Iranian nationals in the city of Homs. They were disguised as garbage collectors but carried Iranian passports, while one had a document identifying him as an officer of the Iranian Revolutionary Guards (*Stern*, 4 January 2012). There have been other incidents in which Syrian rebels claimed to have found evidence of Iranian involvement, and in February 2013 a senior commander of the Iranian Revolutionary Guards was killed in Syria (*Time*, 26 February 2013).

The confessional kinship, which for years played only a minor role in the Iranian–Syrian relationship, has now fully unfolded. It has superseded the eternal enmity with Israel as a common ideological ground. An indication of this might be that Assad's and Iran's ally Hezbollah Secretary General Hassan Nasrallah in April 2013 started to justify Hezbollah's engagement in Syria more on religious than political grounds, referring to those to be fought against as (Sunni) extremists and stressing the right of Hezbolah "to defend Saida Zaineb," the holiest Shiite shrine in Syria.

THE ODD COUPLE: SYRIA AND IRAN

Conclusion: assessing the "Strategic Relationship"

There have been plenty of mutual visits between Iran and Syria, as well as treaties and declarations between the two states proclaiming their mutual support for each other. Essentially, their cooperation boils down to two main priorities: bolstering their regional influence and confronting Israel. With regard to the latter, however, it is remarkable that the alliance has played no role in protecting Syria from occasional Israeli airstrikes. In their political orientation, the two states could not be more different—while at the same time both regimes find themselves on the same, Shiite, side of the great inner-Islamic gap. And, while for many years relations remained rather shallow, what has now made them so durable?

One reason for the pre-revolutionary improvement in the relationship might be, as scholars Hussein Agha and Ahmad Khalidi conclude, that the nature of Syrian–Iranian relations allowed for a high degree of divergence (Agha/Khalidi 1995). Each party accepted that the other acted first and foremost according to its security needs. Therefore, Iran rejected but did not obstruct Syrian–Israeli negotiations or occasional Syrian cooperation with the United States. In turn, while never entirely comfortable with Iran's nuclear aspirations, Syrian officials have publicly defended Tehran, and in a joint effort the two states worked together to try to bring Syria onto the board of the IAEA.

While they have occasionally been in competition with each other regarding their respective regional influence, the benefits of cooperation have proven sufficiently valuable for this not to have become a bone of contention. Furthermore, despite—or as Iran expert Jubin Goodarzi explains—because of their fundamentally different worldviews, they were not competing for leadership in terms of political ideology, eliminating a significant element of competition and thus friction from their cooperation, which has antagonized Syria from states with similar orientations like Saddam Hussein's Iraq (Goodarzi 2013).

Several examples show that external pressure has not driven Syria and Iran apart but has instead pulled them closer together. While in most of these cases there was no real threat for either partner, Iran has come to realize that the Syrian uprising has changed the equation. Based on its own experience in the 2009/10 "Green Revolution," it initially believed that Bashar al-Assad could easily crush the rebellion. The uprising has brought other regional players onto the scene, notably Saudi Arabia—a significant competitor for regional hegemony. If Assad's regime was to disappear, the Shiite axis of Hezbollah–Damascus–Tehran would be fundamentally weakened. Although it was not the intention of the Syrians who flocked to the streets in 2011 demonstrating against dictatorship and corruption, the confessional setting of the Syrian power structure has turned their country into the frontline of the ancient, rapidly escalating Sunni–Shiite antagonism—which has driven the Iranian rulers to support Bashar al-Assad's regime with any means at its disposal.

7

BROTHERLY LOVE

SYRIA'S RELATIONS WITH IRAQ

Syria's relationship with Iraq is reminiscent of the most challenging kind of family dynamic. Not only is there a long-standing enmity and competitiveness between the two countries, but both Damascus and Baghdad have a track record of going to great lengths to undermine or one-up the other. At the same time, Syria and Iraq are connected by a shared history, geography, and demographics, and by family ties, language, and commerce. Despite their myriad cultural and political differences, at the governmental and societal levels each demonstrates a grudging respect for the other, albeit sometimes rather quietly. And through everything, there is an unstated recognition that Syria and Iraq are inextricably linked. What occurs on one side of the border almost always has consequences next door, and each country's attempts to weaken the other carries the risk of creating trouble at home in the long run.

Iraq's policy toward Syria in 2011 shows that it is in a particularly difficult situation, torn between regional and international demands. As a consequence of the 2003 Iraq War, Iran has been able to establish strong networks of influence in Iraq, and under Iraqi Prime Minister Noori al-Maliki relations have become much more substantial. While the Iraqi–Syrian relationship has certainly improved, it is rather the evolving Iran–Iraq axis that determines Iraq's positioning in the current

Syrian domestic crisis. The Iraqi government has adopted a position of neutrality within the Arab League. It is not supporting the crackdown of the Syrian regime but it has not been very outspoken in condemning the Syrian government's actions either, and it is also careful in assisting Syrian refugees of which around 160,000 have now entered Iraq, mainly going to the Kurdish north and Anbar. In July 2011, Prime Minister Noori al-Maliki ordered a UN camp set up for refugees from Syria to be shut down, afraid of Syrian Sunni militants possibly taking refuge there (Reuters, 10 October 2011). The United States has asked Iraq to cooperate and not let Iran deliver weapons to the Syrian regime, which has imposed a strain in Iranian–Iraqi relations.

The uneasy foundations of Syrian–Iraqi relations

Given the nature of this changeable relationship, events in Iraq have historically had a profound impact on Syria's foreign policy. Syria has always been governed by a preoccupation with security in making foreign policy decisions vis-à-vis Iraq, balancing a desire to have a neighbor that is not strong enough to be a threat, but which is not so weak as to pose a danger because of its incapacity. The wars against Iraq in 1991 and 2003 had far-reaching implications for Damascus, and proved to be landmarks in Syrian regional and international relations. Syria's decision to participate in the First Gulf War in support of American-led efforts to curb Iraqi expansionism opened doors for Damascus both regionally and internationally which had, until that point, been firmly closed. A little over a decade later, however, Syrian opposition to the Second Gulf War virtually slammed shut the very same doors and contributed directly to the deterioration of Syria's power position in the Middle East.

In 1991, Syria's decision-making process was relatively straightforward. The United States and its Arab allies characterized the war as necessary to restore balance to the prior regional power dynamics that had been unsettled by Iraq's assault on Kuwait. Syria saw the war as a means to weaken its strongest regional adversary while advancing its own interests in the Middle East. Despite Syrian public opinion against the war, Hafez al-Assad saw that he stood to gain by supporting the United States and chose sides accordingly.

In 2003, the situation was entirely different. For one, the war did not have the legitimacy conferred by international law. More importantly, however, for Syria, was that this time the war was not portrayed as an effort to bring balance to the region as was the case in 1991, but rather as a drive to change a government and an entire system in order to set a paradigm for the rest of the region. While Iraq's alleged development of weapons of mass destruction provided a pretext for the US-led military intervention, it was clear that the goal was much broader than this. American neoconservatives aimed to cause a "domino effect" by toppling Saddam Hussein's regime and installing a democratic state in the midst of neighboring authoritarian regimes. They predicted that success in Iraq would inspire the populations of other regional states to push for democratization in their own countries.

In these circumstances, Syria's defiance of US pressure was not surprising. The Syrian regime viewed American plans for Iraq as an existential threat and suspected that the US administration might not even wait for its Iraq strategy to bear fruit before turning its attention to neighboring countries, of which Syria would likely be the first target.[1] While the "domino effect" could potentially have affected any authoritarian regime in the region, Syria seemed to be under special scrutiny. Glossing over fundamental differences between Syria and Iraq, American neoconservatives focused on the presence of the Ba'th party in Syria as a central pillar of the regime, and after 2001 Syria was increasingly considered a "rogue state."

Under these circumstances, the Syrian government refused to cooperate with the United States in the 2003 attack on Iraq. Other Arab states expressed their discontent with the situation more carefully and maintained a low profile, whereas Syria took a far more provocative stance as soon as it became clear that the United States would go to war even without a UN resolution. In contrast to his father in 1991, Bashar al-Assad played on public opinion and exploited the war to bolster his domestic credentials, and while official rhetoric praised Syria's solidarity with the Iraqi people in their time of need, the regime was primarily concerned with its own survival (Khaddam 1998).

A long-standing enmity

Syria and Iraq have been at odds in one way or another since Saddam Hussein's rise to power in 1968. With the Ba'th party as the central political force in both countries, it might have been assumed that

Damascus and Baghdad would cooperate with one another in furthering their domestic and regional agendas, but the reality was quite the opposite. In fact, it was the rivalry between the Syrian and Iraqi wings of the Ba'th party that initially caused the rift between the two countries, with Syria's decision to support Iran during the Iran-Iraq War serving to widen the divide.

Both Hafez al-Assad and Saddam Hussein wanted to be the unchallenged leader of the Arab world and to speak on behalf of the "Arab nation," and each was convinced that they were best suited for the role. Hostility between Syria and Iraq had never resulted in open warfare prior to 1991, but the tension played out indirectly and mirrored the personal animosity between the leaders. The two countries cooperated with each other's opposition forces and regularly accused one another of attempted assassinations. At the close of the Iran–Iraq War in 1988, Saddam Hussein sought revenge for Syria's backing of Iran by supporting anti-Syrian movements in Lebanon. Meanwhile, Syria became Iraq's most vocal opponent in the Arab League. While no other Arab state objected to Iraq resuming full participation in the Arab League and hosting the 1990 summit in Baghdad, Syria declared it to be unacceptable and, Egyptian mediation efforts notwithstanding, Hafez al-Assad refused to attend the summit.

In the years following the Iran–Iraq War, the Syrian regime maintained a delicate balance of relationships and influence with a wide range of Iraqi figures. Damascus varied its approach according to its objectives and circumstances, at times with questionable results. Syria's multipronged strategy in its relations with Iraq is illustrated particularly well by four key examples: the confrontational approach toward Iraq in 1991; its efforts to destabilize Saddam Hussein through support for Iraqi opposition groups; the resumption and expansion of Syrian–Iraqi relations in 1996; and Syria's response to pre-war rhetoric and the US-led attack on Iraq in 2003. These examples will be discussed in further detail below. While these cases point to Syria's willingness to work on many fronts simultaneously in pursuit of its foreign policy goals, they also highlight Syria's uneven record of foreign policy success.

Confrontation: Syria and the Gulf Crisis of 1990

With the benefit of hindsight, it seems painfully obvious that Saddam Hussein made a serious miscalculation in invading Kuwait in 1990. For

Syria, the invasion made it imperative that Iraq was prevented from imposing its expansionist plans on the region. Hafez al-Assad made it clear that the occupation of Kuwait had to be reversed without delay and put Syrian troops on high alert immediately after the attack. The Syrian president was highly critical of Iraq's actions, joining the international community in characterizing the invasion as a breach of international law. With pressure mounting on Iraq to withdraw from Kuwait, Saddam Hussein attempted to regionalize the situation by making Iraq's withdrawal from Kuwait conditional on the termination of other cases of occupation in the Middle East, namely, Israel's presence in the occupied territories and Syria's hold over Lebanon.[2] Not surprisingly, this tactic touched a nerve and enraged Hafez al-Assad. To him, Syria's presence in Lebanon was not an occupation but a bulwark against further Israeli incursions, and under no circumstances could it be compared to the Israeli occupation of Palestinian and Syrian lands. Syria rejected Saddam Hussein's proposal outright.

In a joint effort, US President George H. Bush and the president of the ailing Soviet Union Mikhail Gorbachev forged an international coalition to oust Iraq from Kuwait. The United States was particularly eager to enlist Arab states in the effort in order to counter Saddam Hussein's portrayal of the crisis as an Arab–Western confrontation and, later on, as a war between Islam and non-believers.[3]

Within the Arab League, the situation created a clash between two of its founding principles: on the one hand, non-interference in the policy of a fellow state, and, on the other, the commitment to defend the autonomy and integrity of all Arab states. It soon became evident that the Arab League would not be able to solve the problem on its own— and it was also clear that the United States was not willing to stand idly by in the case of a crisis that so significantly affected its interests in the region. However, Arab states were concerned at the prospect of heightened US influence and an increased American troop presence in the region. The main question for Syria, therefore, was not whether to oppose Iraq's invasion of Kuwait, but how to justify allying itself with America against a fellow Arab state. In choosing his course of action, Hafez Al-Assad knew that he faced a serious public relations challenge. Saddam Hussein had become immensely popular with the "Arab street" for resisting US pressure and interference in regional affairs. Yet, in Hafez al-Assad's worldview, the advantages of cooperation with the

United States far outweighed the risk of domestic dissent, and he decided to disregard public opinion and deal with the consequences. A dent in domestic popularity was a small price to pay for the potential regional and international gains.

Early in the Gulf Crisis, Syria brought an end to Iraqi influence in Lebanon by ousting pro-Iraqi President Michel Aoun and installing proxies in power, thereby cementing Syria's presence in Lebanon.[4] Newly re-established Syrian–Egyptian relations quickly gained momentum, namely in the attempts to establish an Arab security framework in the Gulf.

For Syria, joining the US-led coalition offered a long-awaited chance to improve ties with Washington and an unparalleled opportunity to assume a leadership role in the region. Iraq, weakened by war and sanctions, was in no position to challenge Syria's regional aspirations. Jordan and the PLO, meanwhile, found themselves marginalized politically— the price they were forced to pay for siding with Saddam Hussein during the war—leaving the field open for Syria to raise its international profile and pursue its own agenda with respect to the peace process.

Syria's position was certainly also motivated in no small measure by a dire need for foreign aid to bolster its deteriorating economy. Financial support from the Soviet Union had decreased rapidly in the latter part of the 1980s under Gorbachev, who made it clear that he would not give Syria grants and loans to the extent which his predecessors had. Aid from Arab states was also on the decline due to Syria's support for Iran during the Iran–Iraq War, which did not sit well with many in the region. Discounted Iranian oil had eased Syria's financial straits somewhat, but by the end of the war in 1988 there was little outside funding available to Syria.[5] Damascus's decision to support the coalition produced the desired results. European funds, off-limits to Syria since the mid-1980s due to concerns over Syrian support for terrorist acts in Europe, now became available, as did aid from the United States, Japan, and even the Gulf States.[6]

As certain aspects of his plan were falling into place, Hafez al-Assad began to grow distressed by the increasingly evident rifts among Iraqi factions inside Iraq which he feared would threaten the country's territorial integrity. Even more, he feared the knock-on effect for Syria and the specter of Kurdish separatism in his own country. With this in mind, al-Assad implemented a two-part containment strategy: providing support and safe haven to Iraqi opposition groups that he wished to see weaken the Iraqi regime, while exerting some measure of control over the various players (including the Patriotic Union of Kurdistan and the Kurdish Democratic Party).

Cultivating the Iraqi opposition

Support for Iraqi opposition movements became a key element of Syria's foreign policy strategy following the First Gulf War. Syria utilized contacts established with Iraqi forces throughout the conflict when both Syria and Iran provided sanctuary to high-ranking opposition leaders, sponsored their activities in Iraq, and provided them with military training and equipment. Prior to 1986, Syria had rather haphazardly sponsored a broad range of terrorist activities all over the world, but once it became clear that this strategy was not yielding the intended results, Damascus chose to focus on neighboring countries, employing a more structured approach to forge alliances with a variety of opposition movements.

The Syrian regime facilitated the transfer of opposition leaders to third countries, encouraged Iraqi parties to set up offices in Syria and develop contacts with domestic security services and with the international community, and permitted the factions to disseminate their own publications. In 1980, the radio station "Voice of Free Iraq" began broadcasting from Syria, providing Iraqis inside Iraq with an alternative to the messages of their state-controlled media.[7]

For Damascus, the ideology and politics of the various Iraqi opposition groups was of little importance. Relations with Kurdish groups were clearly accorded the most importance, given Hafez al-Assad's domestic concerns, but he also supported Shia movements like the Supreme Council for the Islamic Revolution in Iraq (SCIRI) and ad-Da'wa, both of which went on to play key roles in Iraqi politics following the Second Gulf War. In a 2003 interview, Hamid al-Bayati, SCIRI's London representative who later became interim deputy foreign minister of Iraq, described the nature of Syrian support to his party:

We used to have camps in Syria and were trained by the Syrian authorities. Our people were crossing the border, going to Iraq with their arms and they launched attacks against the regime. Syria was one of the countries which gave us support during certain times when they had problems with the Iraqi regime.[8]

Closer to Syrian interests but less relevant in terms of actual power were the pro-Syrian wing of the Iraqi Ba'th party, other nationalist groups, and ethnically based opposition groups like the Turkmen Front and Assyrian Democratic Movement, all of which received Syrian support. The diversity of the Iraqi opposition groups, not to mention their sponsors, prevented the formation of a united front, making joint action almost impossible, although the parties did come to an informal agreement of sorts:

> [A]ll parties agreed to divide Iraq into three fields for operations. Islamist parties would operate in the south, the Kurds in the north, and the Communists and the renegade band (nationalists) in the middle and Ninawa province. But Syria, unlike Iran, allowed the Kurdish parties to open only representative offices. Equally significant, while Syria hosted the nationalist parties, Iran hosted the Islamist parties. Libya also supported the PUK, including training its members, and tried to coordinate between Iran and the PUK. (Rabil 2002)

Following the devastating Anfal campaign,[9] Kurdish opposition groups decided to cooperate with one another and formed the Iraqi Kurdistan Front in 1988, later joined by nationalist and communist forces. Meanwhile, Iran expanded and diversified the scope of its cooperation with Iraqi Shia groups (Rabil 2002). However, all efforts to unite the organizations failed despite a series of meetings sponsored by Syria in 1987, 1991, and 1992 to bring together the spectrum of opposition groups. Through this initiative Syria had hoped to improve coordination between the groups and mold the Iraqi opposition in its own image with a strong pro-Syrian Ba'th party at the head of a front that included all other groups. For Damascus, this would have been the ideal scenario, with Syrian interests being promoted by the Ba'th party, and the inherent divisions among the rest of the groups preventing any one faction or alliance from becoming too powerful. While the united front Syria hoped for never materialized, the meetings did result in concrete discussions, and at the March 1991 meeting in Beirut the representatives of twenty-three Iraqi factions agreed to mobilize support to topple Saddam Hussein.[10]

In April of 1991, Saddam Hussein's troops violently crushed an uprising of Kurdish and Shia opposition forces. The opposition groups had acted in the belief that American support—both political and military—would be forthcoming. The incident served to increase suspicion within the Iraqi opposition about international, and particularly American, policy and intentions for Iraq, although soon after the failed operation a no-fly zone was established in northern Iraq with US assistance. With their security and autonomy now more or less guaranteed, Kurdish groups had little motivation to cooperate with the rest of the opposition. When, eight months later, Syria hosted a meeting of the Iraqi opposition in Damascus, the leaders of the two main Kurdish parties, Masoud Barzani and Jalal Talabani, declined to attend and sent representatives of lower rank. Iraq's neighbors began to voice concern about the impact of the Kurds' growing autonomy and special protected status on their own domestic Kurdish populations. In 1992 Syria, Turkey, and Iran began a series of regular trilateral meetings that aimed to undermine Kurdish aspirations for independence and underscored the need to maintain the territorial integrity of Iraq.[11]

It was obvious to Iraqi Kurdish parties and other Iraqi opposition groups that, despite appearances, Syria was not looking to create a viable and independent opposition movement, but rather one that it could influence or even control, and this may have contributed to Damascus's lack of success in bringing the various parties together. Political, ethnic, personal, and religious differences among groups took care of the rest, with the result that a common strategy was almost impossible to develop, save the only common denominator among them: the need to remove Saddam Hussein from power.

Diverging interests: regime change or enfeeblement?

Despite their support for Iraqi opposition groups, Syria and other regional powers opposed full-scale regime change in Iraq, which they feared would lead to chaos and the eventual disintegration of the Iraqi state, with destabilizing effects on the entire region. Presumably, they were also concerned at some level that any one of them might be next on the list. Damascus aimed to interfere in Iraqi politics and tacitly challenge Saddam Hussein. It was not a Syrian priority, however, to remove him from power. Syria used the opposition as a tool to weaken the Iraqi regime, but with little interest in actually developing or strengthening these opposition forces. Iraqi opposition groups, meanwhile, chafed at their dependence on Syria and other sponsors who evidently did not share their objective of regime change. Omar Sheikhmous, a founding member of the PUK, describes the relationship between Syria and the Iraqi opposition in very pragmatic terms:

For the Iraqi opposition, the Syrian support was very helpful, very effective, they had infrastructure, weapons, ammunitions, they got help with passports.

For Syria the issue of support for the Iraqi opposition was never at the level of regime change, though, it was about creating a nuisance, a headache, but Syria did not want the oppositional groups to become independent actors—it always wanted to keep control. ... For Syria it would have been more desirable if a pro-Syrian wing of the Ba'th Party would have come to power in Iraq.[12]

Iraqi opposition groups welcomed Syrian support, and then went looking for sponsors outside the region who more closely shared their political agenda. They soon found willing backers in the United States and Europe. Al-Assad was not at all comfortable with these relationships, and despite the hostility between the Syrian and Iraqi regimes, vehemently opposed further American interference in his neighbor's domestic affairs. He grudgingly continued Syria's involvement with the Iraqi opposition because he was loath to leave the field completely open to the United States.

By mid-2002, with an impending war in Iraq more a question of "when" than "if," Damascus had become a hub for journalists and diplomats seeking to engage with key Iraqi opposition figures and ascertain their plans for Iraq post-Saddam Hussein. A Western diplomat who maintained regular contact with the spectrum of Iraqi opposition groups in Damascus during that period and was later posted to Iraq describes the party offices, particularly the SCIRI offices in Zahira, as having a "revolving door." Upon her arrival, an American colleague was almost always leaving, and upon departure, Iranian colleagues were frequently on their way in—a foreshadowing of the American–Iranian competition for influence that has characterized Iraq since the war. The Syrian government made no effort to restrict foreigners' access to Iraqi opposition groups, and it was common during that period to see representatives of the various parties at diplomatic events and gatherings.

This engagement policy did not, however, extend to the establishment of civilian ties between Syrians and Iraqis. The regime did not permit Syrian citizens to travel to Iraq, and itself preferred to deal with the Iraqi opposition groups through the intelligence services, as Syrian analyst Ayman Abdel Nour explains:

The Syrian regime harbored them and supported them, but that was just an excuse, a justification. When they were there in Syria, they had contact only with the intelligence, not with the foreign ministry. In the Syrian intelligence there was a branch for Palestine, a branch for Lebanon, and a branch for Iraq. I was in a program on al-Arabiyya with [Syrian Foreign Minister] al-Mouallim, a year and a half ago and he agreed on that. ... They were blaming him, and I said "Don't blame him too much. Don't blame him for relations with Lebanon, don't blame him for the Palestinian groups, don't blame him for Iraq. It was not in the responsibility of the foreign ministry, it was in the hands of the intelligence."[13]

As a result, the relationship between Syria and the Iraqi opposition remained superficial—more about power than partnership. When a number of the same figures took on positions of leadership in the new Iraq, it became clear that an opportunity had been missed.

How not to win friends and influence people

Regime change in Iraq brought with it a new political elite. Several personalities formerly based in Damascus as opposition representatives assumed high-ranking government positions in Baghdad. The former SCIRI representative to Syria and Lebanon, Bayan Jabr, became minister for housing and reconstruction in the first provisional Cabinet, then minister of interior in April 2005, and minister of finance in May 2006. Ibrahim al-Jaafari, prime minister of the Iraqi Interim Government of June 2004, had, in the past, fled Iraq through Syria. Nouri al-Maliki, who in 2006 became prime minister of Iraq, headed the Dawa party office in Syria before the war. But Bashar al-Assad made little attempt to capitalize on these connections or on Syria's history of support for the Iraqi opposition in order to set Syrian–Iraqi relations on the right track or to mend fences with the United States. While the Syrian government could well do without Saddam Hussein, it was not prepared to deal with a new government that had come to power under the auspices of the Bush administration and American military might.

The Iraqi opposition, meanwhile, had achieved its objective of toppling Saddam Hussein. For the new Iraqi political elite, maintaining good relations with their US sponsor was far more important than reconciliation with Syria, which was not a popular idea with the United States and, accordingly, not a priority for the new Iraqi leadership. Ayman Abdel Nour blames Syria's previous arrogance in its dealings with the Iraqi opposition for this state of affairs:

That is the reason why there are no good relations between the former Iraqi opposition and the Syrian government today. It was only pressure. There was no connection between the groups and Syrian society, civil society, universities, artists, NGOs. They were forbidden to contact any civil society group or coop-erate with them. ... They had to talk to these officers who knew nothing and behaved as if they were the most intelligent. It was all pressure, and once you release the pressure it changes, of course, they'll immediately turn away from you. It is not real, the Iraqi opposition did it just because they had to.[14]

Iran, no less concerned than Syria about the potentially destabilizing effects of regime change on the region, employed a very different approach in its dealings with Iraq. In order to maintain influence and safeguard its own interests, Iran utilized its expertise and long-term involvement with the Shia groups that emerged as the strongest players in post-war Iraq—particularly SCIRI and Dawa (ICG Report 2005a). In contrast to the Syrian regime's narrow approach, Iran had established broad networks and deep relationships within the Iraqi opposition and encouraged the development of civilian ties through scholarships and other diverse initiatives. Neither Syria nor any of Iraq's other neighbors could compete with this level of influence, and as it became increasingly clear just how much sway Iran would hold in the new Iraq, regional states began to voice their fear that the real winner of the war would in fact turn out to be Iran.

An "embarrassed" rapprochement

As is so often the case in Middle East politics, official rhetoric provides one version of events while an entirely different story unfolds behind the scenes, and this is also true of the Syria–Iraq relationship. On the inter-national and regional stage, Syria and Iraq were at loggerheads following the First Gulf War, with Syria actively and publicly engaging the Iraqi opposition. However, each soon realized that it needed the other, and a tacit rapprochement began in the latter half of the 1990s when Saddam Hussein was looking to negate the sanctions regime by entering into trade agreements with neighboring states.

Syria meanwhile was watching with concern as Turkey and Israel increased their economic and military cooperation and Jordan moved further into America's orbit. Surrounded by potentially hostile states, Damascus feared an escalation on one front, or worse, from north and south at the same time. In this scenario, Iraq was the only available ally. On both sides, the motivation for rapprochement was self-interest and the need to adapt to changing dynamics. As scholar Flynt Leverett writes: "There was no love lost between Iraq and Syria, or for that matter, between Saddam Hussein and Hafiz al-Assad, but perceived necessity can eliminate hesitation and reluctance."[15]

The Iraqi government signaled that it was ready to resume relations, and Hafez al-Assad agreed provided that political cooperation was not too obvious. With this tacit opening towards Iraq, "a quiet, almost embarrassed rapprochement, coupled with public denials that Syria had changed its stance," (ICG Report 2004a, p. 15), Hafez al-Assad was attempting to turn the tables on the United States and reassert his position as an independent and important regional actor.

Bilateral relations resumed quietly in 1996, starting with trade and parliamentary visits. In November 1997 Deputy Prime Minister Tariq Aziz visited Damascus, the first high-level visit between the two neighbors in twenty years. As a direct result of this visit, the opposition radio propaganda station "Voice of Free Iraq," which had been established by Syria in 1980, was shut down. Two new border crossings were soon opened, and in 1998 Syria and Iraq began to discuss building a second pipeline and agreed to reopen the Banyas–Kirkuk pipeline. Burgeoning Syrian–Iraqi ties raised eyebrows internationally, but by this time the Syrian government was prepared to articulate its position. As Vice President Abdel Halim Khaddam explained in a 1998 interview:

Iraq is facing two serious threats. The first targets Iraq's territorial integrity and the unity of the Iraqi state. Regardless of how good or bad our relations are, we cannot but resist and oppose any attempt to encroach on Iraq's unity, Iraqi territorial integrity, Iraq's national unity, and the unity of the Iraqi state. In fact there have been, and there still are, schemes and plans to fragment Iraq. The second is the Iraqi people's suffering. The Iraqis are a fraternal people, and they are suffering. Why are the Iraqis being punished? This suffering lays the foundation for a future of serious animosities because suffering produces a psychological state of mind which, if established, would be very harmful to inter-Arab relations; therefore, we stated clearly that Arab states must work to alleviate and remove this suffering. We opened the borders to alleviate this suffering. This is the picture of our position toward Iraq. (Khaddam 1998)

In February 2000, Iraq opened an interest section in the Algerian embassy in Damascus, a step that the Syrian government reciprocated in May 2001. Damascus had previously sent a delegation to Baghdad to discuss the implications of Israel's unilateral withdrawal from Lebanon and to explore possibilities for increased economic cooperation.[16] The 1996 agreement between Jordan and Iraq served as the model during these talks. Until 1999, Jordan had been Iraq's primary trading partner, and although the two countries were effectively circumventing the sanctions regime, the agreement remained uncontested.

Syria desired the same preferential treatment and successfully negotiated a trade protocol (ICG Report 2004a, p. 15). With Iraq so isolated in the international arena and very much in need of a partner, Syria had the upper hand in these discussions and shaped the relationship according to its own interests. Soon after the death of Jordan's King Hussein in 1999 the Iraqi regime began to encounter difficulties importing products via Jordan, allowing Syria to assume an even more important role in Iraq's foreign trade (Duelfer Report 2004, I, p. 50). Yet in spite of the many steps taken to further bilateral cooperation, self-interest on both sides kept the relationship between Syria and Iraq cool; it did not become a real detente.

From security to economy

For Hafez al-Assad, security always trumped economics. His son and successor, Bashar, in contrast, viewed economics more strategically, and as a consequence put a great deal of effort into exploring ways to bolster Syria's economic development. The burgeoning relationship with Iraq made it easy for Bashar to increase revenue by expanding business ties. However, these opportunities came at a price. Despite the relatively smooth succession from father to son, the new president needed to consolidate his power and now felt compelled to build loyalties by granting lucrative business deals in Iraq to family members and regime insiders, or to turn a blind eye when he lacked sufficient control to prevent them from simply taking what they wanted. The situation was an ironic turn of events indeed for Bashar al-Assad, who in the late 1990s had earned a reputation for fighting corruption. Money could be made in a variety of ways. At the national level, legal trade under the Oil for Food (OFF) regime generated significant revenue. Iraq was a good market for inexpensive Syrian-made daily use products that could be exported duty free under a trade agreement with Iraq.[17] A number of Syrian officials benefited from kickbacks generated by the OFF through oil vouchers handed out by the Iraqi regime. When in January 2004 the Iraqi daily al-Mada published a list of dignitaries who had received these vouchers, several Syrian names were included, most notably Firas Tlass, the son of then Minister of Defense Mustafa Tlass.[18] At a lower level, profitable smuggling networks facilitated by Arab and Kurdish cross-border tribal connections flourished along a border notoriously difficult to police.

Oil deals that circumvented the sanctions regime were a major source of income for the Iraqi government between 2000 and 2003, also resulting in large revenues for the Syrian regime. During this period it is estimated that Syria imported between 150,000 and 200,000 barrels of Iraqi oil per day, with none of the income generated by this practice reflected in Syria's state budget. The Iraqi State Oil Marketing Organization (SOMO) earned an estimated $US4.9 billion from illicit oil sales to Syria, Turkey, Jordan, and Egypt from 2000 to 2003.[19] The Kirkuk–Banyas pipeline, closed by Syria at the beginning of the First Gulf War, was reopened to facilitate oil exports.[20] Syria bought oil from Iraq at a reduced rate and then exported the same amount of oil at world market prices.[21] This Syrian connection was so important for Iraq that Syria was the only country exempt from a 10 per cent surcharge imposed by Iraq on oil contracts with foreign entities (Duelfer Report 2004, I, p. 42). The Syrian government reaped an estimated $US2.8 billion in profits from this arrangement, and the revenue it generated constituted the primary source of income for both Damascus and Baghdad (Blanchard/Katzman 2005, p. 17).

The United States protested the opening of the pipeline, but the Syrian regime consistently denied that it was being used for commercial purposes. In 2001, when Secretary of State Colin Powell visited Damascus, he raised the issue of the pipeline and once again the Syrians maintained that it was being used only for tests.[22] This often repeated claim led an analyst to remark, "Syria continually denied doing it; they said they were testing the line. Well, they tested the line for two and a half years at the rate of about 150,000 to 200,000 barrels a day."[23] One week after the war ended, the US military closed the pipeline.

A third important source of revenue for Syrian companies and members of the country's political and military elite was derived from Iraqi imports of military equipment and dual-use items through Syrian territory. The 2004 Duelfer Report states that, of Iraq's neighbors, Syria was the most willing to allow prohibited items to pass through its territory. An estimated 70 per cent of illegally imported weapons entered Iraq through the Syrian ports of Latakiya and Tartous, and SOMO records show that between October 2000 and April 2003, Iraq signed contracts with Syria worth $US1.2 billion. Military equipment and dual-use items originated from Eastern Europe, other Western countries, North Korea, and China. This was possible, of course, only with the acquiescence of agencies and persons within the Syrian regime who took a cut of the proceeds in exchange for the unhindered delivery of items to Iraq. The Duelfer Report states that this practice involved "agencies or personnel within the government itself." Foreign companies came to regard the greed of Syrian intermediaries as an increasingly serious problem. So generous was the commission exacted in some of the deals that the suppliers asked their Iraqi partners to consider changing the delivery route (Duelfer Report 2004, I).

Perhaps the most notorious case of Syrian involvement in the transmission of dual-use items to Iraq is a contract for the supply of some $US4.425 million worth of night vision goggles in March 2003. US Defense Secretary Donald Rumsfeld openly accused Syria of "hostile behavior" in this case, but Syrian government spokesperson Butheina Shaaban immediately denied the charges as "an absolutely unfounded, irresponsible statement."[24]

Yet the evidence suggests a very different story, and, once again, complicity at the highest levels of the Syrian regime. The Syrian partner in the night vision goggles deal was a company owned by Bashar al-Assad's cousin and head of presidential security Dhu al-Himmet Issa Al-Shalish. His company, SES International, was heavily involved in the sale of dual-use items to Iraq and signed over 250 contracts worth $US187 million between 2000 and 2003. SES facilitated the transfer of purchased goods with a combination of strategies, including concealing the true nature of the items, forging delivery certificates, and providing fake end-user certificates to suppliers keen to distance themselves from the transactions. In keeping with the theme of regime complicity, it was Defense Minister Mustafa Tlass who issued the end-user certificates, charging between 12 and 15 per cent of the contract value as compensation for his "support." However, others in the supply chain also took their cuts at various points in the transaction. When in 2002 Tlass's son Firas represented his father in a deal to sell weapons to Iraq, he had to buy the acquiescence and protection of Syrian intelligence at a rate of 10–12.5 per cent per transaction to ensure safe passage of the goods through Syria (Duelfer Report 2004, I).

BROTHERLY LOVE: SYRIA'S RELATIONS WITH IRAQ

The Syrian regime was playing a very dangerous game. The illegal activity of Syrian companies, as well as the complicity of government figures at all levels, and the regime's increasingly untenable denials of wrongdoing, left Damascus vulnerable to the scrutiny and censure of the United States and increasingly isolated from the international community, none of which it could afford. But the question is, why? Why would Bashar al-Assad risk his country's security and credibility in such a way?

Experts tend to suggest that Bashar al-Assad's inexperience is to blame for Syria's conduct in the period leading up to the Iraq War. Iraq had turned into a cash cow for Syria, and perhaps Bashar's focus on economic gain, rather than on security, played a role in his decision-making. It is possible he hoped that economic success would bolster his domestic standing and strengthen his authority within the regime. The sheer volume of trade and the number of regime insiders involved may have driven the Syrian regime to pursue illicit deals even when, with the war approaching, doing so was tantamount to political suicide. Neighboring countries, such as Turkey and Jordan, had already recognized this and had scaled back their activities dramatically in the months leading up to the war. Another theory is that Bashar lacked the experience needed to establish control over key regime figures and intelligence agencies in Syria and was thus powerless to stop them from entering into lucrative deals harmful to Syria's security and reputation, which they would never have dared to do while his father was alive.

Whether intentional or the product of Bashar's own weakness, Syria's illicit trade with Iraq leading up to the war had serious foreign policy consequences for Damascus. They were perhaps underestimated or disregarded at the time, but they clearly underscore the crisis of leadership facing the country as the region once again found itself on the brink of war.

The complexity of the 2003 Iraq crisis for Syria

In 2003, Syria found itself in a quandary. In Washington the drums of war were beating, and the United States had clearly set its sights on Iraq, depicting it as a rogue state and member of the newly invented "axis of evil" in the Bush administration's "war on terror." Relations between Syria and the United States, meanwhile, were steadily improving as a result of cooperation in the fight against al-Qaeda. However, as the only Arab nation on the UN Security Council, Syria felt a special responsibility to safeguard regional interests and stability, which meant contesting US policy openly, which Syria could not well afford to do. The Syrian government attempted to strike a middle ground, focusing on the role of UN weapons inspectors and warning against military intervention.[25] But as US plans to implement a regional strategy for the Middle East, and specifically for Iraq, became increasingly bolder, Syria was left with less and less room to maneuver.

Syria had come to rely on the idea of Iraq as a stable albeit toothless neighbor. It also successfully exploited growing international concern over the catastrophic effects of the sanctions regime on ordinary Iraqis in order to establish lucrative bilateral commercial relations. US plans for Iraq threatened to interfere with Syrian interests on both counts, and it became clear that whatever the outcome of a war in Iraq, it would not be favorable for Syria. Not only did Damascus anticipate the regional destabilization that would inevitably follow the toppling of Saddam Hussein's regime, it was also in no hurry to see a pro-American democracy installed next-door which would potentially challenge its own stability and the role of the Ba'th in Syria. The Syrian regime clearly feared it was the next target for an American "intervention." Asked by the Egyptian weekly *al-Usbu'a* whether this fear was the real reason for Syria's opposition to the war, Foreign Minister Farouq al-Sharaa responded immediately that there is no shame in siding with one's brother because one is next in line (al-Sharaa 2002). Although aware that US forces would likely find an easy victory in Iraq, Syria nonetheless went on the offensive; becoming more and more vocal in its rejection of US actions and policy in the region.

The Syrian government was reluctant to push for a diplomatic solution, as it had done in 2000. Syria "took strong issue with last-minute attempts to persuade Saddam to resign or leave Iraq" and allegedly vetoed a Kuwaiti–Qatari proposal to persuade Saddam to step down from office (ICG Report 2004a, p. 17). Washington, meanwhile, faced serious difficulties in enlisting broad international support for "Operation Iraqi Freedom," placing Syria in good company in its opposition to the war. Motivated primarily by self-preservation, Damascus focused its criticism on the lack of justification for US action under international law, aware that if the intervention in Iraq were allowed to proceed as a unilateral effort to combat terrorism, Syria could well be next.

BROTHERLY LOVE: SYRIA'S RELATIONS WITH IRAQ

On 8 November 2002, the UN Security Council voted on Resolution 1441, and Syria came out in favor of the resolution. Butheina Shaaban, head of the Syrian Foreign Ministry's foreign media department, explained that the Syrian government "wanted to show goodwill, to help the region and Iraq avert a war" (ICG Report 2004a, p. 17)· As Zisser writes:

Syria gave its blessing to Security Council Resolution 1441, which included a strong demand that Iraq agree to the renewing of the activities of the international inspectors in Iraqi territory or else suffer the consequences. The Syrians tried to present its vote as a "diplomatic victory" or alternatively as in response to the Arab consensus that Syria is called upon to represent in the Security Council. They even bragged that their vote had succeeded in foiling, or at least, postponing the American attack on Iraq. (Zisser 2007, p. 38)

Meanwhile, in Syria, official rhetoric portrayed the impending war as the latest US–Israeli plot to fragment, subdue, and control the region. The regime hoped to bolster its domestic and regional credibility by playing to the emotions of the Arab street and positioning itself as the steadfast defender of Arab causes. Though slow to start, anti-war demonstrations were soon staged several times a week by a motley crew of opposition figures, human rights groups, and government employees and students directed to attend protests instead of going to the office or to class. My apartment happened to be on the protest route, which was always the same: up Abu Roumaneh Street towards the American embassy. My colleagues and I would observe the proceedings from the balcony, taking in the obviously mass-produced placards written in quite dubious English, and making note of any differences in the mood of the gatherings from day to day.

Despite its vocal opposition to the war, the regime maintained an ambiguous position, not openly siding with Saddam Hussein, so as to safeguard Syria's chances of playing a constructive role at a later stage. When it became clear that war was inevitable, Syria called for solidarity with the Iraqi people and avoided mention of Saddam Hussein altogether. It was soon evident that even in the absence of a broad base of support, the United States intended to proceed with its plans for Iraq along with its "coalition of the willing," and that Syria, regardless of its temporary seat on the Security Council, would not be able to assist in preventing another Gulf war.

Employing a different strategy, Bashar al-Assad focused on boosting his popularity with the Arab street. He sought to capitalize on the growing anti-Americanism in the region, fiercely attacking US foreign policy. The gloves were off. The Syrian president, senior officials, and the state media all had the US administration as their primary target. The provocative rhetoric chosen by representatives of the Syrian regime resonated in the Arab street. Worshippers at al-Azhar mosque in Cairo were reportedly heard chanting "Bashar, Bashar, set the world on fire."[26] However, Syria's tactics did little to improve relations among Arab countries at an official level. On the contrary, the Jordanian and Egyptian governments resented the domestic pressure they felt to emulate Bashar's strong stance, not to mention his outright criticism of the Arab regimes' hypocrisy and unwillingness to support Iraq.[27] In Syria, anti-war demonstrators carried banners reading "Death to Mubarak" and "Death to King Abdullah" (of Jordan), resulting in formal protest from Cairo.

Bashar's vitriolic attacks also strained relations with the United States, which bridled, not so much at Damascus's opposition to the war, but at the sheer extent of the insults leveled at the Bush administration. The Americans dismissed Syria's constant references to the Vietnam War, paying little heed to Damascus's predictions of the obstacles they might encounter in Iraq. Rather than attempting to convince Syria to cooperate, Washington opted for a dual strategy of pressure and isolation, viewing Syria less as a key regional actor and more like an arsonist who portrays himself as the fire brigade.

Bashar's risky populist strategy made little sense in terms of consolidating power or building constructive alliances. Why did he choose this path and what was his aim? Perhaps the answer once again is inexperience. Bashar appears to have been trying to increase his popularity by cultivating a hero-like image of a righteous and dedicated Arab leader attuned to the sensibilities and aspirations of the street, but finally thwarted by international conspiracy and circumstance. It is possible that he recognized how difficult it would be to rally enough support in the Arab world to resist American pressure, and decided to pursue a course of action to destabilize other countries in the region, so that Syria would not suffer the negative effects of war alone. This course of action, however, led Syria away from the foreign policy approach that so characterized his father's rule, that of constantly balancing interests and being prepared to strike a temporary rapprochement in the face of an extra-regional threat. Bashar does not seem to have engaged in any of the same sort of calculated maneuvering to enlist the support of other regional powers and ensure an exit strategy. In failing to do so, Bashar appears to have blatantly risked regional and international isolation for the sake of popular support—indicative perhaps of arrogance or inexperience, or possibly some combination of both.

The rapid and almost uncontested conquest of Baghdad deeply shocked the Syrian regime—and the Syrian people—while the United States saw it as proof positive that Syria's warnings were groundless and inaccurate. The ensuing deterioration in Iraq, however, soon boosted Syria's self-confidence. Initially afraid that the conflict would spill over the border into Syria, the regime now adopted an "I told you so" attitude and made it abundantly clear that it expected to be asked for assistance in resolving the crisis. As Bashar al-Assad said in an interview in 2006:

Two years ago I said: "You will end up swallowed by the Iraqi swamp and one day you will need somebody's help to get out of there." Now all this has turned true. But let's leave all this talk of threats and prophecies. In fact, we live in this region and know it well. History has taught us that power that is based on the power of weapons only does not lead anywhere.[28]

Washington, however, was far more focused on addressing its long list of grievances with the Syrian regime than on asking for help. In addition to smuggling and facilitating the passage of illicit and dual-use items, the United States accused Damascus of retaining Iraqi assets in its Commercial Bank; providing support to the Iraqi insurgency; encouraging and facilitating the travel of foreign fighters to Iraq; sheltering members of Saddam Hussein's regime; and hiding Iraq's weapons of mass destruction. Though Washington failed to produce any evidence to substantiate its WMD claims, the other charges were far more difficult for the Syrian regime to contest.

The struggle over Iraqi assets in Syria

Illicit sales of Iraqi crude oil and petroleum products generated $US3.4 billion in revenue between June 2000 and July 2003.[29] Some 60 per cent of this was deposited in the Commercial Bank of Syria (CBS) to be used for future Iraqi purchases of Syrian goods. The remaining 40 per cent went into a cash account at the Syrian–Lebanese Commercial Bank (SLBC) in Beirut, a CBS subsidiary. When on 22 May 2003 the UN Security Council adopted Resolution 1483 requiring all UN member states immediately to freeze the assets of the former Iraqi regime and senior Iraqi officials and transfer them to the Development Fund for Iraq, Damascus came under strong US pressure to comply.[30] The Syrian government confirmed the existence of Iraqi assets, but claimed that the funds would be required to repay Iraqi debts to Syrian companies.[31]

Eventually, the Syrian regime was forced to adopt a more conciliatory position, and in October 2003 invited a US Treasury Department team to investigate CBS files. The team found that at the time of the US military victory in Iraq, the CBS account held approximately $US850 million and the SLBC account another $US72 million.[32] The US administration acknowledged Syria's cooperation and then demanded that Damascus transfer the funds, $US580 million of which the regime had in the meantime paid out to Syrian companies that allegedly had outstanding claims. In early 2004, Bashar al-Assad announced that Syria would transfer $US200 million to the Development Fund for Iraq but no action was taken (BBC, 9 January 2004). The US responded by designating the Commercial Bank of Syria an organization of "primary money laundering concern" but gave Syria a further opportunity for redemption by sending a Treasury Department team to Damascus to advise how the regime could avoid a complete blacklisting of the CBS.[33] During a series of high-level visits between Damascus and Washington, US officials threatened the Syrian regime with sanctions due to non-compliance; and nevertheless, when Iraqi interim Prime Minister Iyad Allawi visited Damascus in July 2004, Syria made it clear that it had no intention of repatriating funds to Iraq as long as the occupation forces remained.[34] Syria finally did transfer a total of $US121 million to the Development Fund for Iraq, but Washington deemed this merely symbolic and proceeded to impose sanctions on the CBS.[35]

Border security and foreign fighters

In the weeks leading up to the war in Iraq, and well into its first days, foreign fighters made their way to Iraq through Syria in significant numbers, adding to Washington's frustration with Damascus and further increasing tensions between the two countries. Syria was the only one of Iraq's neighbors not to seal its borders during the conflict, thereby providing the easiest point of entry into Iraq for foreign fighters. Syrian authorities were clearly aware of the traffic, but turned a blind eye and made no effort whatsoever to curb the flow of fighters into Iraq during the early days of the war, often even facilitating their passage. There was something quite deliberately provocative about the regime's behavior during this period. In order to travel to Iraq, volunteers were required to obtain visas at the Iraqi Interest Section in Damascus, located inside the Algerian embassy, directly across the street from the American embassy. This was the very same location from which large numbers of would-be fighters left Syria by the busload to assist their brothers in Iraq.

As a young political analyst in Syria, I distinctly remember sitting in my car with a colleague, both of us clutching our mugs of coffee, watching in disbelief as young men, many of whom looked like they had only just started to grow facial hair, gathered at dusk in front of the Iraqi Interest Section, jostling each other to climb aboard the buses that had arrived to transport them. Despite US government protests, the transfers continued for several days although the pick-up location moved to the Iraqi pavilion on the former fairgrounds in downtown Damascus, an area protected by Syrian security personnel. When Sheikh Ahmad Kuftaro, the government-appointed Grand Mufti of Syria, issued a statement explicitly supporting and encouraging martyrdom operations in Iraq, it cemented the impression both in the region and outside that the jihadist movement in Iraq was acting with the blessing of the Syrian regime.[36]

Syria put a stop to the systematic trafficking of fighters before the end of the war. On 21 March 2003, Syrian authorities stated that the border with Iraq had been sealed and that only businessmen registered with the chamber of commerce would receive travel permits. Claims that the Syrian government actively encouraged and recruited volunteer fighters were not verified initially, but officials of other Arab states recounted instances of Syrian intelligence agents in their countries recruiting third-country nationals and bringing them to Syria for training.[37] When in 2007 US forces in the northern Iraqi town of Sinjar, 12 miles from the Syrian border, confiscated a cache of documents and computers, the itinerary and the records of more than 600 jihadis who had previously entered Iraq through Syria became known. They had arrived with the assistance of Syrian security—photos showed them together with high-ranking Syrian officials, and GPS-devices had cities in western Syria as first coordinates. These documents eliminated any doubt about the Syrian government's involvement.

Inside Syria, rumor had it that Abu Qaqa, a sheikh in Aleppo, was actively recruiting and training volunteers to go to Iraq, in cooperation with Syrian intelligence.[38] He allegedly provided lists of those who were sent to Iraq so that they could be arrested in the event that they tried to return to Syria, an unlikely event, as most aimed to become suicide bombers in Iraq.[39] At the time, Damascus-based analysts suggested that Syrian intelligence sought to identify and eliminate militants inside Syria who could pose a domestic threat. Suspicions about Abu Qaqa's role and affiliations increased when the Ministry of Awqaf (Religious Endowments) suspended him from preaching in his mosque. He was soon reinstalled by the security services but killed in 2007 under unclear circumstances.[40] While handled in a more discreet manner, the influx of fighters from and via Syria continued for several years and only came to an end in 2006/7.[41]

Syria's policy on foreign fighters further damaged its relations with its Arab neighbors and with the United States. The regime's course of action suggests that it viewed a certain level of unrest in Iraq as being in its own interest. As long as US forces were embroiled in the conflict in Iraq, they had less opportunity to focus on a new target. Syrian officials also made the most of the chaos next door to discredit foreign efforts to democratize the region, and to stifle any similar aspirations for Syria. The US response to Syria's behavior was, in a word, contradictory. Washington alternately accused Damascus of permitting foreign fighters to cross into Iraq, and praised its efforts to improve border security:

With regard to the infiltration of jihadists into Iraq, a top British official said recently that Syria and Iran, accused by some U.S. officials of subverting efforts to stabilize and rebuild Iraq, had in fact been cooperative. Sir Jeremy Greenstock, the most senior British official in the U.S.-led occupying administration, said a dialogue was under way with Damascus and Tehran to encourage them to back more openly the postwar drive to create a new Iraq. "I think on the whole that they have been quite cooperative," said Greenstock, Britain's former ambassador to the United Nations, when asked if Syria and Iran were actively trying to destabilize Iraq. In the same vein, Gen. David Petraeus, Commander of the 101st Airborne division, acknowledged Syria's cooperation. Syria is providing electricity to northern Iraq, especially the city of Mossul, from its own electricity grid. Gen. Petraeus also lauded Syrian efforts to curb the infiltration of jihadists into Iraq despite Syria's limited resources.[42]

On more than one occasion, Syrian Foreign Minister Sharaa refuted American accusations by comparing efforts to police the Syria–Iraq border to the challenges faced by the US in monitoring its border with Mexico.[43] In reality, however, Syrian efforts at border control were influenced by several additional factors, including traditional cross-border linkages between Arab tribes living on both sides of the border and the willingness of Syrian border officials to supplement their meager salaries by taking bribes. As one tribal leader remarked during a discussion about cross-border trafficking:

There are two possibilities. Either somebody manages to cross the border without being detected—or he doesn't. If he manages, he's fine. If he doesn't, he goes to jail. If he goes to jail, either he has the money to buy his way out or he doesn't. If he does, he's fine. If he doesn't he stays in jail.[44]

Over and above these domestic challenges, Syrian authorities claimed that their efforts were hampered by the US refusal to provide crucial monitoring equipment, such as night-vision goggles.[45] In sum, solemn and consistent promises from the Syrian government notwithstanding, the infiltration of foreign fighters into Iraq continued.

Despite the plethora of American reports and statements regarding Syrian border policy and security, some of which present contradictory findings, the real impact of Syrian activity in Iraq is difficult to assess. There appears to be a consensus among regional analysts and within the US intelligence community that while dynamics in Iraq were influenced by neighboring states, "the involvement of these outside actors is not likely to be a major driver of violence or the prospects for stability because of the self-sustaining character of Iraq's internal sectarian dynamics."[46] It thus remains an open question why at various points US officials so clearly highlighted Syrian cooperation—or blamed Damascus outright for foiling US attempts to calm the situation in Iraq. This somewhat schizophrenic policy may have been a reflection of differences within the American administration about how and with what tactics to deal with Syria.[47] Growing hostility from Washington led Bashar al-Assad to remark in a 2005 interview with *TIME*: "Please send this message: I am not Saddam Hussein. I want to cooperate!" (al-Assad 2005c).

Iraqi refugees in Syria

The Syrian regime's inconsistent approach to the Iraq crisis clearly manifested itself when it came time to decide how to handle the country's preparations for the impending war. Aware that refugees fleeing conflict might seek asylum in Syria, the government began refurbishing camps on its eastern border. When Syrian *al-Hayat* correspondent Ibrahim al-Hamidi reported on this development, he was immediately accused of spreading "false information" and spent the next five months in prison. The mere mention of preparations was deemed an offense, as it could be seen to indicate tacit Syrian support for the war.[48]

Few refugees made their way to Syria during the war, but in the chaos that followed, over 2 million people fled Iraq, most of them to Syria, because the latter and Jordan were the only neighboring countries that kept their borders open. Bashar al-Assad's regime was immediately accused of sheltering high-ranking Iraqi officials and Ba'th party members affiliated with the former regime. Even though Jordan was equally easy to reach, for many Syria seemed a safer option because they were less likely to be subject to American investigation. While Syria was careful not to accept—at least not for long—any of the fifty-two most-wanted officials, it did not impose restrictions on other Iraqi citizens unless they were regarded as threats to the Syrian regime, and it permitted the Iraqi Ba'th party to conduct its activities in Syria openly.

Iraqi refugees arrived in Syria in waves. First came the former Iraqi elite, bringing with them considerable money. Wealthy Iraqis were willing to pay well above market value for properties in Syria, and within a short time Syrians began to talk about a sharp increase in property prices and a shortage of housing. This began to stir trouble in the country, and many Syrians started to see the Iraqi presence as a burden that made their lives more difficult and more expensive. Palestinian refugees living in Syria viewed the situation with mixed feelings; they were frustrated that after more than fifty years in the country, they faced greater challenges buying property than the recently arrived Iraqis.[49]

The majority of the approximately 1.5 million Iraqi refugees who fled to Syria were, of course, far less fortunate than this first group. Leaving their homes, possessions, and family members, they sought to escape the widespread violence and insecurity that followed the war and became almost completely dependent on Syrian government support for their basic needs. To its credit, the Syrian government made an impressive effort to respond to the needs of the Iraqis coming across the border, particularly early on when little support was forthcoming from the international donor community.

Syria's decision to welcome Iraqi refugees was equally a humanitarian and a political gesture on the government's part. Regionally, it allowed

Damascus to position itself as a protector of Arab rights and solidarity despite its vehement opposition to the war and repeated warnings about the likely consequences. On the international front, Syria seized the opportunity to send the message that it was a responsible member of the world community and would come to the aid of those victimized by American interventionism.

The Syrian regime viewed the refugees as a tool to pressure the United States when the time was right. As a non-party to the international Convention on Refugees, Damascus was unhindered by the principle of non-refoulement, leaving the refugees more or less at its mercy. In the event that Syria wished to put pressure on the Americans and make the situation on the ground even more challenging for coalition forces, it could simply send the refugees back to Iraq.[50]

Domestically, the regime used the massive influx of Iraqi refugees to bolster its own standing. Bent on undermining the Syrian opposition's desire for democratization, the government pointed to the chaos and insecurity next door in Iraq as the inevitable result of such aspirations, and sternly warned Syrians against seeking external support. Though almost all opposition figures in Syria were fiercely critical of America's role in Iraq, carefully distancing themselves from talk of similar plans for Syria, the regime did not hesitate to accuse dissidents and pro-democracy groups of advocating regime change, leaving them little room to maneuver. This policy resulted in a more than usually disjointed Syrian opposition, with the very same people and parties criticizing the regime for a lack of political openness one moment, and attending government-sponsored anti-war rallies the next.

Resuming diplomatic ties

Syria's vehement opposition to the Iraq War and reluctance to recognize a government installed by "the forces of occupation" led to a very slow and tentative resumption of Syrian–Iraqi diplomatic relations after the war. Syria participated in discussions on the Iraq situation with neighboring states but refused to acknowledge Iraqi officials as the country's rightful representatives. In November 2003, the Syrian regime hosted a meeting of Iraq's neighbors in Damascus but declined to invite Iraqi Foreign Minister Hoshyar Zebari. More US-friendly Arab states intervened, pressuring Damascus to invite Zebari by threatening to boycott the conference. When the invitation was finally issued, Zebari sent his regrets, annoyed at being included at the last minute. Foreign ministers who did attend issued a statement condemning attacks on civilians, but to Washington's dismay there was no mention of assaults on coalition troops.[51]

Syria's unwillingness to recognize Iraq's interim government met with defiance. In October 2004, an article in *al-Hayat* quoted "Iraqi diplomatic sources" as ruling out any kind of diplomatic relations with Damascus ahead of the January 2005 elections (*al-Hayat*, 12 October 2004), although in previous statements Iraqi officials had highlighted Syria's agreement to a full restoration of diplomatic ties (Leverett 2005, p. 199).

Iran's regional position was undeniably strengthened by the Iraq War. Of all the neighboring states, it had the deepest and most widespread connections within Iraq, and figures close to the Iranian leadership had obtained a remarkable share of power in the new Iraq. With Iran so well positioned to influence affairs in Iraq, and Turkish aspirations to strengthen its hand in the Kurdish-controlled north, the Syrian regime felt marginalized. Yet despite its rather unhelpful stance on Iraq, international experts suggested that Syria still had a constructive role to play in resolving the crisis:

Given how dire the situation has become, it will now take active cooperation by all foreign stakeholders—Syria included—to have any chance of redressing the situation. In this context, Syria would bring important assets to the table. Unlike virtually all other involved actors—whether the US, Turkey, Iran or other Arab states—Damascus is perceived as being relatively neutral by the full range of Iraqi actors; it has old ties with ex-Baathists and tribes that straddle the Iraqi–Syrian border as well as new ones with Sunni insurgent groups; it has significantly deepened its relationship with the Maliki government; and it enjoys a good relationship with Muqtada al-Sadr.[52]

Relations between Syria and Iraq improved, initially due to economic considerations, but a high degree of mistrust persisted. The Syrian regime had reservations about dealing with a government that is so closely linked to the United States, but continued violence and instability in Iraq were not in its interest either, leaving it in something of a quandary about how to engage. Meanwhile, Baghdad had, on several occasions, acknowledged increased Syrian cooperation on various issues, but continued to express frustration with what it alleges is Syrian interference in its domestic affairs.

BROTHERLY LOVE: SYRIA'S RELATIONS WITH IRAQ

In his lengthy 2005 speech at Damascus University Bashar al-Assad rebuffed these allegations, making clear that protracted chaos and violence in Iraq was not in Syria's interest and that "external forces" seeking to drive a wedge between the Syrian and Iraqi people were behind the allegations that Syria was sponsoring terrorist attacks in Iraq:

The first danger threatening Iraq is an elimination of its Arab identity using various pretexts and implications which are at odds with the history of Iraq and its people. The second danger is the political and security chaos which pervades the Iraqi arena and which is directly connected to the question of Iraq's territorial integrity. ... Both threats pave the way leading up to the disintegration of Iraq with its incumbent imminent dangers for Iraq's neighbours. When damage exceeds a country's borders, it is no longer a domestic issue. (al-Assad 2005f)

The bumpy road, 2006–2011

In 2006, and under US pressure, official relations between both states were resumed. Syrian Foreign Minister Walid al-Mouallem paid his first visit to Iraq, and later that year, ambassadors were exchanged. This did not hinder the Syrian regime, however, from continuing to turn a blind eye to the issue of foreign fighters that kept on arriving in Iraq from Syria. The relationship between Syria and Iraq remained superficial and haunted by mistrust. In 2009, Baghdad released tapes on which two members of the Syria-friendly wing of the Iraqi Ba'th party were overheard in a conversation relating to a major Baghdad bomb attack. Iraq asked for an extradition of the two suspects, and for Damascus to expel terrorist organizations. The Syrians took issue with the demand and refused to comply. As a consequence, on 25 August 2009, the Iraqi ambassador was summoned back to Baghdad, a step that was reciprocated immediately by Syria.

The following year saw an improvement in relations that derived from an Iranian initiative which led Bashar al-Assad to support a second term of Prime Minister Noori al-Maliki. The ambassadors returned, and in mutual visits of the respective prime ministers, Syria and Iraq vowed to enhance their cooperation on various levels.

All in the family

Syria's primary underlying objective in its dealings with Iraq has always been the same: at all times it has sought to contain its neighbor's regional influence and power. Over time, Syria has pursued whatever course of action and formed whichever alliance it deemed necessary to further this objective. Yet the facts indicate that Damascus has often made rather dubious policy choices in pursuance of this goal, choices that appear to sacrifice its own long-term interests for the sake of weakening or irritating Iraq in the short term.

Damascus's engagement with Iraqi opposition groups up to 2003 clearly illustrates the failure, or perhaps the disinterest, of the Syrian regime in seeing the big picture. Syria courted and in varying degrees supported Iraqi opposition groups of all political, ethnic, and religious stripes in order to put pressure on Saddam Hussein's regime. Yet, unlike Iran, it never took any of these groups seriously enough to form the kind of lasting relationships with them in their own right that could have placed Syria in a very strong position to influence developments in post-war Iraq. Instead, the Syrian regime kept these groups subordinate, with the clear message that it was not interested in an autonomous and effective Iraqi opposition. This policy guaranteed that as soon as the Iraqi movements found more willing and influential backers, they moved quickly and irrevocably out of Syria's sphere of influence, leaving Damascus marginalized when it came time to dealing with the new Iraq.

The tacit rapprochement between Syria and Iraq in the late 1990s began with Damascus in a strong position. It started at a time when the Iraqi regime was in desperate need of external supplies, and Syria felt safe in the knowledge of its archenemy's weakened state. The arrangement proved highly profitable, not only for the Syrian regime but also for individual Syrian businessmen and members of the security establishment. This source of wealth became the basis on which Bashar al-Assad attempted to consolidate his authority upon his ascension to power. Once again, however, Syria did not heed the bigger picture. It put short-term gain ahead of long-term strategic interests, pursuing economic gain even after it began to pose a significant threat to its own security. Bashar's high tolerance for Syrian involvement in illicit business activities with Iraq—all for the sake of shoring up his own domestic support—put Syria at grave risk from a security perspective, and demonstrates very clearly the shift in priorities from father to son. For Hafez al-Assad, security and an exit strategy were always paramount. Though corruption was a reality under the father, he was careful to keep it within certain limits and, unlike his son, did not encourage the amassing of personal wealth. Bashar, on the other hand, did not subscribe to the same school of thought and led Syria down an uncertain and increasingly isolated path.

When it became clear in 2003 that Washington intended to pursue its plans for Iraq with or without Security Council support, Damascus had a choice to make and it opted for aggressive anti-Americanism. There is no reasonable foreign policy explanation for this behavior. Syria's fear that it was next in line for regime change was palpable; all logic would suggest the need to seek support of fellow Arab governments in the face of an external threat. However, Syria's choice of strategy left it weaker and more isolated, immediately damaging US–Syrian relations and utterly failing to win Syria any support from regional states. Bashar's aggressive tactics did win over the Arab street, but pursuing this populist strategy would only have made sense if he believed that US intervention in Syria was inevitable, rather than preventable by a closing of ranks with other regional actors.[53] Rhetoric notwithstanding, any US intervention in Syria was by no means assured, and Syria's miscalculation left it alone and without friends in a tough neighborhood.

At the moment, however, both countries are so absorbed with domestic issues that there is hardly any room for foreign policy-making. Iraq is concerned with every development in its neighborhood that might create further problems, but at the same time, there seems to be tacit support for the Assad regime despite Damascus's support for the jihadis that had spread terror throughout Iraq only a few years earlier. The rising Sunni–Shiite schism in the entire region has also brought Noori al-Maliki's government and the Syrian regime closer together. Iraq's parliament may be divided about how to deal with the crumbling Syrian regime but confessional loyalty, political pressure from Tehran and the fear of a rising Sunni rebellion in the western Iraqi provinces have induced a rapid effacement of malpractices of the past.

8

BACK TO THE SCENE

RUSSIA

The decision to choose 1990 as a starting point for this book was based on the fact that the decline of the Soviet Union and its eventual disintegration in 1991 was a moment of dramatic change for Syria, given the USSR's previous importance in Syrian foreign relations. The end of the Cold War forced Syria to make a strategic reorientation, for which the First Gulf war in 1991 was a welcome opportunity.

While this helped Syria to establish more positive relations with the United States, these could not make up for what had been at the core of Syrian–Soviet cooperation: arms deliveries and a partner to outweigh the regional impact of US support for Israel. Russia—as the successor state of the Soviet Union—did not play a central role in Syria's foreign policy between 1990 and 2011. Absorbed with its domestic affairs, change in its immediate neighborhood and the priority of re-establishing its relations with Europe, Russia rather passively followed events in the Middle East throughout most of the 1990s. The Soviet Union had co-sponsored the Madrid Conference, but the USSR was dissolved two months after the conference had concluded. Russia was basically absent from the Middle East peace process—and the Middle East as such. When it started to re-engage in the region after 2003, the focus shifted to Iran rather than Syria.

Yet with the Syrian revolution Russia returned to the Syrian scene, and in a more prominent role than it had ever had previously. While Syria became internationally isolated, Russia prevented a UN Security Council resolution against Syria and became its strongest partner. Russian arms deliveries and material support have been the lifeline allowing the Syrian regime to survive. Where does this sudden renewal of Russian interest in Syria come from? What makes relations with a state on the verge of collapse of interest to Russia, when its support might affect relations with the economically much more important Gulf States which are supporting the revolution against the Syrian government?

A rude awakening

The necessity for Syria to adapt its foreign relations did not come out of the blue. In 1986, a year after his election, Mikhail Gorbachev as the new secretary general of the CPSU began to implement a series of political and economic reforms that included a re-assessment of Soviet foreign policy priorities. The Middle East, hitherto an arena where both superpowers had competed for influence, was no longer seen as a primary concern but rather a cost-intensive ideological project with little political revenue. For Hafez al-Assad, hitherto considering himself a close partner of the USSR, the realization that the Soviet Union had little interest in supporting Syrian ambitions came as a surprise. As noted by Swiss scholar Martin Stäheli, in Michael Gorbachev's book *Perestroika*, only three pages are dedicated to the Middle East and Syria is not even mentioned (Stäheli 2000). Adding insult to injury, Gorbachev at the same time resumed the diplomatic contacts with Israel that Moscow had interrupted as a consequence of the 1967 war. There had been "occasional conciliatory gestures" (Karsh 1991), but what the Soviet leader now aimed for was a full normalization of relations. And this warming of relations between the two states took place alongside an increase in Jewish emigration from the USSR to Israel. The Statistical Abstract of the Israeli Central Bureau of Statistics (2006) gives a figure of around 67,000 Soviet immigrants per annum for the years 1990–2005. Hafez al-Assad claims that this was an "act of aggression," alleging that Israel's policy was to settle them in occupied territories (Stäheli 200).

The disintegration of the Soviet Union induced motion in all of the countries of the former Warsaw Pact. What started as a tacit reform process ended in popular revolutions and sweeping change. The toppling of a series of hitherto seemingly stable authoritarian regimes was unsettling for Hafez al-Assad since he noticed the resonance of the Eastern European quagmire in his own country as well. The close relationship between Hafez al-Assad and Romanian dictator Nicolae Ceauşescu inspired the rare graffiti sprayers in Syria to draw parallels between the two authoritarian rulers and threaten Assad with the same fate as Ceauşescu: after the execution of the Romanian dictator in December 1989 writing appeared on walls in Damascus saying "*kull Ceauşescu, biji yomhu*," literally "For every Ceauşescu the day will come," or simply "*Shamşescu*"—"Sham" being the popular form of referring to Syria (Perthes 1995).

Reorientation in times of change

There was always an element of ambiguity in Syrian–Soviet relations. Hafez al-Assad had structured the Syrian political and economic system in a socialist fashion and leaned towards the Eastern Bloc, yet he liked to stress the independence of his regime from Soviet influence. Thus in 1993, with hindsight to the October 1980 Syrian–Soviet "Treaty of Friendship and Cooperation," the standard mechanism used by the USSR for fostering relations with other countries, the Syrian president stated:

We were not in the Soviet orbit. ... We took our own decisions. This was the case from the very beginning in 1970. I used to appreciate the strong Soviet stand on our behalf, but we were not part of the Soviet world system. (al-Assad 1993)

While stressing his independence, Hafez al-Assad still depended on arms deliveries from the Soviet Union. After several visits by Syrian officials to the USSR in 1987 and 1989 failed to change Soviet policy with respect to upholding their prior level of military support to the regime, Hafez al-Assad himself traveled to Moscow in 1990 but also returned with empty hands. After this traumatic experience he would not return to the Kremlin for a further nine years (Stäheli 2000).

In 1990/1, both the Soviet Union and the United States supported the UN resolutions leading up to the Gulf War, which made it easier for Hafez al-Assad to justify joining the US-led initiative. During the war the Syrian army deployed troops to Saudi Arabia but did not participate in the fighting. Hafez al-Assad was in many ways satisfied with the outcome of the war but one aspect troubled him: the swiftness with which the international alliance had accomplished its victory in Iraq led to doubts in Damascus regarding the quality of its own military equipment which, like Iraq's, had been provided by the Soviet Union. Soviet officials were quick to deny the charges, however, saying that no parallels could be drawn since the Iraqi armament—as opposed to the Syrian equipment—was not the latest technology (NYT, 1 March 1991).

Participation in the Gulf War had required a quick and profound adaptation to the new world order. The Syrian government's decision to join ranks with the United States in the intervention was an unprecedented reversal of previous government policy. Hafez al-Assad had recognized a historic opportunity and seized it. Politically, he extracted the maximum from this. The United States committed to a new effort to resolve the Middle East conflict and invited Syria to join. It received a green light for extending its presence in Lebanon. And the regime also achieved a significant improvement in its relations with the United States, which had earlier been strained due to the terrorist activities of the 1980s.

The issue of Syrian payment for the arms deliveries, which the USSR had neglected throughout much of the 1980s, was subsequently brought back to the table later in the decade due to the Soviet economic crisis. Syria, itself in a dire economic situation, was unable to pay. The unsolved debt problem with Russia overshadowed Syrian–Russian relations until 2005, when a debt swap arrangement was finally reached. In exchange for a new arms purchase contract worth $US4 billion, Russia wrote off $US9.8 billion of Syrian debt. This rendered Syria one of Russia's largest arms customers:

With some 4 billion dollars in active contracts, Syria is one of Russia's largest arms customers both globally and in the Middle East. Although Syria's international isolation has provided Russia with a preferential market for arms sales and investment, Russia has invested much more in Libya and its investments in Iran dwarf those made both in Libya and Syria. (Patokallio/Saarinen 2012)

Russian interests in Syria

In 1988, Syria had granted the Soviet Union a lease without term over a naval base in Tartous, the only Soviet base in the Mediterranean. Limited in size and in poor condition, its main value was seemingly symbolic. But there is more to the Russian presence there, as Russian Middle East expert Ilya Bakharev explains:

> The base is small, it is only one pier. What is more important is what is based in the mountains in the Tartous area. Here, Russia has installed anti-aircraft missiles, radar and other heavy equipment. It is a long-term presence and it is much more important than the base itself. For Russia, this is one of the spots from which they can observe Israel and the Mediterranean.[1]

However, this is not the main reason why Russia supports Bashar al-Assad. If its main interest was solely in the naval base, it could have chosen a different approach to the revolution and retained the base under a future government. Syria also lacks economic interest for Russia, which normally offers its support in return for shares in banks and companies, and Syria is currently unable to offer this.

The conflict in Syria has one dimension that Russia is afraid of: Islamism. It projects its own security concerns from its experience in the Northern Caucasus on Syria. Most important for the Russian positioning, however, are strategic considerations with regard to third states.

Cooperation in Unfavorable Times

One determinant of the intensity of Syrian–Russian relations has been the Russian–American relationship, which has experienced a number of highs and lows since 1991. Russia, for example, vehemently rejected the 2003 war in Iraq in 2003, arguing that Saddam Hussein's regime was not a breeding ground for international terrorism. This led to discord in Russian–American relations, which was exacerbated in 2005 when Russia failed to join with the West in placing increasing pressure on Syria due to its interference in Lebanese politics. With regard to UN Security Council Resolution 1559, which was passed in response to the Lebanese issue, the representative of the Russian Federation lobbied for amendments of the resolution and warned that "with tensions high in the region, any wrong step might exacerbate the situation and lead to a new focal point of instability" (UN press release SC 8181, 2 September 2004). These amendments were not accepted, and thus Russia was one of only six states in the Security Council to have abstained from the voting for the resolution on 2 September 2004.

The timing of the debt swap arrangement discussed above is evidently significant in this context, given that it was announced at a time when most of the international community was seeking to isolate and place pressure on the Syrian regime due to its alleged involvement in the assassination of the former Lebanese Prime Minister Rafic al-Hariri. It is consequently hard to avoid the conclusion that the sudden improvement in Syrian–Russian relations after a fifteen-year period of Russian indifference has a great deal to do with Russian–US relations, as well as Moscow's desire to expand its influence in the region more broadly. Indeed, this latter objective was clearly implied in the reaffirmation both states made during a press conference regarding their mutual interest in an expansion of bilateral ties, with particular emphasis being placed on the economic sector where Syria has the potential to act as a gate through which Russia will be able to amplify its engagement in the Middle East.

When the Syrian revolution began, Russia and the United States were at odds with each other due to the intervention in Libya, in which Moscow felt it had been cheated by the United States and in retrospect regretted its decision to support Western policy. As Bakharev explains:

Russia needed something to show that it has some leverage, to demonstrate to the people that it still has power and plays a role in the international arena. The decision to back the Syrian regime was part of its international politics. Russia plays by the international rules: create leverage and then use it.[2]

Russia continues to provide the Syrian regime with arms, even though it is not clear whether its deliveries are being paid for—or by whom. There has been some speculation that Iran has been financing the weaponry. It is clear, however, that Syria no longer has the means to pay. Instead of receiving money from Syria, Russia has taken cash there. According to the investigative website ProPublica, between July and September 2012 there were eight flights from Russia to Syria, each delivering 30 tons of bank notes.[3]

Conclusion

Hafez al-Assad showed impressive flexibility in adapting his foreign policy to a post-cold war order, turning a disadvantageous situation into an opportunity for advancing Syrian external interests in the region. Syrian–Russian relations were never abandoned, however. Syria would have been interested in more profound relations, but this was mainly because of Syria's strategic regional interests rather than a genuine interest in Russia. Russian support is vital for the regime's survival in the current crisis. In recent months, Russia has come to realize that it is unrealistic to assume Bashar al-Assad will regain control over Syria. It has stressed that it is not attached to Assad personally. Syrian intransigence has made it more difficult to defend its position.

From the Russian side, the intensity of interaction with Syria has been closely connected to the quality of relations between Moscow and Washington. This appears to have been the driving force behind the rapprochement of 2004/5 and it also holds true for March 2013. In both cases, rapprochement with Syria offered an opportunity to frustrate Western policy.

9

CONCLUSION

This study of Syria's foreign policy has shown how the government has survived the ups and downs of international politics over the past two decades mainly through a strategy of inertia. The regular change in leadership in those states that pressure Syria most—the United States and Europe—means that their successive governments have set different priorities, leading to a lack of consistency in Western policy. Regardless of how hard Syria is pressured, the regime has learned that sooner or later the other actors involved will change their attitude and policy towards it, even in the absence of a change in Syria's stance. This was the case with the international isolation that came to an end in 1990 with the First Gulf War. Other examples include the strained relations over the 2003 Iraq War, or the isolation Syria experienced in 2005 over Lebanon. All of these crises were ultimately overcome largely by waiting for others to change their policy.

With Syria's limited size and power, one would assume that it might need to capitulate to external pressure, so to a certain extent its perseverance may appear irrational. However, the Syrian government's experience is that it does not need to respond to demands but can simply sit things out. In his speech in January 2013, Assad prided himself on exactly this point:

Syria has always been, and will remain, a free and sovereign country that won't accept submission and tutelage. That is why it has been a nuisance for the West, so they sought to take advantage of internal events to drive Syria out of the political equation in the region to get rid of this irksome problem and to strike at the culture of resistance and turn us into subordinates. (al-Assad 2013a).

The current domestic situation in Syria shows that previous experience is not a guarantor that things will always work out in the same way. The strategy of repression, which had worked in the past, has not silenced the protesters in the current crisis, as is clear from the 245 protests that were held throughout Syria on the second anniversary of the uprising on 15 March 2013.

Yet on the international level, Bashar's policy has thus far been surprisingly successful. As usual, Bashar al-Assad has tried to lie low as long as possible. Framing the protests as a foreign conspiracy emanating from "enemies of the homeland" (al-Assad 2013a), his warnings regarding foreign fighters, Salafists, and al-Qaeda in Syria have formed part of a broader effort to promote his government as a bulwark against extremism. In doing so he has hit the nerve of a Western audience that remains concerned about Islamism and al-Qaeda. Western countries were consequently prevented from throwing their full weight behind the revolution long before Salafists became a significant part of the rebel movement. The Western anxiety of weapons ending up in the "wrong hands" has impeded the opposition from acquiring funds, even when these are intended for humanitarian purposes.

The early concentration of Syrian Special Forces in core areas and the withdrawal of troops from the borders have made it much easier for foreign fighters to enter the country, and the propaganda of the Syrian regime has thus become a self-fulfilling prophecy due to its own policy. Donors like Saudi Arabia or Qatar, who are less concerned with the potential agenda of the revolutionaries, have provided Islamist groups with massive support. Russia and Iran have meanwhile continued to deliver arms and equipment to the Syrian regime. It is only the moderate and secular groups in the revolution who have had difficulties in obtaining even a share of what the radical and regime elements have at their disposal. Even though many Syrians may be more inclined towards moderate political ideas, Islamist and Salafist groups have gained in popularity because it is they, and they alone, who have the means to cater for the people's needs, and after two years of revolution, the Syrian people are exhausted and in many places are in dire need of basic goods.

Another successful regime strategy during the revolution has been to create the impression that the objectives of the rebels and the opposition are too diverse to understand, and that their accounts of events cannot be trusted: journalists, who were hardly free to operate even before the revolution, tend to be hand-picked by the regime for reporting from inside the country, thereby feeding the regime's own narrative—despite extensive research confirming that regime forces were responsible for the massacre in Houla, for example, the government continues to circulate propaganda alleging that the atrocity had been committed by the rebels. The government's media campaign has been well orchestrated—and it has also found a certain resonance among specific groups, notably those on the left who are eager to frame the uprising in Syria as a conspiracy to bring down the "anti-imperialist Assad regime."

The Arab countries have experienced decades of a political setting almost paralyzed by fear. In all of the Arab countries, leaders have remained in power over long periods of time while arranging for succession by sons or other proxies. This might have led Bashar al-Assad to think that change from inside was impossible, and that, accordingly, it was not necessary to deal with the demands addressed to his government. In its efforts to quell the rebellion, it is possible that the regime has followed the example of the 1982 popular uprising that was violently crushed by Hafez al-Assad and his brother. Times have changed, however. Despite all efforts to censor and control the media, modern technology makes it impossible for the regime to hide the atrocities it is committing, and it has also served to give the protesters a forum and a voice that ensures they are seen and heard abroad. Tragically, the Syrian revolutionaries have learned that knowledge about atrocities does not necessarily lead to a reaction: the Syrian regime has repeatedly been able to cross the red lines imposed by the international community, and clearly feels that it is now able to act with impunity.

Buying time—but what for?

Bashar al-Assad's foreign policy has consisted in maintaining strong relations with Russia, Iran, and other entities that unconditionally support the regime's position. He has tried to soothe his adversaries by declaring his commitment to the UN and Arab League efforts to end the violence while not fulfilling any of the requirements. He assured the UN in August 2011 that troops would be withdrawn from the cities, and he made a commitment to the Arab League that he would end the violence, neither of which has happened. At the end of December 2011, Syria admitted an observer mission of the Arab League and also allowed UN observers into the country, yet the regime still continued with its violent suppression of the protests. Domestically, Assad has offered the Syrian people some half-hearted promises of constitutional reform and other long-pending and oft-promised changes.

All of this has been done to delay international action with the aim of buying the Syrian regime more time. But what for? It seems that the political elite has failed to use this period to develop a strategy that would enable it to get out of this situation. Assad announced in March 2013 that he intended to run for the presidency in the 2014 elections (which would allow him to remain in power for another two legislative periods, i.e. until 2028), but considering the level of harm inflicted on civilians and the destruction of infrastructure, it seems as if the regime has simply given up on the idea of regaining control over the country; indeed, from the very beginning of the revolution, Assad's forces are known to have sprayed graffiti throughout the villages they had devastated declaring: "Assad forever or we will burn the country down." As journalist Christoph Reuter writes: "Even for a dictator it is unusual to threaten subjects with destruction of the entire country. Not even former Iraqi dictator Saddam Hussein or his Libyan counterpart, Moammar Gadhafi, did that. It reveals the strange relationship the Assads have with their country. … They have treated Syria like loot to be held onto, to be destroyed rather than surrendered" (Reuter 2013).

The illusion of only two choices

The current understanding of the situation in Syria as a choice between a brutal (but secular and somehow reliable) dictator, and a Somalia-like situation with a heavy Salafist presence, does not reflect reality. The opposition is diverse, and there are without doubt Islamist elements among them. In the majority of the liberated areas, we have witnessed, however, strong technocratic efforts to set up administrative structures, to provide a basic (and not exclusively Islamic) legal system for the transitional period, and a very strong grassroots activism in terms of daily affairs. This gives hope for a future Syria, because what can be seen here—and in some ways this is the positive side of the lack of foreign funds for Syrian civil causes—originates from an authentic commitment to rebuilding a different Syria.

CONCLUSION

It is time to realize that everything Assad and his government may once have been appreciated for no longer exists: the government is neither in control nor is it providing security or stability. While portraying itself as a protector of minorities it has persecuted dissidents, and the regime's aerial bombardments do not discriminate between civilians of different confession. What is worse, the regime has not only failed to protect civilians—in many cases it has deliberately targeted them. In his interview with Barbara Walters for ABC News, Bashar al-Assad, as we have seen, claimed that neither he—who is the highest commander of the army, according to the constitution—nor anybody else was in command of the Syrian army. This might seem to be a poor excuse. But it might unintentionally be true: nobody is in control. The International Crisis Group has concluded that underfinancing and ill treatment have indeed lowered the *esprit de corps* to an extent that the army is not a reliable force for the regime. Fears of revenge due to the cruelties have driven many people out of the country, and the situation on all borders, including on the Golan Heights, has become volatile. Syria might be turning into a threat for its neighboring states—not despite Assad's efforts but because of his policy.

A continuation of the current situation enhances direct and indirect tensions in neighboring states. In Turkey, PKK and Alevite solidarity with the Syrian Alawite community continues to polarize the Turkish population, and Turkey also has to deal with hundreds of thousands of refugees from Syria, a number that is likely to multiply in the future. The latter would also affect Lebanon, whose societal mosaic is similar to Syria's. In the case of Lebanon, the consensus between political leaders regarding the need to avoid a spillover of regional and international conflicts into the country is gradually eroding. The ever more open participation of Hezbollah in the fighting in Syria is a pressing and polarizing issue, and something Assad has tried to encourage—in an article from 23 April 2013, for instance, the Lebanese daily *as-Safir* reported his criticisms of Lebanon's policy of dissociation from the Syrian crisis. As has been conveyed on many occasions by the Syrian Arab News Agency, Syria has repeatedly considered engaging in military action against targets in Lebanon in response to the alleged hosting and support of the armed opposition.

It will not be possible to foresee the consequences of an intervention, regardless of whether the latter takes the form of large-scale arms supplies to the rebels, enforcing a no-fly zone or (highly unlikely) a full military intervention with ground troops. It is beyond doubt, however, that in the absence of an intervention the situation will continue to grow worse, with all the undesired consequences this will inevitably entail.

Patterns and paradigms

To learn from history usually involves studying it as an example, rather than repeating it step by step. The examples analyzed and discussed in this book, however, show that Bashar al-Assad is trying to face the current challenges by doing the latter. He has not effected major reforms since coming to power. While removing a number of members of the political elite that he "inherited" from his father, this has not led to a change in policy. Hafez al-Assad was well known as a shrewd leader and an excellent strategist. In decisive moments—the most important for Syria being the end of the cold war, discussed at the start of the book—he showed a high degree of flexibility in adapting his policy to the situation.

Bashar al-Assad, on the contrary, has not been dealing with challenges as if they need a real answer. He has blindly repeated patterns and paradigms without understanding their mechanisms, hoping for the situation to adapt to his policy rather than vice versa. When deviating from what Leverett dubbed his father's script, it was not for the better, as can be seen in the case of the Iraq War in 2003, when he even went so far as to allow the accrual of personal benefits to certain members of the ruling elite to interfere with a usually security-oriented foreign policy. It is not so much the personality of the leader that matters but, most importantly, the way he manages and controls the state institutions and their personnel. In 2013, the government of one of the most important actors in the Middle East finds itself with its back to the wall, without a vision, without a strategy, and it seems to be more prepared to take everyone and everything down with it than to manage any kind of transition.

In some ways the opposition, admirably courageous in their protests, suffers from a similar problem: for a long period they were overly focused on opposing the regime rather than developing a common agenda and vision of the future. Indeed, even as the protests spread throughout the country later in 2011, one of the leading rebels, Razan Zeitouneh, maintained that it was still too early for that to happen

(Fischer 2011). For the opposition to grow in strength it will be necessary for the disparate groups to overcome their mutual mistrust and divisions in order not only to topple this regime but to move quickly towards a reformed system and a new government. However, the opposition lacks a common vision, the commitment to a joint leadership, and a strategy. Along with the prolonged violence, this has made the opposition vulnerable to foreign influence—the sole consequence that both the government and the opposition prior to the revolution had agreed should be avoided.

There are still members of the opposition who would be willing to negotiate. Indeed, even the head of the National Coalition, Mo'az al Khatib, has made such an offer. Although this was not popular among all sections of the opposition, it did place the ball in the government's field. The regime's conditions for entering negotiations—starting with oppositional armed groups ending their fighting before the government stops fighting—are impossible to fulfill. In the absence of a partner for negotiations, therefore, international support for a political solution is honorable but seems far from feasible.

Outside support

The complexity of the situation, with a high number of regional and international interests at stake, has served as a powerful argument against international involvement. While other interventions might have suffered from being poorly conceived or based on misguided prerogatives, it is unfortunate that the case of Syria seems to be seen exclusively through this lens rather than being judged in its own right and in the context of the current situation.

Any intervention bears the danger of unforeseeable developments and undesired outcomes. However, after two years of futile diplomatic and political initiatives, after more than 100,000 people have lost their lives and with a pending crisis involving millions of refugees having not yet fully unfolded, it is essential that other possibilities are explored to end the situation. That the most desirable option—an organized transfer of power, following the peaceful protests—has been rejected imposes the question of a direct or indirect intervention on the part of the international community. Yet even without an intervention, the West's political efforts to help and protect the Syrian people have fallen, and continue to fall, far short of what is required; the responsibility to protect principle has completely vanished from international discourse, it seemed. Even when news broke about the use of chemical weapons, the discourse was mainly on "punitive measures" or "regime change"—hardly tackling the issue of how either would be addressing the issue of protection of civilians in the aftermath of a strike. European countries have not eased their visa regulations and at the time of writing are still reluctant to accept larger numbers of refugees. The European preference is to keep Syrians in the region. However, neither the refugees nor the neighboring countries have, received sufficient humanitarian aid. Since the National Coalition has not yet been widely recognized as the sole legitimate representative of the Syrian people, substantial amounts of humanitarian aid are still being distributed only in those areas controlled by the Syrian government. These policies should be revised and adapted to the situation. It is important that the international community supports the opposition not only politically, but also through the provision of significant amounts of finance that will enable it to prepare for the transition.

The opposition was and remains divided. Blindly ignoring all of the differences and difficulties among its members and postponing any difficult questions until the collapse of the Assad regime would clearly be a mistake. It is not only legitimate but necessary to ask the opposition the kind of questions it would be asked if it was already in power: what should the future constitution and political system look like? How can minority rights be guaranteed? And how can violence be controlled and stopped? Under the given circumstances it is not feasible to make substantial support for a political transformation contingent on the formation of an "ideal opposition" based outside the country—these kind of demands would simply lead to a deeply flawed transitional regime (as in the case of Iraq and Afghanistan), which, while proving popular with the West, would lack legitimacy among the Syrian people.

Even though it has so far failed to lead anywhere, outside powers should still address those who are either blocking a condemnation of Syria in the UN Security Council (Russia and China) or admonish regional powers to step back from exacerbating ethnic or religious rifts in Syrian society in order to mitigate adversary effects.

And even if it is unpopular and highly controversial, the issue of intervention, whether indirectly through weapon supplies, or directly, with troops on the ground, must be discussed. As former diplomat

CONCLUSION

Ignace Leverrier put it: "Arming the Syrian revolution … do you have a better solution?" (*Le Monde* (blog), 16 March 2013) Objections against providing sophisticated weapons to the hundreds of local and regional groups of Syrian fighters are well reasoned, but there is no optimal solution; the choice instead boils down to choosing the least bad option. From the beginning the regime has clearly indicated that its response to the protests will not change, regardless of whether the opposition is armed or not. In many instances, such as the killing of Daraya's prominent non-violence activist Ghiath Mattar or the shelling of Kafranbel, famous for its sharp caricatures of international politics and Syria, it has shown a tendency to hit much harder on peaceful activism than confront FSA or other militant groups. With the use of chemical weapons, it is not only a US-set "red line" that has been crossed, but one established by the Geneva Protocol in 1925, prohibiting the use of poisonous or other gases. Failure to address it quickly might send a dangerous message. If there were only surgical strikes, weakening the regime but not toppling it, it might be understood that any other form of atrocity is tolerable for the international community, as long as it is not chemical weapons. If there is no decision at all to intervene militarily, it might also signal to other states that despite the ban on non-conventional weapons, they will not be held accountable for their use.

"To be honest, we feel a bit insulted," Syrian activist Mohammad Al-Attar said, "with all the documentation of human rights violations in Syria, we would have expected the international community much earlier to become active, but nothing ever happened. Only when the chemical weapons issue turned up, it was the first time ever an intervention in Syria was seriously discussed. The reason why we would accept an intervention now is: If there is none, we have no guarantee that Assad will not use them again. We knew there were only very few limits before, and this would really convey that there are none at all."[1]

The longer the violence prevails in Syria and the closer the situation comes to a civil war, the higher the burden for any future government will be, and the more dangerous events will become in a larger context.

NOTES

INTRODUCTION

1. In this interview, Assad said Syria had no "policy to crack down or to torture people". He blamed the killings on "individuals" who committed "mistakes". The interviewer insisted on asking whether the army was acting on presidential command, to which Assad answered: "No, no, no. We don't have —nobody —noone's command," and said the institutions did not need any order because they were just performing their normal duties (al-Assad 2011d).

2. See Mohammad al-Attar's interview with Fawaz Traboulsi in Mar. 2013. http://www.lb.boell.org/web/113–1233.html

3. For an interesting compilation of the Syrian Arab News Agency's (and the government's) efforts to spread these allegations, see *LA Times*, 19 July 2012: http://latimesblogs.latimes.com/world_now/2012/07/syrian-media-warn-of-staged-videos-rebels-dressed-as-soldiers.html

4. For cluster bombs, see http://www.hrw.org/news/2012/11/27/syria-evidence-shows-cluster-bombs-killed-children-0. HRW's report on the use of incendiary weapons: http://www.hrw.org/features/syria-incendiary-weapons-used-populated-areas

5. Both politicians' statements were meddled with by the Iranian news agency, eliminating hints at regime responsibility and pointing instead towards the rebels. For Rafsanjani, see *Daily Star*, 1 Sept. 2013. For Rouhani's Tweets, see the United States Institute for Peace, 27 August 2013, http://iranprimer. usip.org/blog/2013/aug/27/rouhani-tweets-chemical-weapons-syria

6. See here a discussion from the village of Kafranbel: http://www.youtube. com/watch?v=z_UVQHIMx88

7. Author's interview with Mohammad Al-Attar, Beirut, 1 Sept. 2013.

1. THE LINKAGE BETWEEN DOMESTIC AND FOREIGN POLICY AND THE REBELLION OF 2011

1. For a detailed and well-written account of Syrian institution-building, see Radwan Ziadeh (2011).

2. In 2005, Khaddam went into exile in France. In a surprising speech on 30 Dec. 2005, he declared his opposition to the Syrian government and now engages in the "National Salvation Front" in order to bring down the regime. Despite having been a core member of the regime for decades, he never revealed any interesting insight and was not taken seriously as the opposition leader he wanted to be.

3. Important persons here are, among others, the late Asef Shawkat (his brother-in-law, former head of military security and deputy minister of defense); his brother Maher al-Assad (head of the Republican Guard and the army's elite Fourth Armored Division), or Mahmoud and Hafez Makhlouf from the other side of the family.

4. The first figure is the result for Bashar al-Assad in his first referendum in July 2000, the second the one of his father in 1999. For the manipulation of numbers, see e.g. George 2003, pp. 90f.

5. The Progressive National Front was established in 1972 and has been enlarged several times. At the moment, it includes the following parties: the Arab Ba'th party, two wings of the Communist Party (the Bakdash wing and the Faisal wing), two wings of the Arab Socialist Movement, the Socialist Unionist Party, the Democratic Socialist Party, the Arab Socialist Party, and the Syrian Socialist Nationalist Party.

6. Seale in a lecture 25 Jan. 2001 as quoted by http://www.mafhoum.com/press/chttam.html. In a lecture published first by *al-Hayat* 26 Jan. 2001, he also uses the term "fossilization."

7. Chief of Staff Hikmat Shihabi had been involved in handling the Lebanese portfolio, too. While Khaddam stayed in office, Shihabi was retired altogether. Khaddam had half-cunningly, half-seriously been dubbed "ra'is lubnan"—the Lebanese president. That he had to turn this file over to Bashar was a sign that Hafez al-Assad intended to limit his influence. For changes in the highest ranks preparing Bashar's accession see also Gresh 2000.

8. Another long-standing politician forced to step down was Prime Minister az-Zubi who previously belonged to Hafez al-Assad's confidants. He was charged with corruption and left in Mar. 2000; he later committed suicide. In the intelligence, Bahjat Suleiman, who was known to be close to Bashar, was upgraded in the internal directorate of General Intelligence; in Feb. 2000, the long-term head of Military Intelligence, Maj. Gen. Ali Duba, was replaced by Hassan Khalil. See Leverett 2005, pp. 62ff.

9. Regarding these revenues, see Economist Intelligence Unit Country Profile of Syria, 2008, p. 14; Binder 1992, pp. 85ff.

10. There are many examples of policy decisions in which it became obvious that Hafez al-Assad did not act on ideological grounds, e.g. his choice to intervene in the Lebanese civil war, thereby disrespecting the Arab norm of non-interference in the domestic affairs of fellow Arab states; Assad's support for Iran in the Iraq War was an even clearer deviation from pan-Arab solidarity.

11. The Syrian intervention in Lebanon in 1976 was allegedly also not in accordance with Syrian public opinion. Only when the success of fighting back Israel gave the Syrian engagement a different notion than being involved in internal fighting did the perspective change.

12. Kissinger 1982, Baker 1995, Ross 2004.

13. Due to the government attitude towards preventing ethnic and religious distinction, there has never been a census. Accordingly these figures are mere estimates and indicate a trend only, not reliable statistics.

14. Author's interview via phone with political analyst Omar Sheikhmous, 1 Nov. 2007.

15. In the government crisis in 1983/4 when Hafez al-Assad suffered a heart attack, Rifa'at tried to stage a coup with the help of this unit but was defeated by loyalists to Hafez al-Assad; the defense squad was dissolved. Author's interview with Omar Sheikhmous via phone, 1 Nov. 2007.

16. The official denomination "Syrian Arab Republic" is only one of various official references to the Arab identity of Syria, and Article 83 of the Syrian constitution states that the Syrian president must be an "Arab Syrian."

17. In 2004, Assad explained it the other way round, stating that in 1962 Kurds immigrated from abroad had been given Syrian citizenship in 1962 but not all, and that those who had not were the Maktumin; *El País*, 12 Oct. 2004.

18. Author's interview with Omar Sheikhmous via phone, 1 Nov. 2007.

19. The first strategy was broadly applied to members of the outer power circles but also to Minister of Defense Tlass, who was retired in 2004, losing his post in the Regional Command of the Ba'th party in its 2005 congress. On the same occasion, Khaddam "voluntarily" resigned. A prominent example for removal through upgrading is former Foreign Minister Sharaa.

20. On this website, Imad Moustapha presented artists from Syria, discussed cultural matters, and talked about recent books he has read, see http:// imad_moustapha.blogs.com. Moustapha was called back to Syria in 2012.

21. According to the CDF Report to the UN Human Rights Committee, 2005, p. 9, a study by the University of Damascus found that about 1,900 decrees, laws, and administrative orders had been signed by Bashar, but most of them have not been implemented; see also ICG.

22. See for example Stephen Plaut's article about Syria's economic situation in 1999: http://www.meforum.org/476/the-collapsing-syrian-economy
23. Dardari left Syria in Mar. 2011 to start working with the UN's ESCWA delegation in Beirut.
24. It has to be taken into account that this reflects public perception, not independent data on corruption.
25. A well-known example is the case of the Egyptian mobile phone company Orascom, which in 2001 obtained the first licenses for the Syrian market. The following year the company was pushed out due to special interests of a relative of the president. Another example is Daimler, where the Syrian government did not accept the company's choice of its representative in Syria and tried to push in somebody else.
26. Sadowski 2001, pp. 143–4; see for example the monopolies Firas Tlass (son of former Minister of Defense Mustafa Tlass) has achieved over the army's food supply; another well-known example is the business interests of former VP Khaddam's offspring.
27. This subject has been discussed on several occasions with the human rights lawyers Anwar al-Bounni (himself arrested in 2006 for the signature of the Damascus Declaration) and Razan Zeitouneh between 2002 and 2005; here she is quoted from an interview on www.syriacomment.com, 4 Oct. 2005.
28. There were further incidents to which the Syrian regime seemed to react heavy-handedly, e.g. a peaceful Kurdish protest in front of the UN offices in Damascus where participants were arrested, as well as later on a student who placed photos of the protest on a Kurdish website.
29. Author's interview with Syria expert Joshua Stacher, Damascus, 2005; for rumors around Abou Qaqa, see also Moubayed 2007.
30. Talks with human rights lawyers Haitham al-Maleh (Human Rights Association of Syria) and Razan Zeitouneh (SHRIL) between 2003 and 2005.
31. Bashar al-Assad in an interview with *ash-Sharq al-Awsat*, 8 Feb. 2001 (official Syrian translation as on www.al-bab.com).
32. The arrest and conviction of ten leading activists, among them political leader Riad at-Turk, economist Aref Dalila, and the MPs Riad Seif and Ma'moun al-Homsi, marked the end of hopes for democratic developments from the grassroots.
33. Ammar Abdulhamid, communication with the author, 25 Oct. 2007; the Syrian Young Entrepreneurs Association (SYEA) was established under the patronage of the president's wife, Asma al-Akhras; FIRDOS was founded and is run by her and the wife of Vice President Shara'a; MAWRED was founded by Asma al-Akhras, and Reem Khaddam, daughter of the former Vice President Abdel Halim Khaddam before she left the country with him.

The only area in which the government has not established competitive organizations is the field of human rights.

34. The Jamal al-Atasi forum was the last one to be shut down. Until then the government used it as a fig leaf. Its whole board was arrested in 2006 and has not held meetings since the release of its members. See al-Atasi 2006.
35. Michel Kilo, one of the founders of the "Committees for the Revival of Civil Society," expressed his appreciation for the regime's open-mindedness and positive attitude in dealing with the statement, *al-Hayat* 14 Jan. 2001.
36. Speech of Bashar al-Assad as quoted in *ash-Sharq al-Awsat*, 8 Feb. 2001.
37. For the text and the signatories of the Damascus Declaration, see www.syriacomment.com, 1 Nov. 2005; for comments on the agreement see Syrian activist al-Haj Saleh on www.syriacomment.com, 28 Oct. 2005.
38. Fourteen people were arrested for signing the declaration, and at least seventeen dismissed. See *al-Hayat*, 20 June 2006.
39. Author's conversations with Wael Sawah in 2004 and 2007 in Damascus; also expressed in an article in *al-Hayat* 2003 about the need to form a liberal party.
40. On the problem of a lack of innovative ideas, see Zeitouneh on Syrian opposition groups being run by "outdated and ideological mindsets to which the youth is no longer receptive"; www.syriacomment.com, 4 Oct. 2005.
41. In case of the Iraq War, the official protest started several days after the opposition protesters had already made their daily march an institution. For the pro-Palestinian protests, see Cahen 2002; another case in which the government has tried to silence oppositional voices by crowding out was the Atassi forum; see Atassi 2006, p. 47. She relates that security forces even told her that it was their strategy to have the whole space occupied by Ba'this.
42. Video available at www.youtube.com
43. Author's interview with Christoph Reuter. Berlin, 7 Jan. 2012.
44. See for example MasasitMati, http://www.youtube.com/watch?v=W5RifYxWr-4
45. Author's interview with Frida A. Nome, 17 Nov. 2011.
46. *Global Post*, 23 Apr. 2001, http://www.globalpost.com/dispatch/news/regions/middle-east/110423/syria-Asad-protests-daraa, accessed 4 Jan. 2012; "Ya Boutheina ya Shaaban, ash-shaab as-suri mu juan."
47. Author's interview with Wael Sawah, 18 Apr. 2011 via Skype.
48. Ibid.
49. Human Rights Watch (2011), "By All Means Necessary"; http://www.hrw.org/sites/default/files/reports/syria1211webwcover_0.pdf
50. http://www.hrw.org/news/2012/08/30 syria-government-attacking-breadlines

51. Author's interview with Doreen Khoury, Beirut, 20 Jan. 2013.

52. Author's interview with a Western journalist, Berlin, 7 Jan. 2012.

53. Author's interview with Wael Sawah, Beirut, 2 Aug. 2011.

54. Interview with journalist Christoph Reuter, Berlin, Dec. 2012. Many of the videos on Youtube were also found on mobile phones of Shabiha who were captured or killed.

55. Author's interview with Norwegian researcher Frida Nome, 17 Jan. 2012 via skype.

56. Author's interview with a Syrian analyst, Damascus, 4 Nov. 2011.

57. Author's interview with a Syrian journalist, Damascus, June 2007.

58. Author's interview with a Western diplomat, Brussels, 26 Mar. 2011.

59. Author's interview with Christoph Reuter, Beirut, Feb. 2012.

60. See for example the article of Ismael Hameh, 31 Dec. 2011, at http://yekiti-media.org/indexLa.php?z=en

2. FROM PUSH TO SHOVE: SYRIA AND THE UNITED STATES

1. See chapter on Lebanon; at the end of the Lebanese civil war, General Michel Aoun established a parallel government that was opposed to the Syrian involvement in Lebanon and in the end declared war on the Syrian government. Iraq was the first country to recognize Aoun's government as legitimate; see FAZ, 11 Oct. 1988.

2. Saddam Hussein was very interested in generating this image because he could exploit it to mobilize the Arab street. See Bengio 1992.

3. President Assad in a radio broadcast on 12 Jan. 1991; see Binder 1992, p. 75.

4. Speech of Saddam Hussein on 12 Aug. 1990. Bengio 1992, pp. 27f., 125.

5. For more on this matter, see the chapter on Iraq.

6. In the beginning, Hafez al-Assad put it as one of four conditions for his participation in the Madrid Conference that it would be held under the auspices of the UN, a condition that would not have worked with Israel. As a compromise, the UN was granted observer status and formally the conference was held under US and Soviet auspices.

7. President Hafez al-Assad interviewed by Patrick Seale; *Journal of Palestinian studies*, XXII (1993), p. 121.

8. Baker 1995, pp. 462–3. The perceived ability of the US to change Israel's behavior remained a popular topic of discussion; see Syrian radio statement on the Powell visit in May 2003: "Hence, we say that the United States is capable of deterring the aggressor [Israel, B.S.] and putting international efforts on the right track in order to achieve a just and comprehensive peace." http://news.bbc.co.uk/2/hi/middle_east/3000513.stm

9. E.g. the compromise on the UN status in the conference, first defied, then

according to US Ambassador Djerejian accepted and later on again denied by Assad, Baker 1995, pp. 460f.; Ross 2004, pp. 73ff.; the same for already reached understandings on the letters of assurance and invitation on 15/16 Oct.; Ross 2004, p. 79.

10. "The phrase which I will forever associate with my sixty-three hours of talks with Assad: bladder diplomacy." Baker 1995, p. 454.

11. As Ma'oz 2004 writes, 1993 was perceived as a lost opportunity; the time was ripe for a breakthrough when US mediator Warren Christopher went on a holiday (Ma'oz 2004, p. 9); Ross blames the missing of this opportunity on Oslo (Ross 2004, p. 114). Both parties allegedly also came close to an agreement in 1995 in Wye.

12. For the Alliance of Palestinian forces, see also Eisenstadt 1993 and Strindberg 2000.

13. It is debatable what effect a statement of Hafez al-Assad would have had since he had shown on other occasions that he could implement unpopular policies; the symbolism to do so in a press conference with the American president should not be underestimated, however, since in this context it could easily have been interpreted as Assad bending under US pressure.

14. Bush 2001a, Bush 2002a, Bush 2002b.

15. Bush 2001b, Cheney 2001.

16. Country Reports on Terrorism, update 30 Apr. 2007.

17. Address to a Joint Session of Congress and the American People, 20 Sep. 2001.

18. See witness Murhaf Jouejati's statement; http://www.9–11commission.gov/hearings/hearing3/witness_jouejati.htm

19. Arar was released and brought back to Canada, with the apologies of the Canadian government in 2005. Zammar was convicted of being a member of the Muslim Brotherhood in 2007 and remains in a Syrian prison.

20. Author's interview with Israeli member of Knesset, 21 June 2006.

21. Address to a Joint Session of Congress and the American People, 20 Sep. 2001.

22. See http://www.whitehouse.gov/news/releases/2002/04/print/20020404–1.html, 4 Apr. 2002.

23. Katzman/Blanchard state in the CRS Report to Congress of 6 Apr. 2005, p. 17 that this earned the Syrian regime an estimated $US2.8 billion; on top of this, there were also benefits for individuals from the oil voucher trade, see the list of beneficiaries published by the Iraqi daily *al-Mada* on 25 Jan. 2004, translated by MEMRI, 20 Feb. 2004. See chapter on Iraq.

24. Lecture of Shaaban in Houston, 10 Dec. 2003, see www.bouthainashaaban.com (accessed May 2008).

25. Farouk al-Sharaa, quoted in *al-Hayat* (London), 28 July 2003.

26. See e.g. remarks of the Syrian ambassador to the United States, Rustom al-Zoubi on CNN, 16 Apr. 2003.

27. Abu Jihad Talaat, as quoted by BBC: "Powell warns Syria of 'Consequences'," 5 May 2003.

28. After the Hamas victory in the Palestinian elections in 2006 Bashar al-Assad did not hesitate to congratulate and meet the leaders of the group in public. Politically he supported a government of national unity for Palestine.

29. See letter of Israeli UN ambassador Dan Gillerman to the UNSC and the GA, 9 Oct. 2003.

30. Letter by the Syrian minister of foreign affairs to the UN, 5 Oct. 2003 http://domino.un.org S/2003/940.

31. According to Syrian and Palestinian sources both attacks were carried out in retaliation for previous assaults in southern Israel, respectively Gaza. The September attack killed Izz ed-Din Subhi Sheikh Khalil. AP, 26 Sep. 2004 and AP 13 Dec. 2004. Khalil had lived in Gaza before being deported to South Lebanon in 1992.

32. After the assassination of the former Lebanese Prime Minister Rafiq al-Hariri, a paragraph was inserted in the country report on terrorism that mentioned the possibility of Syrian involvement.

33. Executive Order 13338 of 13 May 2004.

34. www.treas.gov/press/releases/js1538.htm, issued into a final order on 30 Mar. 2006; this restricted American financial institutions' relations with the Commercial Bank of Syria.

35. Executive Order 1338 of 13 May 2004.

36. By mentioning that Nasrallah met with "at least 10" factions, hinting at the Alliance of Palestinian Forces composed by ten factions including Hamas, and by having Hamas leader Khaled Meshal commenting on the meeting.

3. SYRIA, ISRAEL, AND PALESTINE

1. In March 2013, the Israeli government apologized to Turkey.

2. Originally a term to refer to Israel in its biblical extension (Genesis 15: 18–21), which would reach as far as Syria and Iraq, this term was used by Secretary of State James Baker in his speech to the American–Israeli Public Affairs Committee on 22 May 1989, when he called upon Israel to give up "the unrealistic vision of greater Israel" that would include the territories occupied in 1967.

3. For more about this ideological concept, see Pipes 1990. According to him, Syrian regional policy aims at unifying Syria, Lebanon, Israel, Palestine, and Jordan under Syrian command.

4. Assad never officially recognized the state of Israel. However, since both resolutions ask for Israeli withdrawal from territories occupied in the 1967 war, their acceptance is an indirect recognition of the state of Israel.

5. Astorino-Courtois/Trusty 2000, p. 366; this aspect was also understood by US officials, and the assessment is widely shared among analysts; see also Lawson 1996, p. 153; Rabinovich 1998, p. 131.

6. In fact, Assad saw Clinton as an outstanding US president in this regard, Ross 2004, p. 140; Ross adds: "For someone who had previously met with Presidents Nixon, Carter, and Bush, this was a remarkable statement."

7. At that time, Hafez al-Assad was minister of defense. Therefore it has often been insinuated that bringing this part of territory back under Syrian sovereignty was also a personal interest of the president.

8. While Israel refers to the English version of UNSCR 242 that talks about "withdrawal from territories," Syria prefers the French version in which it reads "withdrawal from the territories."

9. In Gaza, before the 2005 withdrawal, there were 8,000 settlers; in the West Bank there are more than 230,000. For Israeli settlements on the Golan Heights, see also Shalev 1994, pp. 70–81.

10. In 2005, Syria for the first time agreed to the import of products from Israeli occupied territories. BBC, 7 Feb. 2005.

11. See remarks by Foreign Minister Sharaa at the Madrid Conference 1 Nov. 1991 where he elaborated on Shamir's past as a terrorist wanted by the British authorities, www.damascus-online.com/history/documents/madrid. html

12. See Rabinovich 1998, pp. 46f., Ben-Aharon claims that with this policy, Rabin himself was "pulling the rug from under the Israeli delegation's feet," Ben-Aharon 2000, p. 3.

13. The restrictions applied not only to leaving the country but also limited the space in which Syrian Jews could move within the country.

14. For figures on immigration to Israel, see Israeli Central Bureau of Statistics Report 2006, pp. 241/2. When Syria allowed its Jewish community to leave the country, the majority settled in New York, not in Israel; see Tuttle on www.syriacomment.com, 24 Oct. 2005; Darrah 2007, p. 42.

15. For Israel, Arafat was the symbolic figure of the Palestinian struggle against Israel; Arab leaders blamed him for having incited unrest in their countries (Jordan, Lebanon). Within the occupied territories, he had gradually lost backing because the struggle of the PLO did not improve the situation for the Palestinian population. The first intifada, starting in 1987, was neither anticipated nor manipulated by Arafat or the PLO in Tunis. His signaled readiness to negotiate with Israel was seen by some as treason to the Palestinian cause.

16. See e.g. IDF interview with Prime Minister Rabin, 25 May 1995 as on www.mfa.gov.il

17. Author's interview with Gen. Uzi Dayan, Jerusalem 20 June 2006.

18. Due to the secrecy of the commitment and Assad's acknowledgement that it was in the Syrian interest to keep to it, he could not sell this as an achievement. See Ross 2004, p. 113; Seale 2000, p. 74; see also Hafez al-Assad's address to the Syrian Trade Unions Congress 14 Dec. 1992 in which he already remarks that Syria will continue the process "but not indefinitely." *Journal of Palestinian Studies*, 12 (1992), p. 143.

19. Author's interview with Gen. Uzi Dayan, Jerusalem, 20 June 2006.

20. See Seale 2000, p. 75 who believes that Peres was not aware of the "deposit" regarding the commitment to withdraw.

21. In the so-called "Gil affair," Israeli Mossad agent Yehuda Gil reported that Syria had moved considerable amounts of troops into striking range.

22. See Ma'ariv 25 Oct. 1996 as quoted by BBC Summary of World Broadcasts 26 Oct. 1996. US Secretary of State Warren Christopher conveyed this message to the Israeli ambassador to Washington.

23. Ibid.

24. Amatzia Baram in a CNN interview, 9 Sep. 1996.

25. This was on 10 July 1996; see official information on the website of Israeli MFA.

26. It should not be forgotten, though, that Oslo was not a result of US mediation but had been achieved under Norwegian auspices.

27. See Ma'ariv 25 Oct. 1996 as quoted by BBC Summary of World Broadcasts 26 Oct. 1996. Pipes does not mention Djerejian as part of the negotiation team and he focuses on Aug.–Sep. 1998 only, without mentioning the 1996 talks. There have been other private tracks for negotiations as efforts by the American businessman Ronald Lauder published in 2000 and an initiative starting in 2004 to convert the Golan Heights into a leisure park under Syrian sovereignty but open for tourists from both countries; for more on the initiative, see below.

28. See Naveh's Letter to the Editor of *The New Republic*, 2 Aug. 1999, www.danielpipes.org/article/311

29. The summaries were intended to remain confidential, but the Syrian summary was published in *al-Hayat* on 9 Jan. 2000 and the Israeli version in *Ha'aretz* and *Yedioth Akharonot* on 13 Jan. 2000. For a comparison see Reinhart/Katriel 2000.

30. At least in theory it did; in practice, Hezbollah used the Shaaba farms as a last pretext to keep on with the "resistance." Syria and Lebanon both declared the Shaaba farms—from which Israel had not withdrawn—as Lebanese. Israel claims that the disputed territory belongs to Syria and

accordingly could be restored only within the framework of a peace agreement with Damascus. For more about the significance for Hezbollah, see chapter on Lebanon.

31. See www.arableagueonline.org/las/arabic/details_ar.jsp?art_id=1777&level_id=202# for the text of the initiative.

32. For the draft of this proposal of 2004, see http://www.haaretz.com/hasen/spages/813769.html.

33. See for example the address of David Grossman to the Rabin Memorial Assembly, 11 Aug. 2006 (Grossman 2006).

34. The term "bladder diplomacy" was coined by James Baker because of Hafez al-Assad's habit to hold talks in overheated rooms, serving plenty of tea—conditions to which he was used but not the others. Similarly, in one-on-one meetings he would sit next to his counterpart instead of facing each other.

35. Author's interview in Jerusalem, Aug. 2006.

36. Foreign Minister Sharaa speaking on al-Jazeera on 11 Oct. 2001; see also Zisser 2007, p. 163.

37. For the background, the Syrian letter to the Security Council and the position of other countries, see UN Press Release 7887 of 5 Oct. 2003 http://www.un.org/News/Press/docs/2003/sc7887.doc.htm

38. The letter of Sharaa as transmitted to the UNSCR by Ambassador Faisal Mekdad.

39. See remarks of Secretary of State Dean Acheson as quoted by Rabinovich 1991, pp. 90/1; for a remarkable account of Zaim's resettlement plans, see Shlaim 1986.

40. One element of the infrastructure improvements was the integration of the sewer system of two camps into the surrounding Syrian system.

41. At the time of the intervention in Jordan, Assad was not yet president but head of the Air Force.

42. The NSF comprised the Syrian-founded Sa'iqa, Fatah al-Intifada led by Abou Moussa, the PFLP-GC headed by Ahmad Jibril, PFLP and DFLP.

43. In Islamist conceptions, rule is not restricted to a territory defined by borders but by confession. Thus the nationalist concept focused on Palestine is theoretically a contradiction to Islamist ideology. The rapprochement with secular groups was supportive insofar as it permitted to modify this conception as well as to abolish other not so popular issues. See Strindberg 2000, p. 61.

44. The relationship between the Syrian government and the groups is focused on control. The groups can hold events in Syria but not without the acquiescence of the government. For funerals and commemorations, there are often high-ranking representatives of Syrian institutions. See Brian Whit-

taker in *The Guardian*, 5 Nov. 2001 for a commemoration celebration for the above-mentioned Shiqaqi.

45. Hamas, PIJ, PFLP, PFLP-GC, PLF.

4. BACK TO SQUARE ONE: SYRIA AND TURKEY

1. In 1939 France transferred the territory to Turkey, allegedly to enlist Turkey's support in World War II.
2. Foreign Minister Sharaa as quoted by AFP, 5 Feb. 2001, see Daniel Pipes, www.danielpipes.org, 10 Jan. 2005.
3. Other official maps do not include these changes.
4. See "Turkey Singing a New Tune" by Yoav Stern in *Haaretz*, 9 Jan. 2005; on this occasion Gül also remarked sardonically that the cases of Hatay and the Golan Heights were not comparable since in the case of the latter, "the United Nations determined that the territory is occupied."
5. Kohen 1996, p. 2. Syria complained about the poor quality of water due to pollution.
6. Up to the middle of the 1980s, Syria had a long record in providing activists from the most different groups and countries with forged passports, safe haven, and training facilities. In 1986, Syria changed its policy and ever since has only supported groups acting in their neighboring countries whose activities it defines as resistance, not terrorism. This is of course ironic in the case of the Kurdish groups—while repressing its own Kurdish minority, the Syrian government has not had a problem in supporting the other states' Kurdish movements.
7. For a list of other militant groups in Turkey, some of which were also supported by Syria, see Imset 1992.
8. See Öcalan 1999, p. 182; Author's interview with Öcalan's Syrian biographer Nabil Melhem, Damascus, 23 Apr. 2005.
9. Interview with Öcalan's Syrian biographer Nabil Melhem (biography was published in Arabic with the title *Sabat Ayam m'a Apo*), Damascus, 23 Apr. 2005.
10. The large number of Syrian Kurdish participants in the struggle against Turkey is also reflected in the count of the missing, as mentioned by MacDowall 1998, p. 65; According to Montgomery 2005, p. 134, between 7,000 and 10,000 Syrian Kurds have died or disappeared fighting Turkey.
11. Author's interview with Omar Sheikhmous, researcher and one of the leading founders of the PUK in Iraq, 1 Nov. 2007 via skype; here, Sheikhmous also pointed out that in the 1990s Syrian Kurds who tried to return to Syria were arrested at the border and released only on the condition that they would go back to fighting. For the trade-off PKK training vs military service, see also Montgomery 2005, p. 135.

12. Author's interviews with local representatives, 2004.
13. A camp closed down by Syria in late 1992.
14. For the text of the protocol, the minutes, and the Adana Agreement, see Annexes to Soysal 1998–99, pp. 116–23.
15. Prime Minister Benjamin Netanyahu as quoted by Gresh 1998, p. 194. This was the first condemnation of PKK terrorism by an Israeli prime minister.
16. Sayari 1996, pp. 44f.; there have been exceptions to this policy; e.g. Ankara recognized Syria after it left the United Arab Republic, a move for which Cairo broke relations with Turkey.
17. For Turkish relations in the Middle East, see also website of the Turkish Foreign Ministry.
18. For Turkish reservations about the Syrian–Israeli negotiations, see Sever 2001, pp. 1/2; Sayari 1997, p. 50.
19. Kirisci in Rubin/Kirisci 2001, p. 101. Kirisci here also notes that with the death of Turkish President Özal in 1993 there was a change in policy by his successor. Since relations between Israel and Turkey seemed to improve again in the autumn of 1993, it does not seem to have been a change but rather a temporary effect.
20. See the following passages on the security protocols 1987–93.
21. Elekdag 1996. In this oft-cited article the author claims that Turkey should rely on a "2 ½ war strategy," enabling it to fight two external powers (Greece and Syria as most likely military challengers) and an internal war (½) against the Kurds at the same time.
22. Sever 1996/7, p. 124; Turkey also stressed that the agreement was only one in a series it had already concluded with fifteen other countries, among others, with Egypt, Saudi Arabia, and Kuwait.
23. As quoted by Piccoli/Jung 2000, p. 96.
24. NZZ, 9 Apr. 1997; according to Kirisci 1997, the situation became even more complicated by Iran offering Syria a military pact similar to the Turkish–Israeli one.
25. See "Kurden entdecken einen neuen Feind," *Die Welt*, 18 Feb. 1999.
26. Egypt had also been invited to join but decided not to; it also tried to convince Jordan to take the same position. Bengio 2004, p. 150.
27. Olson 2001, p. 105; he also quotes the daily *Hürriyet* of 17 Sep. 1995 on Öcalan saying Hatay "must be turned into a bloody lake," ibid.
28. Author's interview with a Western diplomat, Damascus, Nov. 2005.
29. For the text of the "Agreement concerning PKK and Öcalan" of 20 Oct. 1998, see *Turkish Review of Middle East Studies*, 10 (1998/9), pp. 120–3.
30. Section (d) of the Adana Agreement, ibid., p. 122.
31. Bengio 2004, p. 106; Ostrovsky 1999 quotes a letter that according to him

was sent out by the Israeli embassies underlining that Israel did not participate in the capture of the PKK leader.

32. When about twenty Kurds tried to storm the building, consular personnel opened fire from inside killing three and wounding several of the protesters. In contrast, Israeli officials claimed to have fired only a warning shot and acted in self-defense. For a detailed description of the incident, see ARD television program "Kontraste" of 27 May 1999; *Die Welt*, 18 Feb. 1999.

33. Starting in 2000 the military confrontation between the PKK and Turkish Forces was largely suspended, until 2007, when heavy fighting resumed, and in 2008 Turkish forces invaded northern Iraq.

34. In view of the increased Turkish–Israeli security cooperation, Öcalan had threatened attacks against Israeli targets, but these became a reality only after his arrest. See Aras 2000, p. 155.

35. Fisk 1999; he refers to a lecture of Efraim Inbar in Oct. 1998 mentioning joint Turkish–Israeli listening posts in the southern border; see also Candar in Makovski/Candar/Inbar 2000.

36. US officials stated that the capture was also a result of US cooperation that had provided essential intelligence. *The New York Times*, 20 Feb. 1999.

37. http://news.bbc.co.uk/2/hi/middle_east/3251572.stm; After the Nov. 2003 bomb attacks in Istanbul, Syria quickly handed over twenty-two suspects to Turkish authorities. It turned out that these suspects were not involved in the attacks.

38. In 1992, northern Iraq had become a quasi-autonomous entity ruled and administered by the two major clans and their political parties. For most of the 1990s these were involved in internecine fighting and reconciliation was achieved only in 1999.

39. This Israeli strategy of broadening its access in northern Iraq was dubbed "Plan B" by an Israeli officer, see article of the same title by Hersh, *The New Yorker*, 28 June 2004.

40. The more conservative Islamic orientation of Erdoğan's AKP changed the hitherto prevailing Israel-friendly position of the Turkish government, which played a role in the overall deterioration of Turkish–Israeli relations.

5. LOVE THY NEIGHBOR: SYRIA AND LEBANON

1. When this decision was taken, Syrian troops were already in Lebanon. The Arab League's decision therefore was rather the recognition of a *fait accompli*.

2. See Sayigh 1996. According to the Bureau of Democracy, Human Rights and Labor of the US State Department, in 2003 Palestinians were still

excluded from seventy-two professions in Lebanon. For the report of 2003 (published 25 Feb. 2004), see http://www.state.gov/g/drl/rls/hrrpt/2003/27932.htm

3. See el-Husseini 2012, who states that, in addition to the shared economic benefits tying the political elites of both countries together, there were penalties for those in Lebanon who questioned or criticized Syrian influence.

4. Netanyahu raised the "Lebanon First" option with Clinton in 1996 when progress on other tracks of the peace process seemed to have stalled. It consisted of a unilateral Israeli withdrawal from Lebanon in exchange for security guarantees. The idea was to take Lebanon out of the equation and nullify the foundations of Hezbollah's armed struggle, and, with it, Israel's main threat from the north. The move would also bring Syria under pressure to relinquish its hold on Lebanon.

5. The use of "Jerusalem" as a *pars pro toto* for Israel is not the expression of a political statement but is based on the fact that all political institutions of Israel are based in Jerusalem, not in the capital Tel Aviv.

6. Speech of President Bashar al-Assad at the conference of Syrian expatriates in Damascus, 8 Oct. 2004; printed in *al-Ba'th*, 9 Oct. 2004.

7. Even three years after the withdrawal no diplomatic representations have been established in the other respective capitals.

8. Allegedly, it was Syrian businessmen running these stores. The establishment of huge duty free shops between the borders meant serious competition for the stores at the Lebanese side of the border. Those duty free shops are in the hands of the RAMAK-group, owned by the Syrian president's cousin Rami Makhlouf.

9. Author's interviews with Western and Syrian diplomats, Damascus, Apr. 2004, May 2005.

10. Author's interview with Ziad Haidar, Damascus, 14 June 2007.

11. Author's interview with Syrian analyst Wael Sawah, Damascus, 6 Dec. 2007.

12. Author's interview with former *Daily Star* journalist Robert Bain, Beirut, 11 Aug. 2007.

13. Zisser 2007, p. 191. Two Syrian presidents who preceded Bashar had met with their counterparts on Lebanese soil in the town of Shatura—Syrian President Shukri al-Quatli, who met with Lebanese President Bishara al Khuri in 1947, and Hafiz al-Assad, who met with Sulayman Franjiyya in 1975—but never in Beirut.

14. Author's interview with Lebanon expert and former *Daily Star* journalist Robert Bain, Beirut, 11 Aug. 2007.

15. Geagea was accused of maintaining a militia under the cover of a political party, of having assassinated Lebanese fellow politicians as Dany Chamoun or Rashid Karami, and of having planned to kill Deputy Prime Minister

Michel Murr. Given that he was held responsible for crimes committed during the civil war without it being done in the context of a wider campaign for dealing with civil war crimes and that some of the charges were allegedly trumped up anyway, the trial against Geagea was considered arbitrary.

16. Middle East Intelligence Bulletin (MEIB), 2, 2 (Feb. 2000), "Syria Moves to Control Druze Religious Establishment."

17. See also in the following the issue of Lahoud blocking Hariri.

18. "Hezbollah may be the 'A-Team of Terrorists' and maybe al-Qaeda is actually the 'B'-Team." Remarks at the US Institute of Peace Conference, 5 Sep. 2002; http://www.geosociety.org/geopolicy/news/0209armitage.htm

19. In 1996, he held the first international donors' conference for Lebanon in Washington, DC, chaired by US President Bill Clinton and co-chaired by Hariri; in 2001, there was Paris I.

20. It can be assumed that Prime Minister Hariri's good connections in the international sphere, and particularly his personal friendship with French President Jacques Chirac and the Saudi king, played a role in drawing more attention to the Lebanese issue and building up pressure on Damascus. Hariri's frustrations with the Syrians were not a secret, and neither were the difficulties deriving from the tense relationship with President Lahoud that had blocked or slowed down any progress in the last years. At the same time his excellent relations with influential leaders made the Syrians suspicious of him. They were afraid of his gaining too much independence from them. For this see Blanford 2006, p. 49, and Junblatt as quoted in Blanford 2006, p. 123, referring to Hariri as "Syria's unofficial foreign minister … much more important than the real foreign minister, Farouq al-Sharaa."

21. White House press release, 5 June 2004.

22. The outgoing minister of economy and trade, Marwan Hamadeh, was severely injured and his driver killed by a car bomb in Beirut on 1 Oct. 2005.

23. For the findings of these commissions, see Fitzgerald Report, Mehlis Reports, Brammertz Report.

24. http://www.repubblica.it/2005/b/sezioni/esteri/libano/intervassad/inter-vassad.html, 28 Feb. 2005.

25. See news agencies on 4 Mar. 2005 on talks between Crown Prince Abdullah and Bashar al-Assad; allegedly, Syria had also demanded that at the upcoming Arab summit an official Arab request should be made to have Syrian troops withdrawn from Syria, which would have given the pullback Arab endorsement and cover. This request was also turned down by Saudi Arabia.

26. Ceremony on 26 Apr. 2005 near the border.

27. Author's interview with Detlef Mehlis, Berlin, 10 June 2006.
28. Qassem 2005, pp. 240f.—this meeting was followed by others with Syrian Foreign Minister Farouq al-Sharaa, Vice President Khaddam, and Maj. Gen. Ghazi Kana'an.
29. Picco 1997, p. 224. It was the release of US citizen Jesse Turner that was carried out directly in Beirut. Picco then tried to find Syrian intelligence in the Lebanese capital to arrange the transfer to Damascus and the handling of matters in the usual procedure, which—with some delay—took place in the end.
30. Palmer Harik 2005, p. 46. Syria's support for Hezbollah in Lebanon did not mean that Hezbollah was unpopular: on the contrary, Assad's strategy was to endorse popular Lebanese politicians for the vital positions that agreed with his interpretations of regional affairs.
31. Hamzeh 2004, p. 63; I would add that Iran's spending on the military sector and the Islamic Resistance surpasses expenses for the civilian projects.
32. On various occasions, Bashar al-Assad has stressed that a demarcation will take place only after the liberation, see e.g. his interview with Dubai television as published on SANA on 24 July 2006.
33. Among others, the writer Samir Qassir on 2 June 2005, the popular politician George Hawi (Lebanese Communist Party) on 21 June 2005, and LBC TV journalist May Chidiac who was severely injured and left mutilated by a car bomb on 25 Sep. 2005.
34. According to an EU diplomat familiar with UNIFIL in South Lebanon, it could be seen by the curve the fire took that Hezbollah fighters did not intend to hit anything.
35. It can be assumed, thus, that Hezbollah in the summer of 2006 when actually going into Israeli territory and abducting the Israeli soldier was aware that this would have serious consequences even though the scale this reached was certainly not predictable.
36. And the Palestinian Front for the Liberation of Palestine–General Command in 1996.
37. Later, the president of the Lebanese parliament Nabih Berri declared that the resistance had agreed on a new policy whereupon, every attack against Syrian facilities, whether in Lebanon or in Syria, would be understood as an aggression against Lebanon and an attack against Israeli settlements would be considered as a possible response.
38. Author's interview with Syria expert Doreen Khoury, Beirut, 1 June 2012.
39. See for analysis also Ali Hashem's piece in Al Monitor, 30 Apr. 2013, http://www.al-monitor.com/pulse/originals/2013/05/hassan-nasrallah-speech-hezbollah-syria.html. With regard to the battle for Quayr, Hezbollah for the first time admitted sending fighters to Syria.

40. Leverett 2006 suggests that Bashar had inherited a "script" from his father on how to handle foreign policy matters.

6. THE ODD COUPLE: SYRIA AND IRAN

1. Even though the Iranian Revolution brought a Shia movement to power, it was a highly influential incident for the region, since it inspired an over-all revival of Islamist ideas and encouraged Sunni movements too. The divide between Sunni and Shia at that time seemed less politically impor-tant than today. That the cooperation between Syria and Iran started is remarkable, however, and seems best explained in terms of regional devel-opments that made a rapprochement more attractive. Each state seemed to consider the domestic situation in the other country an internal affair that was not an obstacle to foreign policy decisions.
2. See also Syrian analyst Sami Moubayed as quoted in "Syria, Iran Wild Cards in Mideast Diplomacy: All Things Considered," www.npr.org, 1 Aug. 2006; here he emphasizes that the Syrian government is convinced that its ser-vices will be required for a settlement of the Lebanese crisis.
3. See Lesch 2005, p. 41; Goodarzi 2006, Hinnebusch/Ehteshami 1997.
4. The intensified contacts between Syria and Iran started even before the Iran–Iraq War. Syria was the second country, right after the Soviet Union, to rec-ognize the new Islamic regime. Ehteshami/Hinnebusch 1997, p. 89.
5. For the relevance of the issue of Palestine and anti-Israeli politics, see Sadjadpour 2006/7, who depicts both as an elite-driven policy that does not serve to mobilize the Iranian street.
6. See Norton 2007, p. 72; Hamzeh 2004, p. 102.
7. Not to be confused with the Damascus Declaration of the Syrian opposi-tion in 2005.
8. Ahouie 2004, p. 6. On the Iranian position towards Syrian participation in the peace process, see also Ehteshami/Hinnebusch 1997, pp. 183ff.
9. Khatami met with Ahmad Jibril (PFLP–GC), George Habash (PFLP), Ramadan Shallah (Palestinian Islamic Jihad), and Khaled Mashaal (Hamas). See Iran Report of 17 May 1999; www.globalsecurity.org
10. In the 2006 war on Lebanon as well as after the bombing of an alleged North Korean nuclear site in Syria, Syria and Iran have laid low, which pre-vented a further escalation.
11. See also the chapter on Lebanon.
12. Zisser 2003, p. 10; for protests during the war, see also Businessweek of 21 April 2003, http://www.businessweek.com/magazine/content/03_16/b3829613.htm
13. See also the chapter on Iraq.

14. For a critical assessment of Iranian influence in Iraq, see ICG Report No. 38, 21 Mar. 2005. See also Katzman 2005, Katzman 2008.
15. For the illicit oil trade between Syria and Iraq, see also the chapter on Iraq.
16. See FAZ, 19 Jan. 1998 on the visit of Iraq's Foreign Minister to Tehran.
17. FAZ, 30 June 1994.
18. Hashemi Rafsanjani as quoted by Ansari 2003, p. 89 (SWP paper July 2003).
19. It seems that this tactic, at least for Iran, has paid off: for the first time since 1979 there has been official high-ranking contact between the United States and Iran. In the conflict over Iran's nuclear ambitions the United States has also shown more flexibility than could perhaps be expected.
20. Naylor 2007. In 2008 it was reported that Iranian investments had reached $US1 billion. *Syria Today*, 7 May 2008.
21. The visit took place in late Jan. 2001 and was described by both parties as a landmark in their excellent relations. See BBC news, 24 Jan. 2001.
22. FAZ, 30 May 1997—this was prepared under the former Iranian administration, however.
23. See article by Safa Haery "Iran, Syria Anti-US–Israel Alliance is a Hoax," 21 Feb. 2005 http://www.iran-press-service.com/ips/articles-2005/february/Syria_Iran_21205.shtml; see also BBC, 16 Feb. 2005, http://news.bbc.co.uk/2/hi/middle_east/4270859.stm
24. Moustapha as quoted by MSNBC, 16 Feb. 2005 "Iran and Syria say to build a common front," http://www.msnbc.msn.com/id/6979481/.
25. See *TIME*, 2 Feb. 2002; Beehner 2007. The Iranian government was aggrieved that its handling of large numbers of Afghan refugees in 2001/2 has not been acknowledged or rewarded by the United States and its allies, see Lowe/Spencer 2006, p. 8.
26. Author's interview, 24 Aug. 2007.
27. Al-Mouallim as quoted by Samii 2006, p. 1.
28. Ambassador Robert Kimmitt as quoted by Fox News, 22 Feb. 2005.
29. Author's interview with Christoph Reuter, Beirut, 28 Apr. 2013.

7. BROTHERLY LOVE: SYRIA'S RELATIONS WITH IRAQ

1. This rumor spread in such a way that UK Foreign Minister Jack Straw saw the need to deny it publicly, see BBC 14 Mar. 2003. The fear of this scenario was also reflected in bitter jokes circulating in Damascus during the war: a GI finds a Syrian in Iraq; the latter tells him he would like to return to Damascus but does not have the money. The GI offers to pay the bus fare for him. The Syrian: "But once I'm there, how can I give it back to you?" The GI: "Never mind, we'll come to Damascus next month."

2. See Saddam Hussein's "Initiative on Previous and Subsequent Developments in the Region," 12 Aug. 1990, as quoted by Bengio 1992, pp. 125ff. Saddam Hussein had earlier pushed for a UN resolution on the withdrawal of Syrian troops from Lebanon, an attempt Syria foiled on the Arab League's summit in Casablanca in May 1989. See NZZ 28/9 May 1989.

3. This inspired the Syrian government to give its opposition to Saddam Hussein an Islamic legitimization, see Kedar 2005, pp. 128f.

4. At the end of the civil war, there were two governments in Lebanon that claimed to be the legitimate rulers, one of them led by Michel Aoun, who had been backed by the Iraqi regime. In Oct. 1990, Syria ousted him by force, thus installing a pro-Syrian regime. See chapter on Lebanon.

5. Economist Intelligence Unit Country Profile 13, 2007. For the flow of Iranian oil, see also Goodarzi 2006.

6. According to Binder 1992, p. 89, the frozen European aid now released amounted to $US192 million; he also mentions $US100 million economic aid from the United States, Japanese support for a power plant in Homs of $US200 million, and payments from the Gulf States (an estimated 1.5 billion in Mar. 1991).

7. The Iraqi side established a similar station broadcasting toward Syria ("Voice of Arab Syria").

8. Interview with SCIRI's London representative at that time, Hamid al-Bayati, by MEIB, 5 (2003); www.meib.org

9. "Anfal" was the code name for a violent campaign against Iraqi Kurds between 1986 and 1989 during which the Iraqi regime used chemical weapons and killed almost 100,000 civilians.

10. The convener of the Beirut conference (11–13 Mar. 1991) was Nouri al-Maliki.

11. These meetings ended in 1995 because of intra-Kurdish fighting between the PUK and KDP.

12. Author's interview with Omar Sheikhmous, researcher and one of the leading founders of the PUK in Iraq, 1 Nov. 2007.

13. Author's interview with political analyst Ayman Abdel Nour, via Skype, 1 Dec. 2007.

14. Ibid.

15. Leverett 2005. He sees the main motivation for enhanced cooperation in the economic needs of the Syrian regime and in the Iraqi interest in doing business with a country in which there are not UN monitors.

16. While this was still far from establishing an embassy it was a first step to upgrade diplomatic relations with Iraq. For a more extensive timeline of the cautious rapprochement, see Perthes 2001, p. 38; at the same time the Syrian government lifted the travel restriction for its citizens whose pass-

ports hitherto had contained a note saying they were not valid for travelling to Iraq; see *al-Hayat*, 23 May 2001.

17. ICG Report 2004a, p. 16.
18. For the list, see Iraqi daily *al-Mada*, 25 Jan. 2004.
19. Duelfer Report 2004, I, p. 18; plus an additional $US3 billion from oil sales to Jordan 1991–9.
20. Iran had asked Syria for the closure of this pipeline as a measure for weakening Iraq in the Iran–Iraq War. Syria was remunerated for the losses suffered due to the closure of the pipeline, and preferential oil deals as well as oil deliveries from Iran to Syria were intended to make up for it.
21. The amount of oil Syria imports and resells is estimated to be between 150,000 and 200,000 barrels per day, but the data on the prices vary. The Duelfer Report talks about a price difference of $US6 USD/ barrelwhereas other sources mention much higher figures; see e.g. Katzman/Blanchard 2005, p. 18 who state that Syria obtained the oil at half of world market prices.
22. See prepared statement of Dibbes, Joint Hearing 2005, p. 12.
23. James Placke, oil analyst for the Cambridge Energy Research Associates, as quoted by *The New York Times*, 9 May 2003.
24. As quoted by *The Daily Telegraph*, 29 Mar. 2003.
25. He did so e.g. on his visit to London in Dec. 2002, see cnn.com/world, 17 Mar. 2002.
26. On 11 Apr. 2003. See e.g. Deeb 2004, p. 144. Syria also showed its eagerness to obtain Arab support on other occasions, for example in an Arab League meeting on 25 Mar. 2004, where Assad successfully pushed for a resolution in which fifteen foreign ministers accepted the Syrian aim not to give any support for the coalition forces and to ask for immediate and unconditional withdrawal of British and American forces from Iraq. Nonetheless, the Syrian relation with other Arab countries was disturbed. This was also evident after the 2006 war in Lebanon when Assad called the Saudi and the Jordanian King "half men" because of their cautious positioning before the war.
27. as-Safir 27 Mar. 2003, see also ICG Report 11 Feb. 2004 (Syria under Bashar I), p. 15.
28. Bashar al-Assad in an interview with the Italian newspaper *La Repubblica*, as quoted by *El País*, 16 Dec. 2006.
29. This estimate comes from data of Iraq's State Oil Marketing Organization (SOMO); see Duelfer Report 2004.
30. UNSCR 1483, 22 May 2003.
31. While progress has been made, this issue remains unsettled. See e.g. *International Herald Tribune*, 22 Nov. 2007.

32. For these and the following figures, see statement of Elizabeth Dibble and statement of Dwight Sparlin at the congressional hearing on Syrian–Iraqi trade; in the cash account at the SLBC, $US72 million remained as well as $US3.8 million in the accounts of other Iraqi ministries. Leverett 2005, p. 141.

33. Under section 311 of the Patriot Act.

34. For more on the visit and the points of agreement, see al-Safir 27 July 2004.

35. This was carried out under the provisions of the Patriot Act. See Leverett 2005, p. 141.

36. Kuftaro statement circulated by fax on 26 Mar. According to long-term observers of Sheikh Kuftaro's statements, this was a very unusual position for him to take.

37. Background talks with foreign diplomats in Syria, summer 2005, summer 2006. It should be noted here that these fighters did not take part in the fighting during the war but entered Iraq much later to join guerrilla action against the US troops and the newly established Iraqi authorities.

38. The sheikh, Abou Qaqa, who had been trained in Afghanistan in the 1980s, used to preach in a mosque in Aleppo. He was allegedly provided with facilities in Aleppo to undertake training for the Iraq volunteers. In 2007 he was killed under unclear circumstances.

39. Family members of those who died in Iraq as well as records of some who returned related that the often willing but unprepared foreign fighters were not always welcome in Iraq where they were not trained for the mission or died at the hands of Iraqis. Author's interviews, Damascus 2003.

40. Author's interviews with Syria expert Joshua Stacher, Damascus, summer 2004; 15 Sep. 2008.

41. Author's interview with Western journalist, Berlin, Dec. 2011.

42. Murhaf Jouejati in his testimony in the Senate; 30 Oct. 2003.

43. Foreign Minister Farouq al-Sharaa in *The Sunday Telegraph*, 26 Oct. 2003; this comparison was frequently repeated by Syrian officials.

44. Author's interview with an Arab tribal leader in Syria in Mar. 2004.

45. Ever since the Syrian listing as a state sponsor of terrorism in 1979, military material and dual-use goods could not be exported to Syria legally. Ironically, the proliferation of night-vision equipment at the same time was the main Syrian breach of the Iraq sanctions that US Secretary of Defense Donald Rumsfeld seemed aware of because this was the only violation he accused the Syrian leadership of.

46. National Intelligence Estimate, Jan. 2007, p. 8.

47. Particularly John Bolton, Paul Wolfowitz, and Donald Rumsfeld publicly considered a more assertive course vis-à-vis Syria underlining the necessity to hold Syria responsible. The State Department was more moderate, and

President Bush initially even opposed the sanctions demanded by Congress, to maintain a certain latitude for a flexible policy with Syria.

48. Ibrahim al-Hamidi was arrested on 23 Dec. 2002 and released on bail on 25 May 2003.

49. Author's interviews with Palestinian community in Syria, summer 2003.

50. This has been evident in repeated but never implemented Syrian announcements of a more restrictive refugee policy.

51. Author's communication with American officials in Damascus after the conference.

52. Malley Testimony, 8 Nov. 2007, p. 2.

53. Yet it should be noted that in a similar situation, after the Lebanon war of 2006, the Syrian regime has reacted in a similar fashion.

8. BACK TO THE SCENE: RUSSIA

1. Author's interview with Ilya Bakharev, 11 Apr. 2013 via skype.

2. Ibid.

3. http://www.propublica.org/article/flight-records-list-russia-sending-tons-of-cash-to-syria

9. CONCLUSION

1. Author's interview with Mohammad Al- Attar, Beirut, 1 September 2013.

BIBLIOGRAPHY

Abdel-Latif, Omayma (2004), "Unsavoury Alliance: How Strong is the Alliance between Israel and the Kurds?" *al-Ahram Weekly*, 24, 30 June.

Agha, Hussein J. and Ahmad S. Khalidi (1995), *Syria and Iran: Rivalry and Cooperation*, London: Royal Institute of International Affairs.

Ahouie, Mahdi (2004), "The Middle East Peace Process from the Perspective of Revolutionary Iran: Will Tehran Ever Take Part?" *Iran Analysis Quarterly*, 1, 4 (Sep.–Nov.).

Ajami, Fouad (2012), *The Syrian Rebellion*, Stanford: Hoover Institution Press.

Alaçam, Fahir (1994/5), "The Turkish–Syrian Relations," *Turkish Review of Middle East Studies*, 8, pp. 1–18.

Alagha, Joseph (2003), "Hizbullah, Terrorism, and September 11," *Orient*, 3.

——— (2006), *The Shifts in Hizbullah's Ideology: Religious Ideology, Political Ideology, and Political Program*, Amsterdam: Amsterdam University Press.

al-Assad, Bashar (2000), Address to the People's Assembly, Damascus (Inaugural Speech), 17 June.

——— (2004a), Interview with *El País*, 12 May.

——— (2004b), Interview with al-Jazeera, n.d., MEMRI Special Dispatch 714, 14 May.

——— (2005a), Address to the Annual Convention of the Lawyers' Union, Damascus, 21 Jan.

——— (2005b), Speech at the People's Assembly in Damascus, 5 Mar.

——— (2005c), Interview with *Der Spiegel*, 29 Aug.

——— (2005d), Interview with Christine Amanpour on CNN, 12 Oct.

——— (2005e), Address at Damascus University, 10 Nov.

——— (2005f), Interview with Russian TV as quoted on www.arabicnews. com, 12 Dec.

——— (2006a), Interview with Dubai Satellite TV Channel, 23 Aug.

BIBLIOGRAPHY

——— (2011a), Speech in the Syrian Parliament, 30 Mar. (English Translation by SANA; http://www.al-bab.com/arab/docs/syria/bashar_assad_speech_110 330.htm

——— (2011b), Speech in Front of the Cabinet, 16 Apr. (English Translation by SANA; http://www.al-bab.com/arab/docs/syria/bashar_assad_speech_11 0416.htm

——— (2011c), Speech at Damascus University, 20 June (English Translation by SANA; http://www.al-bab.com/arab/docs/syria/bashar_assad_speech_110 620.htm

——— (2011d), Interview with Barbara Walters on ABC, 7 Dec.

——— (2013a), Speech at Damascus Opera House, 6 Jan. English Translation by SANA; http://www.sana-syria.com/eng/21/2013/01/06/460536.htm

——— (2013b), "Europe's Backyard Would Become a Terrorist Haven." Interview with the *Frankfurter Allgemeine Zeitung*, 17 June.

al-Assad, Hafez (1993), "Interview with Syrian President Hafiz al-Asad," *Journal of Palestine Studies*, 22 (Summer), pp. 111–21.

al-Atasi, Suhair (2006), "Innenansichten einer Diktatur," *INAMO*, 46 (Summer), pp. 46–8.

Allaf, Rime (2004), "Point of no Return?" Nov., www.rimeallaf.com http://www.rimeallaf.com/articles/article.php?d=08&m=11&y=2004; accessed on 5 Sep. 2011.

Aras, Bülent (2000), "Turkish–Israeli-Iranian Relations in the Nineties: Impact on the Middle East," *Middle East Policy*, VII, 3 (June), pp. 151–64.

al-Sharaa, Farouq (1991), "Closing Remarks at the Conference of Madrid," www.damascus-online.com/history/documents/madrid.html, 1 Nov.

——— (2002), Interview with al-Usbu'a, 25 Feb.

Astorino-Courtois, Allison and Brittani Trusty (2000), "Degrees of Difficulty: The Effect of Israeli Policy Shifts on Syrian Peace Decisions," *The Journal of Conflict Resolution*, 44, 3 (June), pp. 359–77.

at-Taqi, Samir (2004), "In the Eye of the Storm: Syrian Foreign Policy in the Aftermath of the Occupation of Iraq," 22 Mar., www.all4syria.org

Aydin, Mustafa (2005), "Political Conditionality of Economic Relations between Paternalist States: Turkey's Interaction with Iran, Iraq, and Syria," *Arab Studies Quarterly*, 27 (Winter/Spring).

Baker III, James (1989), "Principles and Pragmatism: American Policy Toward the Arab–Israeli Conflict," Speech at the American–Israeli Public Affairs Committee on 22 May 1989, published by the US Department of State Bulletin, July.

——— (1995), *The Politics of Diplomacy: Revolution, War and Peace 1989–1992*, New York: Putnam.

Baltissen, Georg (2011), "Syrien braucht ein Zeichen des Westens" [Syria Needs a Sign from the West], *die tageszeitung*, 31 Oct.

BIBLIOGRAPHY

BBC World Debate (2011), "Have the West's Policies Failed North Africa & the Middle East?" Brussels Forum, 25 Mar.

Beehner, Lionel (2007), "Is Iran Abetting the Taliban?", Council on Foreign Relations, 14 June.

Ben-Aharon, Yossi (2000), "Negotiating with Syria: A First-Hand Account," *Meria*, 4, 2.

Bengio, Ofra (1992), *Saddam Speaks on the Gulf Crisis: A Collection of Documents*, Tel Aviv: The Moshe Dayan Center for Middle Eastern and African Studies, Tel Aviv University.

———— (2004), *The Turkish–Israeli Relationship: Changing Ties of Middle Eastern Outsiders*, New York: Palgrave Macmillan.

Binder, Frank-Martin (1992), "Die Haltung Syriens in der Golfkrise," in Ferhad Ibrahim and Mir A. Ferdowsi (eds), *Die Kuwait-Krise und das regionale Umfeld. Hintergründe, Interessen, Ziele*, Berlin: Das Arabische Buch.

Blanford, Nicholas (2002), "In US 'War on Terror,' Syria is Foe and Friend," CS Monitor, 14 May; http://www.csmonitor.com/2002/0514/p01s04-wome.html; accessed 5 Sep. 2011.

———— (2003), "Syria Waffles On Militant Groups Despite U.S. Pressure," Christian Science Monitor, 6 May.

———— (2004), "Kurdish Hopes Rise, Spark Riots," Christian Science Monitor, 17 Mar.

———— (2006), *Killing Mr. Lebanon: The Assassination of Rafik Hariri and its Impact on the Middle East*, London/New York: I.B. Tauris.

Brand, Laurie (1988), "Palestinians in Syria: The Politics of Integration," *Middle East Journal*, 42, 2 (Autumn), pp. 621–37.

———— (1990), "Asad's Syria and the PLO: Coincidence or Conflict of Interests?" *Journal of South Asian and Middle Eastern Studies*, XIV, 2 (Winter), pp. 22–43.

Bush, George H. (1990), "Towards a New World Order," Address of the President to the Congress, 11 Sep.

———— (1991), "Inaugural Speech at the Madrid Conference," www.mfa.gov.il, 30 Oct.

Bush, George W. (2001a), "Remarks on Arrival at the White House," 16 Sep., as quoted by John T. Woolley and Gerhard Peters, University of California at Santa Barbara at http://www.presidency.ucsb.edu/ws/print.php?pid=63346

———— (2001b), "Address to a Joint Session of Congress and the American People,"20Sep.,http://www.whitehouse.gov/news/releases/2001/09/20010920-8.html

———— (2002a), "State of the Union Address," 29 Jan. (http://www.whitehouse.gov/news/releases/2002/01/20020129–11.html).

———— (2002b), "Remarks on Homeownership," 18 June, as quoted by http://www.hud.gov/news/speeches/presremarks.cfm

BIBLIOGRAPHY

Byman, Daniel and Matthew Waxman (1999), "Defeating US Coercion," *Survival*, 21, 2 (Summer), pp. 107–20.

Cahen, Judith (2002), "Hinter jedem Geschäftsmann ein General. Syriens alte Garde behält die Oberhand," *Le Monde Diplomatique* (deutsche Ausgabe), 15 Nov.

Central Bureau of Statistics (2006), "Statistical Abstract of Israel, 2006," http://www.cbs.gov.il/reader/shnaton/shnatone_new.htm?CYear=2006&Vol=57

Cheney, Richard (2001), Interview with CBS, 14 Nov.

Chubin, Shahram (2000), "Iran's Strategic Predicament," *Middle East Journal*, 54, 1 (Winter).

CIA World Fact Book (2000), Syria, https://www.cia.gov/library/publications/the-world-factbook/

Darrah, Felix Osama (2007), "Zur Geschichte der syrischen Juden," *INAMO*, 51, pp. 41–4.

Duelfer Report (2004), "Comprehensive Report of the Special Advisor to the Director of Central Intelligence on Iraq's Weapons of Mass Destruction," vols I–III, 30 Sep.; as published 6 Apr. 2004 on https://www.cia.gov/library/reports/general-reports-1/iraq_wmd_2004/index.html

Economist Intelligence Unit, EIU Country Profile 2010, "Syria Country Profile," yearly volumes, Economist Intelligence Unit LTE.

Ehteshami, Anoushiravan and Raymond A. Hinnebusch (1997), *Syria and Iran: Middle Powers in a Penetrated Regional System*, London: Routledge.

Eisenstadt, Michael (1993), "Syria and the Terrorist Connection," *Jane's Intelligence Review*, Jan. pp. 33–5.

Elekdag, Sukru (1996), "2½ War Strategy," *Perceptions—Journal of International Affairs*, Ankara, 1, 1 (Mar.–May).

Fischer, Joschka (2007), "U.S. Should Not Leave Iraq before Establishing Regional Consensus. Interview, 04.12.2007," in *New Perspectives Quarterly*, 25, 2 (Spring 2008).

Fischer, Susanne (2011), "Das Ende der Angst. Syriens junge Generation kämpft für den Sturz des Assad-Regimes," *Internationale Politik*, 23 Aug.; http://www.internationalepolitik.de/2011/08/23/das-ende-der-angst/; accessed 5 Sep. 2011.

Fürtig, Henner (1992), *Der Irak-Iran-Krieg 1980–1988, Ursachen, Verlauf, Folgen*, Berlin: Akademie Verlag.

———— (2002), *Iran's Rivalry with Saudi Arabia between the Gulf Wars*, Reading: Ithaca Press.

Gebauer, Matthias (2013), "Gas Attack: Germany Offers Clue in Search for Truth in Syria," *Der Spiegel*, 3 Sept. 2013, http://www.spiegel.de/international/world/german-intelligence-contributes-to-fact-finding-on-syria-gas-attack-a-920123.html

BIBLIOGRAPHY

George, Alan (2003), *Syria: Neither Bread nor Freedom*, London/New York: Zed Books.

Ghalioun, Burhan (2011), "Stop the Killing Machine," Interview with *Wall Street Journal*, 2 Dec.

Goodarzi, Jubin (2006), *Syria and Iran*, London/New York: I.B. Tauris.

——— (2013), "Syria and Iran: Alliance Cooperation in a Changing Regional Environment," *Ortadogu Etütleri*, 4, 2 (Jan.), pp. 31–54.

Gordon, Philip H. (2003), "Syria Hears the Sound of Rattling Sabers," in Brookings Iraq Report, 15 Apr.

Gresh, Alain (2000), "Der Aufstieg des 'Doktor Bashar'. Syriens junger Präsident sichert seine Macht," *Le Monde Diplomatique* (German Edition), 14 July.

Grossman, David (2006), "For the Love of this Land: Address to the Rabin Memorial Assembly," 8 Nov. as quoted by the Council on Foreign Relations. www.cfr.org

Haery, Safa (2005), "Iran, Syria Anti-US-Israel Alliance is a Hoax," Iran Press Service, 21 Feb.

al-Haj Saleh, Yassin (2012), "The Syrian Shabiha and their State," www.lb.boell. org/web/52–801.html, first appeared in *Kalamoon Magazine*, 5 (Winter Edition).

Haj Yahya, Layla (2012), "Damascus by Night," www.qantara.de, 4 Jan. 2012.

Hamzeh, Ahmad Nizar (2004), *In the Path of Hizbullah*, New York: Syracuse University Press.

Harris, William (1997), *Faces of Lebanon: Sects, Wars, and Global Extension*, Princeton: Markus Wiener Publishers.

——— (2005), "Bashar al-Assad's Lebanon Gamble," *Middle East Quarterly*, XII, 3 (Summer).

Hatina, Meir (2001), *Islam and Salvation in Palestine*, Tel Aviv: The Moshe Dayan Center.

Hersh, Seymore M. (2005), *Chain of Command: The Road from 9/11 to Abu Ghraib*, New York: Harper Perennial Editions.

Hinnebusch, Raymond A. (1984), *Authoritarian Power and State Formation in Ba'thist Syria: Army, Party and Peasant*, Boulder: Westview Press.

——— (1996), "Does Syria Want Peace? Syrian Policy in the Syrian-Israeli Peace Negotiations," *Journal of Palestine Studies*, 26, 1 (Autumn), pp. 42–57.

——— (2009), "Syrian Foreign Policy and the United States: From Bush to Obama," St. Andrews Papers on Contemporary Syria, 2009.

Hinnebusch, Raymond and Anoushiravan Ehteshami (eds) (2002), *The Foreign Policies of Arab States*, Boulder, Colorado/London: Lynne Rienner Publishers.

Hoyng, Hans and Christoph Reuter, "Assad's Cold Calculus," *Der Spiegel*, 26 Aug. 2013, English version: http://www.spiegel.de/international/world/

syrian-chemical-weapons-attack-western-intervention-draws-nearer-a-918 667.html

el-Husseini, Rola (2012), *Pax Syriana: Elite Politics in Postwar Lebanon*, Syracuse, NY: Syracuse University Press.

Ibrahim, Ferhad and Mir A. Ferdowsi (eds) (1992), *Die Kuwait-Krise und das regionale Umfeld. Hintergründe, Interessen, Ziele*, Berlin: Das Arabische Buch.

Imset, Ismet G. (1992), "The PKK: A Report on Separatist Violence in Turkey (1973–1992)," Ankara: Turkish Daily News Publications.

Inbar, Efraim (2001), "The Strategic Glue in the Israeli–Turkish Alignment," in Barry Rubin and Kemal Kirisci (eds), *Turkey in World Politics: An Emerging Multiregional Power*, Boulder/London: Lynne Rienner Publishers, pp. 115–28.

Indyk, Martin (1999a), "I Must Be Optimistic about Arab–Israeli Relations," interview in *Middle East Quarterly*, pp. 67–75.

——— (1999b), Interview on al-Quds Radio London, as quoted by MEMRI, 21 Aug.

International Crisis Group (ICG Report 2004a), "Syria Under Bashar: Domestic Policy Challenges," Part I, 11 Feb.

——— (ICG Report 2004b), "Syria Under Bashar: Foreign Policy Challenges," Part II, 11 Feb.

——— (ICG Report 2005), "Syria after Lebanon, Lebanon after Syria," Middle East Report, 39, 12 Apr.

——— (ICG Report 2013), "Syria's Kurds: A Struggle within a Struggle," Middle East Report, 136, 22 Jan.

Jouejati, Murhaf (2003a), "A Syrian Perspective on the Arab Peace Initiative," Common Ground News Service, 23 Aug.

——— (2003b), Testimony in Front of the Senate, 30 Oct. http://www.gpo. gov/fdsys/pkg/CHRG-108shrg93068/html/CHRG-108shrg93068.htm

Jung, Dietrich and Wolfgango Piccoli (2000), The Turkish–Israeli Alignment: Paranoia or Pragmatism?" *Security Dialogue*, 31, 1, pp. 91–104.

Karam, Joyce (2011), "Hezbollah's Winter," *The Majallah*, 19 Dec., http:// www.majalla.com/eng/2011/12/article55228326

Karsh, Efraim (1991), *Soviet Policy towards Syria since 1970*, New York: St. Martin's Press, 1991.

Kattouf, Theodore, Martha Neff Kessler, Hisham Melhem, and Murhaf Jouejati (2007), "When We Meet with Syria, What Should We Hope to Hear?" *Middle East Policy*, 14, 2, pp. 1–21.

Katzman, Kenneth and Christopher M. Blanchard (2005), "Iraq: Oil-For-Food Program, Illicit Trade, and Investigations," CRS Report for Congress RL 30472, updated 6 Apr. 2005.

Kedar, Mordechai (2005), *Asad in Search of Legitimacy: Messages and Rhetoric*

BIBLIOGRAPHY

in the Syrian Press under Hafiz and Bashar, Brighton/Portland: Sussex Academic Press.

Khaddam, Abdel Halim (1998), "Syrian Vice President Abd al-Halim Khaddam, Interview on the Peace Process, Damascus, Syria, 20 March 1995 (excerpts)," *Journal of Palestine Studies*, 3, pp. 161–5.

Khatib, Lina (2011), *Islamic Revivalism in Syria: The Rise and Fall of Secular Ba'thism in Syria*, London: Routledge.

Kienle, Eberhard (1990), *Ba'th versus Ba'th: The Conflict between Syria and Iraq 1968–1989*, London/New York: I.B. Tauris Publishers.

———— (ed.) (1994), *Contemporary Syria: Liberalization between Cold War and Cold Peace*, London: British Academic Press.

———— (1998), "Beyond the Lion's Reach: External Factors and Domestic Change in Syria," in Volker Perthes (ed.), *Scenarios for Syria: Socio-Economic and Political Change in Syria*, Baden-Baden: Nomos.

Kirisci, Kemal (1997), "Post Cold-War Turkish Security and the Middle East," *Middle East Review of International Affairs*, 2.

Kissinger, Henry (2001), *Does America Need a Foreign Policy? Toward a Diplomacy for the 21st Century*, New York: Simon & Schuster.

Knudsen, Erik L. (2003), "Syria, Turkey and the Changing Power Configuration in the Middle East: An Analysis of Political, Economic and Regional Difference," in Tareq Y. Ismael and Mustafa Aydin (eds), *Turkey's Foreign Policy in the Twenty-First Century: A Changing Role in World Politics*, Aldershot: Ashgate Publishing, pp. 199–218.

Kohen, Sami (1996), "A Thirsty Syria May Make Turkey's Water Price of Peace," Christian Science Monitor, 88, 30.

Kumaraswamy, P.R. (2005), "The Cairo Dialogue and the Palestinian Power Struggle," *International Studies*, 42, 1, pp. 43–59.

Kut, Sule (2001), "The Contours of Turkish Foreign Policy in the 1990s," in Barry Rubin and Kemal Kirisci (eds), *Turkey in World Politics: An Emerging Multiregional Power*, Boulder/London: Lynne Rienner Publishers, pp. 5–12.

Landis, Joshua, Syria Comment: Syrian politics, history and religion, Blog at Joshualandis.com

Lesch, Ann Mosely (1995), "Israeli Negotiations with Syria, Lebanon and Jordan: The Security Dimension," in Robert O. Freedman (ed.), *Israel under Rabin*, Boulder/San Francisco/Oxford: Westview Press, pp. 111–28.

Lesch, David W. (1999), "Is Syria Ready for Peace? Obstacles to Integration in the Global Economy," *Middle East Policy*, 2, pp. 93–111.

———— (2005), *The New Lion of Damascus: Bashar al-Assad and Modern Syria*, New Haven/London: Yale University Press.

———— (2012), *The Fall of the House of Assad*, New Haven/London: Yale University Press.

Leverett, Flynt (2004), "Why Libya Gave Up on the Bomb," *New York Times*, 23 Jan.

———— (2005), *Inheriting Syria: Bashar's Trial by Fire*, Washington, DC: Brookings Institution Press.

Leverrier, Ignace (n.d.), "Un œil sûr la Syrie. Etudes sûr la Syrie et revue commentée de l'actualité syrienne," available online at http://syrie.blog.lemonde.fr/

Lowe, Robert and Claire Spencer (eds) (2006), "Iran, its Neighbours and the Regional Crises: A Middle East Programme Report," London: The Royal Institute of International Affairs.

Ma'oz, Moshe (1988), *Asad: The Sphinx of Damascus*, London: Weidenfeld and Nicolson.

MacDowall, David (1998), "The Kurds of Syria," Kurdish Human Rights Project, London.

Maila, Joseph (1994), "The Ta'if Accord: An Evaluation," in Deirdre Collings (ed.), *Peace for Lebanon? From War to Reconstruction*, Boulder, CO/London: Lynne Rienner Publishers, pp. 31–44.

Makovsky, Alan (1999), "The New Activism in Turkish Foreign Policy," *SAIS Review*, 19, 1, pp. 92–113.

Makovsky, Alan, Cengiz Candar, and Efraim Inbar (2000), "The Turkish–Israeli–Syrian Triangle," Peace Watch, 249, Washington Institute for Near East Peace, 15 Mar.

Masalha, Salman (2011), "Israel's Favorite Dictator," *Haaretz*, 29 Mar.

Mishal, Shaul and Avraham Sela (2000), *The Palestinian Hamas: Vision, Violence, and Coexistence*, New York: Columbia University Press.

Montgomery, Harriet (2005), *The Kurds of Syria: An Existence Denied*, Berlin: Europäisches Zentrum für Kurdische Studien.

Moore, James W. (1994), "An Israeli–Syrian Peace Treaty: So Close and yet So Far," *Middle East Policy*, 3, pp. 60–82.

al-Mouallim, Walid (1997), "Fresh Light on the Syrian–Israeli Peace Negotiations," *Journal of Palestine Studies*, 26, 2 (Winter).

Moubayed, Sami (2007), "An anti-US, anti-al-Qaeda voice is silenced,". *Asia Times*, 2 Oct.

Nakkash, Aziz (2013), "The Alawites of Homs," FES Library, March 2013.

Nasrallah, Fida (1994), "Syria after Ta'if: Lebanon and the Lebanese in Syrian Politics," in Eberhard Kienle (ed.), *Contemporary Syria: Liberalization between Cold War and Cold Peace*, London: British Academic Press.

Naveh, Danny (1999), "Bibi's Secret Deal," Letter to the Editor, *The New Republic*, 2 Aug., http://www.danielpipes.org/311/the-road-to-damascus-what-netanyahu-almost-gave-away

Naylor, Hugh (2007), "Syria, Seeking Investors, Turns Cautiously to Iran," *New York Times*, 4 Oct.

BIBLIOGRAPHY

Niethammer, Katja (2006), *Vertrackte Golf-Spiele. Die Staaten des Golfkooperationsrats und der Iran*, Berlin: Stiftung Wissenschaft und Politik, SWP Aktuell, Juni.

Norton, Augustus Richard (2007), *Hezbollah: A Short History*, Princeton/Oxford: Princeton University Press.

Norton, Augustus Richard and Jillian Schwedler (1994), "Swiss Soldiers, Ta'if Clocks, and Early Elections: Toward a Happy Ending?" in Deirdre Collings (ed.), *Peace for Lebanon? From War to Reconstruction*, Boulder, CO/London: Lynne Rienner Publishers, pp. 45–65.

Olson, Robert (1997), "Turkey–Syria Relations since the Gulf War: Kurds and Water," *Middle East Policy*, V, 2 (May), pp. 168–93.

Ostrovsky, Victor (1999), "Capture of Kurdish Leader Ocalan Recalls Mossad's Collaboration with both Turkey and Kurds," Washington Report on Middle East Affairs, April/May. http://www.wrmea.com/backissues/0499/9904060.html

Oudat, Bassel (2011), "Daraa under Siege," *al-Ahram Weekly*, 1046, 5–11 May.

Özcan, Gencer (2001), "The Military and the Making of Foreign Policy in Turkey," in Barry Rubin and Kemal Kirisci (eds), *Turkey in World Politics: An Emerging Multiregional Power*, Boulder, CO/London: Lynne Rienner Publishers, pp. 13–30.

Palmer Harik, Judith (2005), *Hezbollah: The Changing Face of Terrorism*, London/New York: I.B. Tauris, 2005.

Patokallio, Mikko and Juha Saarinen (2012), "On the Wrong Side of the Arab Spring: Russia's Syria Policy," Diplomaatia, available online at http://www.diplomaatia.ee/en/article/on-the-wrong-side-of-the-arab-spring-russias-syria-policy/

Perthes, Volker (1991), *Regionale Auswirkungen des zweiten Golfkrieges. Probleme der Sicherheit und Zusammenarbeit im arabischen Raum und die Optionen europäischer Politik*, Bonn: Stiftung Entwicklung und Frieden.

——— (1995), *The Political Economy under Asad*, London/New York: I.B. Tauris.

——— (1996), "Syrian Predominance in Lebanon—Not Immutable," in Rosemary Hollis and Nadim Shehadi (eds), *Lebanon on Hold: Implications for Middle East Peace*, London: Royal Institute of International Affairs.

——— (1997), "Syria's Involvement in Lebanon," *Middle East Report*, 203 (Spring), p. 18.

——— (ed.) (1998), *Scenarios for Syria: Socio-Economic and Political Change in Syria*, Baden-Baden: Nomos.

——— (2000), *Vom Krieg zur Konkurrenz: regionale Politik und die Suche nach einer neuen arabisch-nahöstlichen Ordnung*, Baden-Baden: Nomos.

Picco, Giandomenico (1999), *Man Without a Gun: One Diplomat's Secret*

Struggle to Free the Hostages, Fight Terrorism and End a War, New York: Times Books/Random House.

Pipes, Daniel (1990), *Greater Syria: The History of an Ambition*, New York/Oxford: Oxford University Press.

——— (1996), "Syria beyond the Peace Process," Washington, DC: The Washington Institute for Near East Policy, Policy Paper no. 40.

——— (1999), "The Road to Damascus: What Netanyahu Almost Gave Away," *New Republic*, 5 July, www.danielpipes.org

Qassem, Naim (2005), *Hizbullah: The Story from Within*, London: Saqi Books.

Rabil, Robert (2001), "The Maronites and Syrian Withdrawal: From 'Isolationists' to 'Traitors'?" *Middle East Policy*, VIII, 3 (Sep.).

——— (2002), "The Iraqi Opposition's Evolution: From Conflict to Unity," *Middle East Review of International Affairs*, 6, 4 (Dec.)

Rabinovich, Itamar (1986), "The Changing Prism: Syrian Policy in Lebanon as a Mirror, an Issue and an Instrument," in Moshe Ma'oz and Avner Yaniv (eds), *Syria under Asad: Domestic Constraints and Regional Risks*, Sydney: Croom Helm.

——— (1991), *The Road not Taken: Early Arab–Israeli Negotiations*, New York/Oxford: Oxford University Press.

——— (1998), *The Brink of Peace: The Israeli–Syria Negotiations*, Princeton, NJ/Oxford: Princeton University Press.

——— (2004), *Waging Peace: Israel and the Arabs, 1948–2003*, updated and revised edn, Princeton and Oxford: Princeton University Press.

Reinhart, Tanya and Irit Katriel (2000), "How Barak Failed the Peace with Syria," Mit'an, July 2000 [Hebrew]; the English translation is available at http://www.tau.ac.il/~reinhart/political/HowBarakFailedWithSyria.html

Rémy, Jean-Philippe (2013), "Chemical Warfare in Syria," *Le Monde*, 27 May 2013, http://www.lemonde.fr/proche-orient/article/2013/05/27/chemical-war-in-syria_3417708_3218.html

Report of the International Independent Investigation Commission Established Pursuant to Security Council Resolution 1595 (2005), S/2005/662 (1st Mehlis Report), 20 Oct.

Report of the International Independent Investigation Commission Established Pursuant to Security Council Resolution 1595 (2005), S/2005/775 (2nd Mehlis Report), 12 Dec.

Reuter, Christoph (2000), "Und plötzlich droht Frieden," *Die Zeit*, 5, 3 Feb.

——— (2013), "A Two-Years Travelogue from Hell," *Der Spiegel* (English version), 4 Jan.

Risse, Thomas (2000), "Let's Argue," *International Organization*, 54, 1, pp. 1–39.

Robins, Philip (1992), "Turkish Policy and the Gulf Crisis: Adventurist or

BIBLIOGRAPHY

Dynamic?" in Clemens Dodd (ed.), *Turkish Foreign Policy: New Prospects*, Huntingdon: Eothen Press.

———— (2003), *Suits and Uniforms: Turkish Foreign Policy Since the Cold War*, London: Hurst.

Roshandel, Jalil (2000), "Iran's Foreign Policy and Security Policies: How the Decisionmaking Process Evolved," *Security Dialogue*, 31, 1, pp. 105–17.

Ross, Dennis (2004), *The Missing Peace: The Inside Story of the Fight for Middle East Peace*, New York: Farrar, Straus and Giroux.

Rubin, Barry and Kemal Kirisci (eds) (2001), *Turkey in World Politics: An Emerging Multiregional Power*, Boulder, CO/London: Lynne Rienner Publishers.

Sadjadpour, Karim (2006/7), "How Relevant is the Iranian Street?" *The Washington Quarterly* (Winter), pp. 151–62.

Sadowski, Yahya (2001), "The Evolution of Political Identity in Syria," in Shibley Telhami and Michael Barnett (eds), *Identity and Foreign Policy in the Middle East*, Ithaca: Cornell University Press, pp. 137–54.

Salhani, Claude (2003), "Syria at the Crossroads," *Middle East Policy*, X, 3 (Fall), pp. 136–43.

Samii, Abbas William (2006), "Syria and Iran: An Enduring Axis," *Mideast Monitor*, 1, 2 (Apr./May).

Savir, Uri (1998), *The Process: The 1100 days that changed the Middle East*, New York: Vintage.

Sawah, Wael (2013), "Change in Flavor: Women back off when Fighters Proceed." Beirut: Perspectives Middle East, 5 (forthcoming).

Sayari, Sabri (1997), "Turkey and the Middle East in the 1990s," *Journal of Palestine Studies*, 26, 3 (Spring), pp. 44–55.

Scham, Paul (2004), "Israeli–Turkish Relations: New Directions," Middle East Institute Commentary, 20 Aug.

Seale, Patrick (1987), *The Struggle for Syria: A Study in Post-War Arab Politics 1945–1958*, New Haven/London: Yale University Press.

———— (1988), *Asad of Syria: The Struggle for the Middle East*, London: I.B. Tauris.

———— (2000), "The Syrian–Israeli Negotiations: Who is Telling the Truth?" *Journal of Palestine Studies*, 29, 2 (Winter), pp. 65–77.

Seale, Patrick and Linda Butler (1996), "Asad's Regional Strategy and the Challenge from Netanyahu," *Journal of Palestine Studies*, 1, pp. 27–41.

Sela, Avraham and P.R. Kumaraswamy (2001), "The Perils of Israeli–Syrian Diplomatic Stalemate," *Security Dialogue*, 32, 1, pp. 11–25.

Sever, Ayşegül (1996/7), *The Arab–Israeli Peace Process and Turkey since the 1995 Agreement*, Istanbul: Foundation for Middle East and Balkan Studies, pp. 111–38.

BIBLIOGRAPHY

——— (2001), "Turkey and the Syrian–Israeli Peace Talks in the 1990s," *Middle East Review of International Affairs*, 5, 3 (Sep.).

Shaaban, Buthaina (2003), Lecture at Ann Arbor University, Michigan, 17 Dec.

Shalev, Aner (2012), "Keeping Fingers Crossed for Assad," *Haaretz*, 19 Jan.

Shalev, Aryeh (1994), *Israel and Syria: Peace and Security on the Golan*, Boulder, CO: Westview Press.

Shlaim, Avi (1986), "Husni Za'im and the Plan to Resettle Palestinian Refugees in Syria," *Journal of Palestine Studies*, 15, 4 (Summer), pp. 68–80.

Shue, Henry (2004), "Limiting Sovereignty," in Jennifer M. Welsh (ed.), *Humanitarian Intervention and International Relations*, Oxford: Oxford University Press.

Shukri, Muhammad Aziz (1991), *International Terrorism: A Legal Critique*, Brattleboro, Vermont: Amana Books.

Sidki, Bakr (2012), "The Syrian Revolution and the Role of Turkey," available online at www.lb.boell.org

Singh, K. Gajendra (2004), "Iraq: A Perplexing Predicament," *Asia Times Online*, 10 June.

Somer, Murat (2005), "Failures of the Discourse of Ethnicity: Turkey, Kurds, and the Emerging Iraq," *Security Dialogue*, 36, 1, pp. 109–28.

Stark, Holger (2005), "Der vergessene Gefangene," *Der Spiegel* 47, 21 Nov.

Starr, Stephen (2012), *Revolt in Syria: Eye-witness to the Uprising*, London: Hurst.

Staudigl, Robert (2004), *Die Türkei, Israel und Syrien zwischen Kooperation und Konflikt*, München: Herbert Utz Verlag.

Strindberg, Anders (2000), "The Damascus-Based Alliance of Palestinian Forces: A Primer," *Journal of Palestine Studies*, XXIX, 3 (Spring), pp. 60–7.

Tabler, Andrew (2011), *In the Lion's Den: An Eye Witness Account of Washington's Battle with Syria*, Chicago: Chicago Review Press, 2011.

Taheri, Amir (2006), "Syria: The Clock is Ticking," *New York Post*, 13 Jan.

——— (2006a), "How Iran Became Syria's Master," *New York Post*, 6 Nov.

Telhami, Shibley and Michael Barnett (2001), *Identity and Foreign Policy in the Middle East*, Ithaca: Cornell University Press, 2001.

Traboulsi, Fawaz (2013), "Syrian Revolutionaries Owe Nobody an Apology," Interview with Fawaz Traboulsi by Mohammed Al Attar in Beirut, 20 Feb., http://www.lb.boell.org/web/113–1233.html

Tuéni, Gibran (2005), "When Will the Syrians Come to Their Senses?" *al-Nahar*, 3 Dec.

Usher, Graham (1997), "Hizballah, Syria, and the Lebanese Elections," *Journal of Palestine Studies*, 2, 7, pp. 59–67.

Van Dam, Nikolaos (2011), *The Struggle for Power in Syria: Politics and Society Under Asad and the Ba'th Party*, London/New York: I. B. Tauris, 4th ed.

BIBLIOGRAPHY

Van Wilgenburg, Wladimir (2013), "Clashes Break Out between Kurdish Groups in Syria", Al-Monitor, 4 April 2013,, http://www.al-monitor.com/pulse/originals/2013/04/kurdish-clashes-syria-pyd-kdp-pkk-ocalan-barzani.html

Wieland, Carsten (2012), *Syria: A Decade of Lost Chances*, Seattle: Cune Press, 2012.

Williams, Paul (2001), "Turkey's H_2O Diplomacy in the Middle East," *Security Dialogue*, 32, 1, pp. 27–40.

Ziadeh, Radwan (2011), *Power and Policy in Syria: The Intelligence Services, Foreign Relations and Democracy in the Modern Middle East*, Library of Modern Middle East Studies, London/New York: I.B. Tauris.

Zisser, Eyal (1998), "Appearance and Reality: Syria's Decisionmaking Structure," *Middle East Review of International Affairs*, 2, 2 (May).

——— (2003), "Syria and the War in Iraq," *Middle East Review of International Affairs*, 7, 2 (June).

——— (2007), *Commanding Syria: Bashar al-Assad and the First Years in Power*, London: I.B. Tauris, 2007.

Zunes, Stephen (1993), "The U.S.–GCC Relationship: Its Rise and Potential Fall," *Middle East Policy*, II, 1, pp. 103–12.

——— (1997), "The Function of Rogue States in U.S. Middle East Policy," *Middle East Policy*, pp. 150–67.

——— (2003), *Tinderbox: U.S. Middle East Policy and the Roots of Terrorism*, Monroe, Maine: Common Courage Press.

Newspapers and Magazines

al-Ahram Weekly
al-Ba'ath
Daily Star
El País
Frankfurter Allgemeine Zeitung (FAZ)
Guardian
Ha'aretz (English Version)
al-Hayat
The Independent
Le Monde Diplomatique
Middle East Media Research Institute (MEMRI)
Middle East Review of Middle Eastern Affairs (MERIA)
The National (Abu Dhabi)
Neue Züricher Zeitung (NZZ)
New York Times (NYT)
The New Yorker

BIBLIOGRAPHY

Süddeutsche Zeitung (SZ)
Der Spiegel
al-Sharq al-Awsat
al-Thawra
Time Magazine
Tishreen
Turkish Daily News
Die Zeit

INDEX

INDEX

INDEX

Bir, Çevik: 111; Turkish Chief of
  Staff, 110
Bkhtiar, Hisham: assassination of
  (2012), 40
Brahimi, Lakhdar: 5
Brammertz, Serge: resignation of
  (2008), 139
Burns, William: US Under Secretary
  of State for Political Affairs, 62;
  visit to Syria (2009), 62
Bush, George H.W.: address to
  Congress (1990), 50; foreign
  policy of, 54, 173
Bush, George W.: 136; administra-
  tion of, 61; foreign policy of,
  55–6, 61, 63, 139, 179, 185;
  political rhetoric of, 56–7; visit to
  Normandy (2004), 137

Camp David Accords (1979): 73,
  106
Carter, Jimmy: foreign policy of, 54
Ceauşescu, Nicolae: execution of
  (1989), 203
China: 62, 216; arms sold by, 184
Christianity: 7
Chubin, Sharam: 162
Clinton, Bill: 71, 77, 83, 92;
  electoral victory of (1992), 54;
  foreign policy of, 76, 163;
  meeting with Binyamin Netanyahu (1996), 81; visit to Damascus (1994), 54
Clinton, Hillary: US Secretary of
  State, 63
Cold War: 49, 206; end of, 201
Commercial Bank of Syria (CBS):
  money from sales of Iraqi crude
  oil and petroleum in, 189–90;
  subsidiaries of, 189; targeted by
  US Treasury Department (2004),
  62

Communist Party of the Soviet
  Union (CPSU): members of, 202
Convention relating to the Status of
  Refugees: non-parties to, 195
Cyprus: 106

van Dam, Nikolaos: 6
Damascus Declaration (2005):
  signatories of, 30
Dardari, Abdullah: 24, 40
Davutoğlu, Ahmet: Turkish Foreign
  Minister, 118
ad-Da'wa: 175, 180; offices of, 179
Dayan, Major General Uzi: Head of
  Planning Branch of IDF General
  Staff, 78
Demirel, Süleyman: Turkish Prime
  Minister, 103; visit to Damascus
  (1993), 104
Democratic Union Party (PYD):
  Popular Defense Units (YPG), 43;
  Syrian relationship with, 11, 42
Djerejjan, Ed: US Ambassador to
  Syria, 82
Duelfer Report (2004): findings of,
  183–4

Economist Intelligence Unit (EIU):
  profile of Syria, 25
Egypt: 118, 139, 156, 159–60;
  Cairo, 67, 92–3, 99, 106, 188;
  expulsion from Arab League, 152;
  government of, 92; military of,
  67; oil imports of, 183; Revolution (2011), 32, 120, 165
Ehteshami, Anoushiravan: 6
Erdoğan, Recep Tayyip: diplomatic
  efforts of, 85–6, 117; Turkish
  Prime Minister, 116
European Union (EU): 13, 99;
  members of, 115

INDEX

nationalism: 20, 90, 143; Arab, 21, 30

Naveh, Danny: 82

Negroponte, John: US Ambassador to UN, 60

Netanyahu, Binyamin: 81, 104; electoral victory of (1996), 80, 110, 145; foreign policy of, 67, 80–2; Israeli Prime Minister, 86; meeting with Bill Clinton (1996), 81

Nixon, Richard: foreign policy of, 54

Nome, Frida A.: 34

non-governmental organisations (NGOs): 29; quasi-(QNGOs), 29

North Atlantic Treaty Organization (NATO): members of, 106

North Korea: arms sold by, 184; nuclear facilities provided by, 85

Norton, Augustus Richard: 128

Norway: Oslo, 77

Nour, Ayman Abdel: 178–80

Obama, Barack: administration of, 3–4, 62, 65; foreign policy of, 63–4

Öcalan, Abdullah: 103–4, 112, 114; capture of (1999), 111, 113, 116; leader of PKK, 22, 43, 100–2

Oslo Accords (1993): 70, 93–4; opposition to, 90, 94; provisions of, 76; signing of, 76, 109

Ottoman Empire: 105; Armenian refugees from, 20

al-Otri, Naji: Syrian Prime Minister, 163

Özal, Tugut: President of Turkey, 106

Palestine: 11, 75; Gaza, 68, 72;

refugees from, 21, 87–8; Second Intifada (2000–5), 84; West Bank, 72, 81

Palestinian Authority (PA): 91–2

Palestinian Islamic Jihad (PIJ): 90; members of, 91; supporters of, 91

Palestinian Liberation Organization (PLO): 18, 54, 71, 157, 174; aims of, 88–9; camps of, 124; co-operation with ASALA, 100; members of, 76, 89; presence in Lebanon, 122; recognised by Arab League, 76

Paris II (2002): purpose of, 136–7

Patriotic Union of Kurdistan (PUK): 175; members of, 22, 177; support for PKK, 116

Peres, Shimon: 144; background of, 79; electoral defeat of (1996), 80; Israeli Prime Minister, 79

Persian Gulf War (1990–1): 203; belligerents of, 50–1, 76, 89, 106, 120, 127, 148, 155, 170, 173–4, 204; Iraqi Invasion of Kuwait (1990), 49–51, 57, 127, 155, 170, 172–3; regional political impact of, 18, 21, 115, 180, 201, 209

Perthes, Volker: 6, 25, 129

Picco, Giandomenico: UN Chief Negotiator, 141

Pipes, Daniel: 82

Popular Front for the Liberation of Palestine—General Command (PFLP-GC): 90; support for Syrian government in Syrian Civil War, 93; training camps run by, 87

Powell, Colin: US Secretary of State, 59, 86, 183; visit to Syria (2003), 59, 86, 183

INDEX

Progressive National Front (PNF):
16
Progressive Social Party: members
of, 140

al-Qaeda: 55, 57, 86, 186; members
of, 163; presence in Syria, 210
Qaseem, Na'im: 141; Deputy
Secretary General of Hezbollah,
159
Qatar: 2, 186, 210; Doha, 5, 118;
government of, 39

Rabin, Itzhak: 77; assassination of
(1995), 79, 104; political career
of, 74–5
Rabinovich, Itamar: 75; Israeli
Ambassador to USA, 144; Israeli
Chief Negotiator with Syria, 79
Rafasanjani, Akbar, Hashemi: 4,
160
Rahim, Taufiq: 47
Reuter, Christoph: 10
Revolutionary Committee of Homs:
members of, 33
Rouhani, Hassan: President of Iran,
4
Ross, Dennis: 18; US Special Envoy
to Syria, 17
Rumsfeld, Donald: US Defense
Secretary, 184
Russian Federation: 4–5, 41, 62,
201–2, 210, 216; arms supplied
by, 166, 204, 206; Moscow,
206–7; navy of, 205

Sadjadpour, Karim: 157
Sa'iqa: 124
Salafism: 6, 39, 210, 212
Samaha, Michel: arrest of (2012),
148

Saudi Arabia: 39, 99, 113, 139–40,
165, 167–8, 203
Sawah, Wael: 9, 30, 34–5, 132
Schwedler, Jillian: 128
Scobey, Margaret: recalled to
Washington DC (2005), 138; US
Ambassador to Syria, 138
Seale, Patrick: 7, 77
Second World War (1939–45):
belligerents of, 97
Senegal: Dakar, 156
SES International: role in sale of
dual-use items to Iraq (2000–3),
184
Sfeir, Cardinal: 135
Shaaban, Boutheina: 34–5, 184
Shabiha: 7; Alawite members of,
149; role in escalation of violence,
37–8
Al-Shalish, Dhu al-Himmet: family
of, 184; President of SES
International, 184
Shamir, Itzhak: 74; presence at
Madrid Conference (1991), 73
al-Sharaa, Farouk: 40; alleged
defection of (2012), 40; Syrian
Foreign Minister, 15, 58, 60, 78,
83, 86–7, 97, 145, 186, 192;
Syrian Vice President, 15, 34, 40
Sharon, Ariel: 84; Israeli Prime
Minister, 145; visit to Ankara
(2003), 116; visit to Temple
Mount (2000), 84
Shawkat, Asef: assassination of
(2012), 40; family of, 46
Sheikhmous, Omar: 101; founding
member of PUK, 177–8
al-Shiqaqi, Fathi: 91
Shue, Henry: 3
Sidki, Bakr: 42
Six-Day War (1967): 74; territory
occupied by Israel during, 71–2